The Animated Bestiary

The Animated Bestiary

Animals, Cartoons, and Culture

PAUL WELLS

RUTGERS UNIVERSITY PRESS

NEW BRUNSWICK, NEW JERSEY, AND LONDON

LIBRARY OF CONGRESS CATALOGING-IN-PUBLICATION DATA

Wells, Paul, 1961–
 The animated bestiary : animals, cartoons, and culture / Paul Wells.
   p. cm.
 Includes bibliographical references and index.
 ISBN 978-0-8135-4414-4 (hardcover : alk. paper)—ISBN 978-0-8135-4415-1
(pbk. : alk. paper)
 1. Animals in motion pictures.   2. Animated films—History and criticism.
I. Title.
 PN1995.9.A5W45 2009
 791.43662—dc22   2008007764

A British Cataloging-in-Publication record for this book is available from the
British Library.

Jo Shapcott's "Tom and Jerry Visit England" from *Her Book: Poems 1988–1998*,
© 2000 by Jo Shapcott, is quoted by permission of Faber and Faber Ltd.

Visit our Web site: http://rutgerspress.rutgers.edu

Manufactured in the United States of America

CONTENTS

ACKNOWLEDGMENTS

Leslie Mitchner and Rachel Friedman for patience and support beyond the call of duty.

Animation Academy Staff and Research Students, Loughborough University

Aardman Animation

Tim Fernee

Vivien Halas

Nick Park

Simon Pummell

Joanna Quinn

Irene Rose

Karen Scott

Karolina Sobecka

Suzie Templeton

Run Wrake

The Animated Bestiary

Introduction

The Kong Trick

King Kong's Penis

Early in my academic career, I enjoyed an incredible naiveté and ignorance, awesome in its limits and simplistic premises. When first investigating *King Kong* (Merian C. Cooper and Ernest B. Schoedsack, USA, 1933), for example, I sought only to know how King Kong had been done; my scholarly intrigue piqued only by the stunning stop-motion animation of Willis O'Brien. There seemed no other question. It was beauty killed the beast, after all, and there seemed to be no other suspects. Similarly, if you weren't interested in Kong himself, what was the point? All you were left with was a screaming woman and an air show.

I was soon made aware of an altogether different set of perspectives, however. Kenneth Bernard's question "How Big Is Kong's Penis?" (Bernard 1976, 25) came as a bit of a shock, as I had never even considered that he might have a penis; indeed, the thought of a complex ball-and-socket arrangement was about as close as I got on this issue. Further, Bernard's view that "Kong is the classic myth of racist and imperialist repression and anxiety" (Bernard 1976, 129) also went over my head. I had not equated Kong with being a "black" man, largely because I had not seen him as anything but a large gorilla, "an animal," and any stray thought that I might have had relating race issues to the story I vetoed on the basis that it was politically incorrect. Naive I may have been, but I was nevertheless "right on."

So why this trip down the avenue of scholarly memory? Like many formative experiences, it provides the platform for the more engaged and, I hope, more conscious inquiry that I would like to make in this book. *King Kong,* for me, anyway, was more an animated film than it was a live-action spectacle, and it prompted my interest and investment in animation as a form. It was the first instance, too, of my recognition of the presence of animals in animated films. Simply put, the following discussion seeks to explore the representation of animals in cartoons, 3D stop-motion puppet and clay animation, computer-generated movies, and, more independent, fine art–based works throughout the history of animation. It is perhaps surprising that, given the ubiquity of the animal in animation since its early beginnings, it has not been a consistent preoccupation for analysis. There is an almost a taken-for-granted sense about animals in animation such that their status as the leading dramatis personae of the cartoon has scarcely been questioned. Arguably, the animal is an essential component of the language of animation, but one so naturalized that the anthropomorphic agency of creatures from Winsor McCay's Gertie the Dinosaur to PIXAR's Nemo has not been particularly interrogated.

I should be grateful, then, that I stumbled upon Bernard's analysis of Kong:

> The impossible union between Fay and Kong is symbolic of mankind's fatal impasse, the dream of paradise lost irrevocably. However, this particular symbolic inference is complicated by several other factors, notably the idea that Kong is a black man violating American womanhood and that Kong is the emerging (and rampant) Third World nations. With the first we suffer from colossal penis envy and ego collapse for we sense Fay's attraction in despite of herself. In the latter we have violated Kong's sanctuary and brought him back for profit and display, and now he threatens (literally) to screw us. (Bernard 1976, 29)

Bernard, as many film scholars have done, sees such a narrative at a highly metaphoric, subtextual level, and usefully provides a range of perspectives from which the film might be interpreted. He is able to read Kong as a black man on the basis of the representational tropes about race current in 1930s America, and can make his assumptions about the particular imperatives of sexuality and political economy on this basis. Further, he teases out a psychoanalytic layer, which leads him to conclude that the implied (male) audience can only be threatened by Kong's masculine credentials. The more literal-minded of us cannot quite make this leap, even if Kong's attraction to Fay is self-evident, and her pity for him affecting. This is not, however, a facetious undermining of Bernard's position, but rather a desire not to read Kong as a man but as an animated animal, and to therefore problematize the narrative on different terms and conditions. The essential questions, in another kind of formation, therefore, become those about the status and implication of the use of animation, and the symbolic assumptions about animals in relation to humankind. One immediate observation is the fact that in the film it is crucial that Kong functions as a persuasive character able to support the imperatives of the narrative, and that he is not seen as an animated effect. Simultaneously, he must be invisible as animation but consciously present as the vehicle for spectacle—arguably, to see him as an animated character fails his textual purpose, and the suspension of disbelief collapses. At the same time, however, this also renders Kong's status as a puppet and as a gorilla equally invisible, and it is this level of meaning that I wish to recover, as well as addressing the sociocultural, historical, and mythic agenda suggested in Bernard's work.

Beauty and the Beastly

I have suggested elsewhere (Wells 2002a, 1–14) that I see animated characters in the first instance as phenomena and, consequently, able to carry a diversity of representational positions. At one and the same time, such characters can be beasts and humans, or neither; can prompt issues about gender, race and ethnicity, generation, and identity, or not; and can operate innocently or subversively, or as something else entirely. This sense of ambiguity or ambivalence in the language of animation will be at the core of my discussion here. The use of animation can dilute the implications of meaning—after all, this is the artifice of drawings, puppets, objects, virtual simulacra, etc.—or it can amplify it—the illusionism providing exaggeration and fabricated emphasis, throwing the ideas and issues into relief. Let us take Kong once again. Arguably, Bernard is a little coy in his suggestion about a "fatal impasse" and some notion of a "paradise lost," when actually the literal (if unimaginable!) bond between Fay and Kong is to suggest bestiality. It has always been one of my less charitable thoughts that the "Beauty and the Beast" narrative—especially when played out in the Disney version, for example—offers the perverse notion of an intelligent young woman wanting to go out with a buffalo. Yet somehow, the fact that these narratives emerge from the surreal realms of the fairytale and function as animation apparently makes this albeit implied bond innocent and acceptable. This merely draws into relief that animated narratives can accommodate cross-species coupling without radical complaint or intervention.

Cross-species coupling is an endemic and unnoticed currency of the animated cartoon—innocent, innocuous, banal—or looked at another way, shocking, boundary-pushing, camp, queer, subversive. As Donald Duck drunkenly cavorts with a live-action Latino beauty in *Saludos Amigos* (Bill Roberts, Jack Kinney, Hamilton Luske, Wilfred Jackson, USA, 1943), or a wolf kisses a cow in *Little Rural Riding Hood* (Tex Avery, USA, 1949), or Belle dances cow-eyed with the hybrid bear/buffalo/ape creature in *Beauty and the Beast* (Kirk Wise and Gary Trousdale, USA, 1989), are they like Kong and Fay? Or does something occur that prevents them from being animal or, indeed, human, when singularly located within an animated form? On this basis, elsewhere, I have posed the question "Is Jerry a girl?" in the popular Hanna-Barbera "Tom and Jerry" cartoons, simply to illustrate how open and potentially challenging the animated text can be (see Wells 1998, 208–215; Cohen 1997.) It proved to be one of the most controversial questions I could have posed: I received a shoal of letters, some listing cartoons in which Jerry was "definitely" a boy; others noting that Jerry was the "queerest" animated character after Bugs Bunny; and a few suggesting that I was a pervert for asking the question in the first place! (It has always been my argument that Bernard started it.)

Clearly, though, by addressing the specificity of the language of animation, it is possible to evaluate its enunciative distinctiveness in the address of animal stories. At a very simple level, whenever an audience is confronted with an animated film, it recognizes that it is different from live action—its very aesthetic and illusionism enunciates difference and potentially prompts alternative ways of seeing and understanding what is being represented. Bernard starts to suspect something of this order, though, when he notes of Kong: "It is obvious that no mere beast provoked such a depth of response in Fay and others, but rather the intimations of something other, within, something frightening, incredible, even transcendent" (Bernard 1976, 130). In this remark, Bernard's suspicion of "the intimations of something other," represented in Kong, provides a clue for the ways in which it is possible to view animation as an approach that inevitably facilitates a representational difference, and that intrinsically interrogates orthodox positions, embedded ideology, and epistemological certainty per se. Knowledge of and about apparently specific creatures or objects or even human figures is challenged and potentially redefined. Further, allowing a space for characters, or phenomena, to operate on more symbolic or metaphoric terms and conditions invites a greater degree of possibly highly charged emotive or abstract interpretation. It offers, too, the opportunity for such phenomena to embrace a number of complex or contradictory ideas in narrative or representational flux. The animated bestiary embodies the openness of debate and not the fixedness of conclusion.

Cynthia Erb begins to get closer to this point of view when she acknowledges Kong's animated status:

> The film is an animated feature, and . . . much of its visual pleasure derives from the pleasure of watching King Kong move. In a surrealist aesthetic, King Kong is both primitive and automaton—a doubly coded figure of the uncanny, invested with the power to inspire in the civilized spectator a memory of the archaic realm of nature. (Erb 1998, 12)

Kong is defined here within aesthetic parameters, viewed as a manifestation of the surreal, in which Freud's notion of the uncanny is recalled to name Kong as a figure that effaces imagination and reality, yet that prompts recognition of primal feeling, pre-human or nonhuman codes of expression, and, most significantly, notions of "the animal" and/or "the automata." This formation has been largely inscribed in creatures within the horror genre, and is in many senses a partial and not fully theorized version of the "interstitial" condition Noel Carroll has argued is the central premise of the horror monster (Carroll 1990, 31–35). Here he insists upon the "formlessness" or mixed formation of the creature as inherently transgressive. Within such generic infrastructures, this is seen as inevitably frightening in its resistance to orthodoxy. Such monsters inevitably challenge cultural boundaries, but in the context of this discussion the "phenomenology" that I have argued is the inherent state in animation possesses this interstitial condition as its norm. While in the horror genre the interstitial condition is frightening, in animation it merely offers the possibility of transgressive difference, and is not necessarily used for scare effects. Indeed, transgression in animation can be viewed in a number of ways, more of which I explore below, but normally it is recognized as an aspect of the American animated cartoon, inherent in the antics of animal characters, almost invariably described as "anarchic" in clichéd TV listings.

Animation historian William Moritz has taken issue, however, with the notion that comic animals operate in this way:

> Endless chase and mayhem cartoons (Bugs Bunny, Tom and Jerry, etc.) . . . attempt to revive the exhausted vocabularies of the silent film comedians, from Méliès and Linder to Laurel and Hardy and The Three Stooges, by substituting animals for humans. Now, the convention of animal fables is ancient and honorable, and whether it be classical Greece's Aesop, medieval Europe's Reynard the Fox or Heian Japan's Choju Scrolls, the use of animal personae allows the storyteller to say something that could not be said by talking about humans due to political, religious or social taboos. But watching a drawn coyote crash through walls, fall down stairs, be crushed by falling objects or burned to a crisp by the explosives he holds is certainly not as amazing or funny as seeing Buster Keaton or Charlie Chaplin or Harold Lloyd or the Keystone Kops do those same stunts live right before our "camera never lies" eyes. (Moritz 1988, 21)

In this context, Moritz is essentially exasperated at the dominance of animal cartoon, and the ways that it has taken popular precedence in a fashion that marginalizes what is, in his view, the purest form of animation—nonlinear, non-objective, abstract works, by the likes of Oscar Fischinger, Berthold Bartosch, and Norman McLaren. This position equally fails to acknowledge, however, the myriad forms of animation that fall outside the comic aesthetic, and are not necessarily experimental either. Further, it resists the ways in which the freedoms of animated vocabulary interrogate and redefine representational conditions, and all the sociocultural and historically determined ideological currencies associated with dominant forms of expression.

One final observation on Moritz is that it might equally be the case that this kind of physical comedy is made yet funnier by casting the comic protagonists as animals, and defying all physical laws in a way not possible in live action, even in despite of the great comic stunts performed by Chaplin, Keaton, and their ilk. More pertinent, then, is Moritz's recognition of the ways in which animal personae within literary contexts have been used to sidestep the overt engagement with political, religious, and social taboos more usually explicit in any human-centered, realist mode of storytelling. Linking the animated film to this body of work also recalls the illustrative tradition associated with it, and consequently the aesthetic tendencies that have been hugely influential on the look and style of later cartoons. In recalling, among others, Griset, Daumier, Busch, Doré, Rackham, and Tenniel, this prompts a pertinent connection with previous uses and interpretations of the animal in other visual contexts. Of particular significance in the conceptual framework I am developing is the work of Grandville, who published the "Public and Private Life of Animals" between 1840 and 1842. As John Berger has remarked:

> At first sight, Grandville's animals, dressed up and performing as
> men and women, appear to belong to an old tradition whereby
> a person is portrayed as an animal so as to reveal more clearly
> an aspect of his or her character. The device was like putting on
> a mask, but its function was to unmask. The animal represents
> the apogee of the character trait in question: the lion, absolute

courage; the hare, lechery. The animal once lived near the origin of the quality. It was through the animal that the quality first became recognizable. And so the animal lends it his name. (Berger 1980, 16)

I explore this idea of the animal as the point of access to older knowledge later in my discussion. Berger, though he was to change his mind about Grandville, suggests the illustrations were but exaggerations of moral and social traits, and did not point to some original or even alternative social knowledge; rather, he epitomized a banal peopling of situations, which saw its apogee in Disney films. Berger's view of the Disney canon is unfair, and a fuller recognition of the ways in which Disney's animals actually interrogate both humanity and animality, echoing the unmasking process of the mature Grandville, sits at the heart of the argument I develop.

Robin Allan has fully addressed how the European illustrative tradition has informed Disney works:

Like Disney's, the world of Busch [for example] is a rural one, his characters and situations rooted in a popular tradition of peasant and lower bourgeois culture. The cruelty in Busch (Max and Moritz are ground up as corn and eaten for their naughtiness) is reflected in the ruthless Schadenfreude of the early Disney. Mickey makes a violin out of a cat in *Steamboat Willie* and hangs on a cow's udder when the latter becomes airborne in *Plane Crazy* (both 1928). The early Mickey Mouse and Donald Duck parallel Busch's harsh conflict between safe and repressive authority and the yearning for self-assertion. (Allan 1999, 18)

These visualizations do not merely signal a relationship to other caricaturial traditions of animal representation, but, as Allan implies, a particular attitude about the tensions in the modern world. Even though the early Disney shorts are remembered for a certain degree of barnyard humor—the term itself a reference to the coarse or vulgar practices associated with a non-urbane animality—the engagement with machine culture and the topical narratives of contemporary life begins to illustrate the rapid changes that characterize modernity in America. Indeed,

Steamboat Willie. Mickey Mouse in his early guise was a barnyard animal, employed to deliver vulgar humor. This represented animality as a pure, direct, bodily form uninhibited by urban rules and modern ideas.

the emergence of the cartoon—not merely in the United States, but clearly most prominently there—provides a continuity by which animal animation might be recognized as a modernist form; a suggestion that will become a key aspect of this discussion. As Akira Mizuta Lippit has noted, "Modernity can be defined by the disappearance of wildlife from humanity's habitat and by the reappearance of the same in humanity's reflections upon itself: in philosophy, psychoanalysis, and technological media such as the telephone, film and radio" (Lippit 2000, 2–3).

Jonathan Burt has questioned such analyses, however:

These themes of emptiness and the disappearance of the animal not only describe a sense of loss in modernity but reinforce this loss by the very terms of analysis. . . . The disengagement from the animal, its reduction to pure sign, reinforces at the conceptual

> level the effacement of the animal that is perceived to have taken
> place in reality even whilst criticising that process. . . . These
> theories of loss, as a version of mourning, in fact turn out to be
> another flight from the animal. (Burt 2002, 29–30)

The issues about the "disappearance" of the animal, replaced only by forms of representation and the advance of late capitalist industrial modernity, are inevitably problematized further by addressing the intrinsic artifice of the animated form. It is my contention, however, that the confluence of a singularly modernist idiom—animation—and the consequences of modernity—major social development—produces a discourse specific to animation as a form and particular to animals in its content.

This chimes with another of Burt's observations: he urges that "rather than seeing animals purely as semiotic devices it makes more sense to see them as dynamic and fluid agents that are integral to passages of change" (Burt 2002, 83). Though Burt is predominantly talking about the presence of real animals in live-action contexts, his point does not merely hold true for the animated bestiary, but becomes a literal as well as metaphorical or metaphysical principle. Animals in animation are "dynamic and fluid" and *facilitate* "passages of change" both through the processes of visualization, in narrative itself, or through deliberate symbolic effects in the creation of meaning. Though this might be viewed as another distanciation from the presence or credibility of the animal, this is not so, as I seek to demonstrate in my analysis. The processes of visualization in animation are an important factor. Concentrating on understanding animals through visual representation rather than the language that might describe them (see Burt 2002, 88), there is an immediate recollection of a range of significant illustrative depictions of animals that are pertinent to, and revealing about, their condition. Animation operates in a similar way. Its fluent visual parameters operate as an important vehicle by which insightful aesthetic, political, and cultural statements are being made on behalf of animals.

Crucially, what might be termed the legitimacy of the illustration tradition enables contemporary animation to be seen in a more consciously artistic light and within a politicized modernist context. It is possible, therefore, to refute both Moritz's misgivings and, indeed, those of anthropologist Desmond Morris, who has argued, for instance, that the "cartooning of animals" is a clear example of humankind's sense of superiority over them, and that "to make them safe we make them into amusing caricatures, as if they were ridiculous imposters worthy only of our derisive laughter" (Morris 1990, 37). There are a number of issues here worthy of address. Arguably, rather than embodying superiority over animals, it is the case that animation demonstrates an intrinsic respect for animals, and rather than making them safe through humor, it actually begins to articulate relevant narratives to support their cause. Further, rather than seeing animals in animation as "imposters," it is useful to recognize their status as phenomena embodying the relationship between animal and humankind. Effectively the cartoon functions, therefore, not as an oppressive, misrepresentative, undermining vehicle for animals, but a discourse about animals, and animal identity, that requires a degree of theorization that will be the preoccupation of later chapters.

"Animals-in-the-Making"

In order to prefigure the analysis to follow—one that essentially seeks to extend the parameters of representational analysis into a model where animated animal narratives are viewed as vehicles for progressive, transformative agendas—it is worthwhile engaging with the question of why animals became the central dramatis personae of animated film in the first place. Jeff Rovin has suggested:

> The number of drawings needed to produce an animated cartoon . . . dictated a "look" that was simpler than the illustrative technique used by Tenniel for *Alice's Adventures in Wonderland* or the realistic paintings of Beatrix Potter. Figures and expressions were caricatured and, freed from the more "realistic" treatment of animals in the past, writers came up with plots that were equally exaggerated. Moreover, because the comic and theatrical cartoon presentations were by necessity shorter, they tended to

> be gag driven rather than dependent on a great deal of plot. That
> made animal stories more comical than they'd been in the past,
> and in a world soon to be engulfed with world wars and a fiscal
> depression, funny animals became a beloved and much-needed
> respite. . . . Cartoons are now the accepted lingua franca of ani-
> mals, the media of greatest impact and widest appeal. (v)

Rovin usefully identifies the highly specific relationship between the
technique required to facilitate animation, the cultural context in
which animation was produced, the role animal stories already played
in the public imagination, and particularly in the formative years of
childhood. Simply, the complexities of animal caricature in the grand
tradition of the illustrators and artists cited earlier could not be readily achieved in animation. It is one thing to render a complex design
as a single image, but it is quite another to create a design that can be
moved persuasively over twenty-four frames per second.

It was important, however, to continue to embrace animal stories and fairytales because of their intrinsic popularity with adults
and children alike, so it was necessary to create less realistic designs,
which in their graphic realization were based on simpler forms—
"ropes" and "circles." Ub Iwerks's rope-based creatures in the early
"Silly Symphonies"—which Sergei Eisenstein considered the epitome
of "plasmaticness" in the animated form (Leyda 1988, 21)—gave way
to the "squash 'n' stretch" circular designs of Fred Moore, while Disney was embarking on creating the hyperrealist approach that would
eventually lead to *Snow White and the Seven Dwarfs* (David Hand, USA,
1937) and the apotheosis of the aesthetic in *Bambi* (David Hand, USA,
1941). In their early incarnations in the short form, rope and circle
figures were intrinsically performative and *coincidentally* comic. The
cartoon short became, therefore, a vehicle by which characters played
out gags and amusing riffs in specific situations, embedding the animal in an innovative, progressive, and popular art form, but making
the animal intrinsically funny. This shift in representational emphasis
was compounded by the emergent role of the cartoon as comic relief
and morale-raiser-in-chief during increasingly troubled times; it is no
coincidence that Preston Sturges employs Disney's cartoon short *Playful*

Pluto (Burt Gillett, USA, 1934) in *Sullivan's Travels* (USA, 1941) to illustrate its effectiveness in lifting the spirits of even those most disempowered in Depression-era America. With all this in place, the animal, particularly in the dominant American model, attained a naturalized role as a phenomena seemingly immune from the vicissitudes of experience and, perhaps more important, as the embodiment of resilience and continuity. The cartoon animal could always bounce back. Rosalind Krauss cites Walter Benjamin on this very point, discussing his address of Mickey Mouse in the first draft of his seminal "The Work of Art in the Age of Mechanical Reproduction":

> Specifically, Benjamin's recourse to Mickey Mouse revolved around the effects of collective laughter, which he saw as the antidote to the deadening of individual experience under the assaults of modern technology. To the individual anaesthetized by the shocks of contemporary life, this laughter would serve as a kind of counter-shock, a form of the same assault only now converted into 'a therapeutic detonation of the unconscious.' In this sense sufferers from the effects of technology could be protected by that same technology. (Krauss 2005, 118)

Simply put, funny animals in modern cartoons were a cure for the ills of modern life.

It should be remembered, though, that the animal in other traditions was taking on a different form—one need only note the ways in which Ladislaw Starewicz, initially in Russia and thereafter in France, depicted insects and creatures in his 3D stop-motion puppet animation to see that his work speaks more specifically to darker fairytale codes and conventions, and an essentially amoral universe in which the ambivalences and apparent brutalities of the natural world are mapped onto the conscious manipulations and contrivances of human conflict. Nevertheless, in some respects, Starewicz's approach is as much allied to technique as those artists working with the American cartoon, and it is this which once more returns me to Kong.

Willis O'Brien had established a reputation with his animated 3D stop-motion dinosaur spectacle *The Lost World* (USA, 1925), but fell out of fashion with the rise of the talkie, only once again finding a pertinent context to explore his skills when the initial studio-bound pictures gave way to outdoor action adventures. Merian C. Cooper and his partner, Ernest B. Schoedsack, were well placed to embrace and advance such filmmaking, having specialized in anthropological adventures, making *Grass* (USA, 1925) and *Chang* (USA, 1927). Cooper, the director of *King Kong,* was particularly insistent that O'Brien work on the film in a particular way:

> "I want Kong to be the fiercest, most brutal monstrous damned thing that has ever been seen," Cooper demanded. O'Brien argued that it would be impossible to win audience sympathy for a monster ape lacking any human qualities, but Cooper was adamant. "I'll have women crying over him before I'm through, and the more brutal he is the more they'll cry at the end." Cooper returned to his office and called the American Museum of Natural History in New York City, requesting the exact dimensions of a large bull gorilla. (Goldner and Turner 1975, 56)

In 1929, Cooper, a World War I fighter ace, Polish freedom fighter, and explorer, had met with kindred spirit W. Douglas Burden, a trustee of the American Museum of Natural History. Through its president, Henry Fairfield Osborn, the museum had led a filmed expedition in the discovery and capture of the now famous Komodo "Dragons," primeval lizards on a faraway island. The parallels with *King Kong* are not hard to see. Specimens were also brought back for mounting in the "Hall of Reptiles" at the museum—an aspect to which I return later—where Cooper also encountered African hunter Jimmie Clark and gorilla experts Harry Raven and Harold Coolidge (Cotta Vaz 2005, 188). Cooper later recalled a conversation he had with Burden: "When you told me that the two Komodo Dragons you brought back to Bronx Zoo, where they drew great crowds, were eventually killed by civilization, I immediately thought of doing the same thing with my Giant Gorilla. I had already established him in my mind on a prehistoric island with prehistoric monsters and I now thought of having him destroyed by the most sophisticated thing I could think of in civilization, and in the most fantastic way" (Cotta Vaz 2005, 194–195). While Burt has argued "most human-animal relations in modernity are [often viewed] in various ways wrongful—either sentimental or hollow, or a disconcerting combination of the two" (Burt 2002, 25), Cooper sees Kong as part of the discourse of modernity that neither sentimentalizes the gorilla as an animal nor questions his power and inevitable affect, but in a distinctly unsentimental way sees him as an inevitable victim of the modern world. This necessarily required that Kong be understood as an animal, but one not absorbed into modern discourses of welfare, domesticity, or control. Perhaps somewhat ironically, only animation could deliver this authenticity.

As Cooper became increasingly insistent on demanding as persuasive an animal as possible in *King Kong,* O'Brien realized he would have to create a technique and an aesthetic that simulated jungle environments reminiscent of the work of Doré. To authenticate the shifts in body weight and distribution in animal movement, he provided animators with footage of walking elephants and Eadweard Muybridge's sequential action studies (Goldner and Turner 1975, 61–62). Cooper was unambiguous that "the secret of our success with animals in these pictures was that we first found out what the animal would do and then incorporated this into the action of the story. This is quite different from trying to force something to happen as dreamed up by some dope behind a typewriter in Hollywood who has had no experience with the actual things he's writing about" (Goldner and Turner 1975, 80). Cooper clearly expected that O'Brien would create Kong first and foremost as a convincing animal, but it would be the relationship with Fay that would invest him with humanity.

This narrative accords usefully with the work of Donna Haraway on the role of taxidermy and the creation of the African Hall dioramas, opened in 1936, in the American Museum of Natural History (Haraway 2004, 151–197). Interestingly, Cooper was interested in Africa from his youth, citing Paul Chaillu's "Explorations and Adventures in Equatorial Africa" as influential in his desire to be an adventurer (Cotta Vaz 2005, 14–17). He was clearly aware of the research conducted on safaris in Africa and the preeminent presence of Carl Akeley in the field. Akeley is the subject of Haraway's analysis and the creator of the dioramas she describes as follows:

The animals in the dioramas have transcended mortal life, and hold their pose forever, with muscles tensed, noses aquiver, veins in the face and delicate ankles and folds in the supple skin all prominent. No visitor to a merely physical Africa could see these animals. This is a spiritual vision made possible only by their death and literal re-presentation. Only then could the essence of their life be present. Only then could the hygiene of nature cure a sick vision of civilized man. Taxidermy fulfils the fatal desire to represent, to be whole; it is a politics of reproduction. (Haraway 2004, 157)

Haraway immediately privileges a view of the animals as essentially "re-presented"; their realism enhanced by the act of conscious presentation as a vision *of* nature, informed by an authored idea *about* nature. Ironically, Akeley felt that he was preserving wildlife through taxidermy, and justified hunting as the necessary process in attaining the evidence for a scientific discourse designed for public exhibition, education, and consumption. In reality, Akeley was creating public artifacts (arguably, artworks) that offered a unified and sanitized view of the natural world and, perhaps more important, hid the complex process of their creation and the political agenda concerning race, gender, class, and social economy that informed it. In many senses, the *aesthetic* and *technical* issues involved in making the dioramas overwhelmed more significant discourses, and these were problematized further when Akeley photographed his subjects. As Haraway points out, "Both sculpture and photography were subordinate means to accomplishing the final taxidermic scene. But photography also represented the future and sculpture the past. Akeley's practice of photography was suspended between the manual touch of sculpture, which produced knowledge of life in the fraternal discourses of organicist biology and realist art, and the virtual touch of the camera, which has dominated our understanding of nature since World War II" (Haraway 2004, 170–171).

If sculpture and photography served only to be invisible aspects in the confirmation of supposedly objective, verifiable, and proven ideas about animals and nature when fixed in the dioramas (and indeed, in wildlife photography), it is valuable to think about the ways in which the animated form embraces sculpture (among other methods) and photography as vehicles by which to create subjective, open, and suggestive ideas about animals and nature. This provokes discourses rather than embedding, rationalizing, and fixing them. Rather than being subject to any notion of technological determinism, animation uses its resources to invoke its self-evident artifice as a challenge to any model of established social relations, and even at its most conservative it operates as a self-conscious representation of received knowledge. This is crucial, and relates to another aspect of Haraway's work when she suggests,

> Neither gender nor science—or race, field and nation—preexist the heterogeneous encounters we call practice. "Gender" does not refer to pre-constituted classes of males and females. Rather, "gender" (or "race" or "national culture," etc.) is an asymmetrical power-saturated, symbolic, material, and social relationship that is constituted and sustained—or not—in heterogeneous naturalcultural practice, such as primate studies. Doing science studies, my eye is as much on "gender-in-the-making" or "race-in-the-making" as on "science-in-the-making." Category names like "gender" or "science" are crude indicators for a mixed traffic. (Haraway 2004, 208)

At the heart of this observation are some significant factors in the development of my own discussion. Essentially, animation best identifies and illustrates—often literally in the processes of metamorphosis and condensation—codes and conditions "in-the-making," and best exemplifies the "mixed traffic" of cross-disciplinary and inter-disciplinary ideas and representational forms. It resists any predetermined social and cultural construction, constantly pointing up—again, often literally—its engagement with pre-constituted formulations and its interpretation of them. This interpretation is fundamentally related to the aesthetic distinctiveness of all animated phenomena, and the enabling difference in the variety of techniques and approaches that can be employed.

In essence, this discussion is concerned with "animals-in-the-making" and how their creation is a consequence of these conditions, and speaks readily to Haraway's conflation of nature and culture in the term "naturalcultural." The "naturalcultural" is effectively the creative and intellectual environment in which the representations of animated animals exist; consequently, this raises fundamental questions about the relationship between nature and culture. These issues underpin how animals are constructed to perform, their function in these performances, and the meaning that is played out accordingly. Again, Merian C. Cooper was fully aware that it was only a highly conscious immersion in native culture and animal life that would bring authenticity to what he called his "Natural Drama." This led him to embrace, for example, the concept of man-eating-tigers as demonic "spirit-horses" in Nan (Cotta Vaz 2005, 142–152); writing an 800-page monograph on baboons (Cotta Vaz 2005, 167); and making his quasi-ethnographic studies with Schoedsack. As Burt has pointed out, "It is easy to lose sight of the historical perspective when concepts of the animal are associated with ideas of naturalness, emotional directness and simplicity; terms which are themselves important cultural constructs" (Burt 2002, 21). It was this sense of a historical perspective embedded in cultural myth that Cooper wished to recover and to reposition amidst the complacencies of modern culture in the West. This was a culture, somewhat contradictorily, committed to progress while harboring conservative notions of ideological certainty and a sense of self-evident "rightness" in its misplaced convictions.

Of additional relevance here is Gilles Deleuze and Felix Guattari's concept of "becoming animal" (Deleuze and Guattari 2004, 256–351), a philosophic treatise aligning the animal with the process of creativity. It effectively defines the artist engaging with or depicting the animal as subject to a transcendent empathy that enables the essence of the animal to find representation outside orthodox social categories or literal artistic models. While such an idea is much more complex than I have described here, and sometimes so philosophically opaque as to render it beyond my comprehension, there are elements pertinent to this discussion, especially in regard to the ways in which animators engage with the representation of animals. As Steve Baker has noted of Deleuze and Guattari's perspective, "The artist and the animal are, it seems, intimately bound up with each other in the unthinking or undoing of the conventionally human" (quoted in Rothfels 2002, 80), and it is this central premise that I wish to apply to animators—and by extension, writers and directors like Cooper—creating the phenomena in animated films that pertain to humans and animals but nevertheless "unthink" or "undo" conventional notions of either and both. This will be particularly addressed when looking at the ways practitioners facilitate their work through the use and deployment of animal imagery, and will take into account more of Deleuze and Guattari's definitions of animal culture. At a basic level, though, this "unthinking" or "undoing" of convention calls particular discourses about animals into narratives that can provoke significant difficulties.

The *Madagascar* Problem

The core paradigm in many narratives engaging with nature and culture—seemingly the key contextual grounding of the human/animal discourse—is largely based upon a construction of the natural world as wild and the recognition of culture as a model of apparently civilized social order. Such a paradigm often embraces, too, the polarity between urban/pastoral, town/country, and present/past, and, indeed, many other dialectic principles associated with these terms. It is important to restate, then, that even though these oppositional tensions offer a useful guide to the implicit symbolic or dramatic conflicts in the narrative, they are nevertheless simplistic at the level of defining nature and culture as supposedly unified and known entities. Clearly, however we choose to define nature or culture, it will inevitably be complex, historically and culturally specific, and "in-the-making," and will refuse complete resolution. This is not to say that every animated animal narrative should be viewed as an incoherent text, but rather that a more open critical model may be required to engage with the shifts in narrative, theme, motif, and so on in the light of their representation *in animation*. I cannot overstress the difference this makes, as in many respects the animated form is intrinsically various in its illusionism—an important aspect addressed throughout this discussion. A brief analysis of the very clear deployment of the civilized/wild dichotomy in Dreamworks SKG's *Madagascar* (Eric Darnell and Tom McGrath, USA, 2005) will serve to point up these issues when looking at the representation of animals, and help to articulate the core aspects that require interrogation and hopefully will enable the creation of analytical tools that may be helpful in engaging with all animal narratives.

Four animals—Alex, a lion; Marty, a zebra; Melman, a giraffe; and Gloria, a rhinoceros—find themselves in the wilds of Madagascar, having been transported back to Africa when their escape from their comfortable habitat in the Central Park Zoo in New York is misinterpreted as a desire to return to their native environments. Marty, who often daydreams of the freedoms of the wild—comically played out in the acrobatic opening sequence to the lyricism of "Born Free"—complains that the animals have no real knowledge of anything outside the zoo walls, and, in having such thoughts, draws attention to the ways in which the animals have essentially been conditioned to the idea of performing as animals. Alex, the lion, and the zoo's star attraction, is the epitome of this idea, self-consciously aware of his own merchandising, playing out his show business persona, and, most significantly, knowing the conditions of his relationship to the people—"you don't bite the hand that feeds you." He encourages Marty to refresh his performance, which he does with feats of water-spitting and catching and making flatulent sounds with his armpits while stressing that "you don't see that on Animal Planet." This kind of gag is particularly legitimized by the film's deliberately cartoon-like aesthetic, and its clear antecedents in the work of Tex Avery and Bob Clampett. Further, the idea of performing animals is, of course, the staple of such cartoons. In some senses, then, there is a self-consciously foregrounded notion of deliberate "play." There is also recognition of irony in moments such as when Alex holds a steak and argues that "you don't get this in the wild," or in the relationship between two monkeys, one of whom is a champion of culture and the work of Tom Wolfe and the other who "throws poo" but, though mute, is able to read and engage in sign language. These jokes inevitably throw into relief discourses about the perception of animals and the natural world, but they necessarily sustain the limits of the narrative to those traits and tropes readily known and acknowledged in the public domain.

Once the film segues into the wild, however, the limits of the narrative are strained by moving beyond the realms of self-reflexive discourses about animals and into modes of representation that cannot maintain the satisfactions of irony. Leaving aside the fact that Madagascar is apparently evacuated of humankind, has no social problems, and is populated by animals who are wholly self-conscious about their place in the animal hierarchy, the film makes much of the fact that Alex, the lion, recovers his primal instincts in this environment, perceiving his fellow creatures purely as food. "We are all steaks," says King Julian, the lemur, while the former zoo denizens, in a curious sequence set to Louis Armstrong's "What a Wonderful World," confront a number of instances of animals devouring other animals. This law of the jungle sits uneasily with the claims of urbanity so engrained in the animal immigrants, made emblematic in Alex and Marty's signature buddy song, "New York, New York," which reminds the couple of "home." Alex fights his primitive urges, though, in what is essentially presented as a dark night of the soul, desperate to preserve the dignities of his identity as a tamed zoo animal. Most significant, from the point of view of a "family film," he seeks the opportunity to resolve his seemingly amoral, primal needs by finding purpose in love and friendship and, by implication, a disinterest in the naturally preordained food chain. As Martha Nussbaum confirms, apropos of her analysis of animal capabilities in relation to the tiger, "to deny a tiger the exercise of its predatory capacities may inflict significant suffering":

> A tiger's capability to kill small animals, defined as such, does not have intrinsic ethical value. . . . Zoos have learned how to make that distinction. . . . Should they give a tiger a tender gazelle to munch on? The Bronx Zoo has found that it can give the tiger a large ball on a rope, whose resistance and weight symbolize the gazelle. The tiger seems satisfied. Whatever predatory animals are living, under direct human support and control, such solutions seem the most ethically sound. (Nussbaum 2007, 35)

Alex, like the tiger addressed here, is pacified with a substitute resolution that speaks to the ethical necessity of family entertainment.

Ultimately, he returns to the safe context of his performance of the King of Beasts as his intrinsic identity; is educated to eat sushi (in a self-evident disdain for fish in the animal kingdom!); and resolves his predicament through the recognition that "his heart is bigger than his stomach." While this offers some notion of closure, it remains unsatisfactory, both because it reduces a complex animal discourse—*which the film has introduced as its core dramatic problem*—merely to the notion of polite eating, and because a ravenous primal appetite, with its accompanying instincts and violence, is reduced to a matter of social decorum and culinary taste. Although this outcome is inevitable, given that the film is considered family entertainment, an animation, and a mainstream vehicle, it continues to leave unresolved the question of how these human/animal discourses may be best read and for what purpose.

My own brief critique of the film effectively confirms that an analytical model is required that resolves the incoherence of the discourses, because as is often the case in animated animal narratives—and is something that may hereafter be called "the Madagascar Problem"—it is clear that having called these discourses into the narrative, few filmmakers/animators know how to properly use or resolve them, beyond their ambiguous use as a vehicle for jokes. This is not to say that animal narratives need to be equally self-conscious about their political or ideological agendas, nor indeed radically change the ways in which animals are presented, but in principle such narratives might take greater account of the implications of using animals in the same way as they might particular human beings. This merely proves in some ways that (animated) animals have provided a convenient vehicle by which the imperative for a coherent narrative and thematic vision may be compromised, which once more presses the case for addressing these supposedly more neutral, potentially invisible, or more willfully arbitrary narratives with greater rigor. Indeed, it is this very issue that prompted me to consider when animal narratives are successful and when they seem to fail more explicitly. My instincts leading me to conclude that animated animal narratives essentially remain coherent and plausible so long as they retain the inner logic that informs the anthropomorphic intentions and outlook of the characters, but they fail more readily if they do not manage to accommodate what simplistically may be called recognizably true animal actions, behavior, and primal motivation. This mixture of possible meanings and intentions must be viewed, however, in a way that does not polarize cartoon logic and animal authenticity, but rather evaluates the outcome of how they function together. How, then, can we solve the *Madagascar* Problem?

It is important to understand the problem from a number of perspectives, from the point of view of both those who make animated films and those who seek to understand, enjoy, and analyze them. The key discourses, then, are how animals are represented from the point of view of animators (scriptwriters, directors, filmmakers, and so on), that is, *as a practice phenomena and a creative paradigm,* and how animals are represented from the point of view of critical and cultural interpretation, that is, *as a created phenomena and a paradigm to evaluate in the eyes of "the audience."* Further, to create narrative and thematic coherence in narratives such as *Madagascar,* and to embrace meaning "in-the-making" or the idea of the artist as "becoming animal," as I mentioned earlier, it is necessary to view the animal in whatever way it may be defined, as in a state of operational and symbolic flux in virtually every narrative. This is inevitably aided and abetted by the malleability and liminal nature of animation as vehicle of expression. As such, it becomes clear that it is necessary to build a critical paradigm that at one and the same time enables an interpretation that speaks to the fundamental relationships between human and animal, nature and culture, and art and reality, while taking into account the aesthetic and technical variations so distinctive to the animated film. This is the purpose of the following discussion.

A Happy Feat

Following a series of largely disappointing computer-generated animated features during 2006, the status of talking animal movies was once more at the heart of debates about animation. *Barnyard* (Steve Oederkerk, USA, 2006) came under particular attack: "This could be the film that snaps everyone's patience with Hollywood animations which have a Dell computer chip where their heart should be. It's a comedy about animals in a barnyard who can talk and walk upright when the humans aren't watching" (Bradshaw 2006, 9). Aside from recalling the hackneyed idea of the cold computer producing work—a mythology long established before *Toy Story* (John Lasseter, USA, 1995) proved that artists make movies, not computers—this critique starts to question what one might view as the core conventions of the talking animal film, and the surreal playfulness that normally attends it. Particularly troubling for all critics was the fact that bulls had udders:

> Cows who are guys? I kid you not. These cows are trans-gendered. They have udders—udders!—that poke out front as they stride manfully about. Speaking in male voices. Huh? Now, the last time I checked, udders are the exclusive preserve of the female. (One of these is pregnant, incidentally. I wonder how that is supposed to have happened.) Do the city slickers making this animation have the smallest clue what a cow is—in real life, that is, and not one they have seen in other cartoons? (Bradshaw 2006, 9)

This curious rant at one and the same time wants to make a point about consistency yet abandons the terms and conditions upon which such consistency might be grounded. Animals don't talk at all (except in their own established languages and modes of communication) and cartoons readily blur and play with gender boundaries, but the film's lack of reference to a real cow and the orthodoxies of procreation is apparently its core failure. In reality, the key flaw in the film is unrelated: there is no essential reference to the animal-ness of the characters save their caricaturial representation, the setting of the film in a barnyard, and a set of predictable gags. In not drawing upon an animal discourse, however, the film still lends itself to an arguably bizarre metaphorical interpretation: "I suppose this is an allegory of sorts. Ben is Bush senior fighting the first Gulf War, Otis is Bush Junior, revenging his father after 9/11, and the coyotes are the terrorists. Unlike the astringently pessimist *Animal Farm,* this feel-good movie is Orwell that ends well" (French 2006, 17). Though this is a highly forced grounding of the film in a political discourse, it does at least suggest that animated films can carry seriousness of purpose or a pertinent subtext.

Bradshaw's desire to recall "the animal" to the critical agenda, however, only came about later in the year with the release of *Happy Feet* (George Miller, Australia/USA, 2006), which was explicit in its placement of animals within an ecological discourse. In Britain and elsewhere, this prompted a review in popular criticism of the talking animal animation as the bearer of political messages (see Williams 2006). Exploring the normal liberal tensions between individualism and conformism common to most American (animated) movies, *Happy Feet* tells a left-leaning tale of humankind's deliberate exploitation and abuse of the oceans and the ways in which a fundamentalist rhetoric is employed to blame liberal thinkers or nonwhite groups for *not* being faithful, middle-class Republicans, committed to trusting the government and the political status quo. Crucially, it is only by recalling the reality of the animal discourse in the film that the surreal and playful idioms of the "animated feature for children" may be addressed as a more engaged text actually speaking to significant issues. Without it, the film is a masterpiece of motion-captured dancing penguins and amusing jokes, but not the ideologically charged animation it actually is. Fundamentally, then, it is only when the animal discourse is self-consciously used and managed that the *Madagascar* Problem is adequately resolved, recalling films such as *One Hundred and One Dalmations* (Wolfgang Reitherman, Hamilton Luske, Clyde Geronomi, USA, 1961), in which the anti-fur message is supported by the direct action of the animal resistance; *Antz* (Eric Darnell, Tim Johnson, USA, 1998), which works as a clear antifascist parable, underpinned by a metaphoric reading of real ant colonies; and *Ice Age* (Chris Wedge, USA, 2002), which emerges as a survivalist narrative—exemplified by the animals—in the face of inevitable climate change. The reading of animals then becomes highly significant in deducing meaning and affect from narratives that would otherwise be dismissed or marginalized for their status as animation or from the sheer invisibility of the animal, despite its omnipresence in many animated shorts and features. Ironically, this is the very subject of an intrinsically adult feature, *Free Jimmy* (Christopher Nielsen, Norway, 2006), which addresses the idea of animals in forced captivity. The film features a drugged elephant who upon his escape from a circus becomes the focus of the comic and ideological struggle between animal activists, hunters, the circus owners, and the mafia, essentially defining the animal discourse as complex, oppositional, and subject to dialectic tensions. The following chapters define and explore this issue.

1

The Bear Who Wasn't

Bestial Ambivalence

The Animal/Human Divide

In Chuck Jones's adaptation of Frank Tashlin's children's book *The Bear That Wasn't* (Chuck Jones, USA, 1967), a bear emerges out of hibernation into a *Metropolis*-style factory, where he is viewed as "a silly man, who needs a shave, and wears a fur overcoat." Though he maintains he is a bear, his protestations are ignored and he is put to oppressive, repetitive work in the factory, until he too denies his own identity. Finally, reminded of his intrinsic place in the natural order by the passing of a flock of migrating geese and the onset of autumn, he escapes the human world and goes back to hibernation. Tashlin's pessimistic tale was written in 1946, and in its depiction of an inhumane hierarchy of foremen, managers, vice-presidents, and presidents, and even downbeat zoo animals, it shows a hopeless view of humankind as it seeks to rebuild the postwar world. Jones's kinder, inevitably counterculture-tinged adaptation in the 1960s shows the same degree of alienation between human and animal, but when the bear returns to hibernation adds the punch line that "he wasn't a silly man; he wasn't a silly bear either."

This critique of authoritarian regimes and urban modernity shows humankind in a poor light precisely because it has become divorced from any notion of the natural world. The president of the company, like all those who work for him, cannot recognize a bear and conceives that "bears are only in a zoo or a circus." This fundamental lack of contact draws the line between nature and culture on the most severe terms and conditions, rendering human and animal as absolutely separate. While this is clearly a false distinction, and the terms nature and culture demand much closer scrutiny and definition, such an assumed divide provides the opportunity to interrogate the ways in which such an intrinsic difference can be both maintained and reconciled. If Tashlin and Jones, not surprisingly, signal that such a schism leaves humankind all the poorer, and present animals with a greater degree of dignity and resolution, then it becomes clear that the animal/human divide and the nature/culture divide are key thematic aspects of cartoon narratives. Animated films address these apparent divides in a variety of ways. The model in Figure 1.1 shows how these seemingly oppositional tendencies can be engaged with.

It is important to address some of the tensions between perceptions and definitions of animal and human. At its most extreme, on the one hand, this acknowledges the seemingly irreconcilable difference of animals, while on the other, its opposite, the sociocultural assimilation of animals as pets, man's best friends, and quasi-humans. Deleuze and Guattari distinguish three types of animals:

> First, individuated animals, family pets, sentimental oedipal animals each with its own petty history, "my" cat, "my" dog. These animals invite us to regress, draw us in to narcissistic contemplation, and they are the only kind of animal psychoanalysis understands, the better to discover a daddy, a mommy, a little brother behind them (when psychoanalysis talks about animals, animals learn to laugh): *anyone who likes cats or dogs is a fool.* And then there is a second kind: animals with characteristics or

Animal	Human
Irreconcilable "difference"	Assimilation
"The other dimension"	Totemism
Wild systems	Anthropomorphism
Nature	Culture

FIGURE 1.1. The Animal/Human Divide

attributes; genus, classification, or State animals; animals as they are treated in the great divine myths, in such a way as to extract them from series or structures, archetypes or models (Jung is in any event profounder than Freud). Finally, there are more demonic animals, pack or affect animals that form a multiplicity, a becoming, a population, a tale. . . . Or once again, cannot any animal be treated in all three ways? (Deleuze and Guattari 2004, 265)

These definitions represent the view that animals can operate as highly domesticated creatures, endowed with quasi-human qualities and histories, while also being symbolic or metaphoric creatures (which are ahistorical yet tied into a historiography of human evolution and development); and purely abstract creatures (which are wholly "other" in their "lived" experience, and in the ways that they are experienced by humankind). At the representational level, it is clear that art has attempted to embrace all three aspects, and crucially, particularly in relation to the animated film, it has sought to potentially present these formations simultaneously, and mutually exclusively in any one text. Inevitably, the key issues that are raised by animated films emerge from various positions which emerge in between these conceptual polarities and definitions of animals, and have been addressed by a range of writers and critics across disciplines. It is necessary to embrace the broader discourse, then, about the essential sameness/difference in the human/animal divide, and how this has been interpreted, often in a spirit of either maintaining the divide for radicalized political ends, or in collapsing it for the sake of a social convenience. In the same way as Carl Akeley's taxidermy, cited earlier, this hides significant discourses of exploitation or abuse. In evaluating the implications of the human/animal divide it is thus possible to avoid the ultimate Kong Trick of only seeing and accepting the material and ideological split between nature and culture.

Helpful in understanding this further are Erica Fudge's categories in defining notions of animal "history": "intellectual history," "humane history," and "holistic history" (see Fudge 2002, 3–18). The first, "intellectual" history of animals essentially locates them historically as a way of reading human attitudes and formulations; the second, "humane" history of animals addresses their material presence and their use by humans in a social, political, and economic infrastructure; and the third, "holistic" history properly takes into account the status of the animal on its own terms and conditions, in what Fudge notes is a "redrawing of the human" (Fudge 2002, 11). I am attracted, of course, to the ambiguity of the term "redrawing" in Fudge's formulation, as it so literally matches the animation enterprise. Further, "holistic" history allows for the ways in which the representational interpretation of animals draws upon period, context, material existence, and the *essential* relationship with human beings in defining the very identity and outlook of humankind that makes it a purposive model. As Fudge concludes, "By rethinking our past—reading it for the animals as well as the humans—we can begin a process that will only come to fruition when the meaning of 'human' is no longer understood in *opposition* to 'animal'" (Fudge 2002, 16). In engaging with the human/animal divide, and its presence and resolution within a range of disciplines, most specifically within animated film, such a discussion contributes favorably to this historiographic ambition.

The Other Dimension

In many senses, the idea of the irreconcilable difference of animals is outside discourse—essentially it leaves very little to talk about for the animation studies critic, though much to embrace for those engaging with a more objective, scientific study of animals. Strict animal behaviorists and cognitive psychologists effectively share this view, allowing perhaps for a degree of cognition in animals, but refusing the notion of consciousness or complexity in communication. This can create a paralysis of inquiry, but following the lead of cognitive ethologist Donald Griffin, I wish to follow the view that "analysis of behavioral versatility can certainly lead to improved understanding of animal cognition. This cognitive approach to animal behavior can also serve as constructive compensation for the unfortunate tendency of many scientists to belittle nonhuman animals by underestimating the complexity and capabilities of the animals they study" (Griffin 1992, ix). From the point of view of this discussion, therefore, it is quite useful to establish the idea that in any understanding of "otherness" in animals, it has to remain within the remit of interpretation, and throughout this analysis I seek out appropriate links to the study and interpretation of animals that might be enabling, and service the closure of the "oppositional" context that humans and animals are often viewed within.

I partially employ, for example, Griffin's notion of "critical anthropomorphism," which embraces the idea that not all animal behavior is "unconscious." He argues that animals possess a "perceptual consciousness" engaged with memory, anticipation, and sensory prompts; and also, more provocatively, that animals have a "reflective consciousness" signaling awareness of their own actions. Further, he says that animals exchange "rich repertoires of communicative signals" (essentially their own "languages") and that they adapt to novel situations with versatility, physiologically charged "thought," and revelation (see Griffin 1992, 1–27; Burghardt 1997, 254–276). This acknowledges not merely cognition in animals but consciousness, and in doing so allows that levels of mediation may be occurring in animal behavior, which signal their own engagement with the world and, crucially, humankind's relationship to it. Biologist Marc Bekoff uses a "biocentrically anthropomorphic" approach:

> My research and that of others begins with the question, "What is it like to be a specific animal?" So, when I study dogs, for example, I try to be a dog-o-centrist and practice dogmorphism. Thus, when I claim a dog is happy, for example, when playing, I am saying it is dog-joy, and that dog-joy may be different from chimpanzee-joy. . . . As humans studying other animals we cannot totally lose our anthropocentric perspective. But we can try as hard as possible to combine the animals' viewpoints to the ways in which we study, describe, interpret, and explain their behavior. (Bekoff 2007, 74)

Though this begs major questions about the overall function of anthropomorphism—not merely about the overall function of anthropomorphism, which is addressed throughout my discussion, but the fundamental roles verbal, textual, visual, physical, and material "language" plays in determining rational, functional, and social identity—it is not unreasonable to assume that animals may have languages which permit communication in ways that may be parallel to the complexities of human exchange. Griffin and Bekoff's outlook about animal sentience is reflected, for example, in Marcus Bullock's observation on the central issue of choice in the human or animal decision-making process:

> Animals may not choose as we do, and cannot change their lives as we can, but they do choose in their own way. We can watch an animal in a situation where its desire for an attractive morsel of food lures it on, while the risk of exposure to a possible predator holds it back, and perhaps its awareness of us taking in its quandary and a nearby rival also act together to inhibit its decision. These desires and awarenesses manifest themselves in the signs of its attention to each, small motions to direct its senses, listening, looking, sniffing the air, the readiness of its body quivering with contrary eagernesses. Then, out of all this inner response and bodily reaction, it reaches a decision. . . . The difference in our choice remains, because we do have the capacity to recollect and replay the process within larger and larger fields of meaning, but the basis of the moment, filled with the experience of interacting desires, remains a characteristic of life we share with the animal. (Bullock 2002, 116)

This sense of sameness and sharing offers the possibility, then, of interpretation and relationship. Such a relationship is often denied in sustaining the schism between humankind and animals, which Lippit argues was the consequence of Modernity: "Modernity represents a crucial moment in the consolidation of metaphysics during which the superiority of humanity is achieved from the lowest ranks of being . . . [and] as a result, animality ceases to occupy a proper space apart from the humanity that succeeds, appropriates and enframes it" (Lippit 2000, 53). In challenging this entrenchment, by permitting animal "thought," however differentiated or unknown, it allows an analogous position that at least draws humans and animals into a model which promotes enquiry and evaluation. Such a model resists hierarchies and merely sees difference, though inevitably this is complex. Bullock adds,

"In the context of modernity, this returns us to animals as a very powerful source for the meaning of freedom, just as we can imagine that paleolithic cave paintings represented a liberating source of power to their creators. In both cases we understand that this may well not change the world, but it does change us who live in it, and this understanding has a real benefit of giving us pause before we continue the great enterprise of modernism that threatens to destroy the world in the process of changing it" (Bullock 2002, 114). This observation is important in implicitly championing art that empowers humanity by realizing the place of animals and readily engages with their pertinence to modernity and modernism, and which is best expressed through the most intrinsically modernist art, animation. The address of modernity is at the heart of the nature/culture divide, and is essentially played out through the dynamics of the human/animal model in animated film.

The bond between human and animal is a relationship that has challenged and defied many, including, for example, English novelist and essayist D. H. Lawrence, who could be looking at King Kong himself when he describes his response to a chimpanzee:

> If you come to think of it, when you look at the monkey you are looking straight into the other dimension. He's got length and breadth and height all right, and he's in the same universe of Space and Time as you are. But there's another dimension. He's different. There's no rope of evolution linking him to you, like a navel string. No! Between you and him there's a cataclysm and another dimension. It's no good. You can't link him up. Never will. It's the other dimension. (Lawrence 1981, 9)

Compare this once more to Donna Haraway's engagement with Akeley's dioramas in the African Hall in the American Museum of Natural History :

> Each diorama has at least one animal that catches the viewer's gaze and holds it in communion. The animal is vigilant, ready to sound an alarm at the intrusion of man, but ready also to hold forever the gaze of meeting, the moment of truth, the original

encounter. The moment seems fragile, the animals about to disappear, the communion about to break; the Hall threatens to dissolve into the chaos of the Age of man. But it does not. The gaze holds, and the wary animal heals those who look. There is no impediment to this vision, no mediation. The glass front of the diorama forbids the body's entry, but the gaze invites the visual penetration. The animal is frozen in a moment of supreme life, and man is transfixed. No merely living organism could accomplish this act. The specular commerce between man and animal at the interface of two evolutionary ages is completed. (Haraway 2004, 156–157)

Compare this also to the perspective of art critic John Berger:

The eyes of an animal when they consider a man are attentive and wary. The same animal may well look at other species in the same way. He does not reserve a special look for man. But by no other species except man will the animal's look be recognized as familiar. Other animals are held by the look. Man becomes aware of himself returning the look. (Berger 1980, 2–3)

While Lawrence acknowledges the relationship with the monkey, he ultimately cites a dimension of difference that does not enable any real sense of realizing the possible connection between them. His fascination with such "otherness," however, prompts an underlying question of how such an alien creature should be reconciled with humankind as a mutual presence, and as a phenomenon seemingly outside knowledge. Haraway, in contrast, engages with this question immediately, suggesting an implied communion of mutual acknowledgment that comes from "the original encounter," a lost primordial moment of human/animal engagement, here represented not as an adversarial or exploitative encounter but as the embodiment of a pure, unstated, yet unproven bond. Berger confirms this bond in the self-conscious way humankind recognizes itself in the implication of the look it shares with animals. Professor of zoology, geology, and biology Stephen Jay Gould explores this notion further from the perspective of natural historians:

Natural historians have dedicated themselves to the noble and fascinating task of trying to understand, in the deepest way accessible to us, the amazing variety of life on our planet. The best possible procedure immediately runs into Tennyson's limit of proximity with impossibility. I go eyeball to eyeball with some other creature—and I yearn to know the essential quality of it markedly different vitality. I cry to God the gatekeeper of scientific knowability: Give me one minute—just one minute—inside the skin of this creature. Hook me for just sixty seconds to the perceptual and conceptual apparatus of this other being—and then I will know what natural historians have sought through the ages. . . . I am stuck with a panoply of ineluctably indirect methods—some very sophisticated to be sure. I can anatomize, experiment, and infer. I can record realms of data about behaviors and responses. But if I could *be* a beetle or a bacillus for that one precious minute—and live to tell the tale in perfect memory—then I might truly fulfill Darwin's dictum penned into an early notebook containing the first flowering of his evolutionary ideas during the late 1830s: "He who understands baboon would do more towards metaphysics than Locke." (Gould 1998, 376–377)

While it is clear that Gould both acknowledges Lawrence's "other dimension," Haraway's sense of need for an explanatory source of human/animal engagement, and Berger's notion of a shared "gaze," he ultimately seeks out a scientific method that is properly informed by empathetic evidence—an oxymoronic agenda in this case. On the other hand, and fundamental to my argument here, it may be the case that animators have a specific and particular engagement with animals and a special sense of the ways in which animals are used to both represent and relate to the human condition. The particular "gaze" of the animator chimes with the perspective of renowned animal scientist Temple Grandin, who grounds her work in her own experience of autism. She argues:

The reason we've managed to live with animals all these years without noticing many of their special talents is simple: we can't see those talents. Normal people never have the special talents animals have, so normal people don't know what to look for. Normal people can stare straight at an animal doing something brilliant and have no idea what they're seeing. Animal genius is invisible to the naked eye.

And, she adds provocatively,

> Animals are like autistic savants. In fact, I'd go as far as to say that animals might actually *be* autistic savants. . . . Animals can use their amazing ability to *perceive things humans can't perceive, and to remember highly detailed information we can't remember,* to make life better for everyone, animals and people alike. (Grandin 2006, 8 [emphasis in original])

Grandin's claims to this knowledge are based on the idea that her own status as an autistic person, combined with her research in neuroscience and animal behavior, enables her to have direct supra-empathy with the animal, because, like animals, she only thinks in pictures, and like animals, is *only* attuned to the visual environment. The absence of verbal or conscious language means that "autistic people and animals are *seeing* a whole register of the visual world normal people can't or don't" (Grandin 2006, 24). Animators in part share this ability to see a different model of the world, and in literally thinking in pictures demonstrate a greater degree of empathy and understanding of the animal in representational terms. Further, the language of animation may, in turn, provide a point of access for audiences where they have the opportunity to view the animal—and indeed, all other aspects of existence—in a different way accordingly. In other words, some dimension of the "autistic savant" may characterize both the animator and the viewer when the animal is presented through the visual filter of animation. In many respects, the animated animal film is a constant— sometimes highly conscious, oftentimes unconscious—attempt to engage with the world on different terms and conditions, and it is the animal which is the chief vehicle by which this is played out. It remains to explore how.

As early as 1924, this fundamental idea was being addressed—again through humankind's engagement with the ape—in Pat Sullivan and

Otto Messmer's Felix the cat cartoon *Felix Doubles for Darwin* (Otto Messmer, USA, 1924). It is worthwhile remembering, first, at this juncture, the importance of Felix as an animated animal. As Donald Crafton has noted, "The rise of the character series, at the expense of such older forms as lightning sketches, gradually redefined the animated genre as an artificial folkloric tradition. Animals emerged as heroes. Felix was the ruler of this bestiary, and to some extent it was his success that encouraged other animators to develop their own animal heroes" (Crafton 1993, 321). Interestingly, Felix is only nominally a cat, especially given that his upright stance and signature pacing portray him as intrinsically human, but nevertheless, Felix's identity, reinforced by many Felix toys and dolls, became one of domestic familiarity. Felix, inspired by Rudyard Kipling's "The Cat That Walked by Himself," walks a fine representational line between being a thinking, sentient animal, driven by the consistent imperative to find food and survive in a harsh, competitive world, and his status merely as a graphic mark, manipulated to create surreal metamorphoses in the developing narratives. Further, his representational status also becomes indicative of the ways in which a character may be read both as a practice-led paradigm and as a critically led paradigm. At one level, then, in practice, Felix is "black" because of the simple demands of mass production, and the ease of reproducing simple graphic forms and designs, while at another critical level, he may be read as informed by racial tropes, and potentially read as a black character. I retreat to my view, though, that like all other animated characters, Felix works as a phenomena first, and as such operates with a high degree of representational flux even in despite of his dominant form as a cat, and this racial undertow. This may be a particularly important consideration in relation to the film now under discussion, as it is explicit in its depiction of racial stereotypes, but that is to look ahead. First, *Felix Doubles for Darwin* must be read as an animal narrative.

Felix's pursuit of food—"I'd give eight of my lives for a square meal"—leads him to fish for his supper, but in a neat reversal of the cat/fish, hunter/hunted scenario, a shark-like fish casts a line from beneath the waves and hooks Felix. This is but the first reversal of expected animal relationships, and while this is once again about the pursuit of a gag, like the nine lives reference, it acknowledges the folkloric and socially determined ideas about animal relationships. Felix stumbles upon a man reading a newspaper in the company of a monkey, each eyeing the advertisement run by "the Evolution Society," which is offering a reward for anyone who can prove if man comes from apes. Felix signs up to find out, offering to share the reward with the man, and immediately turns his attention to how he might get to South Africa. In true cartoon style, especially of this "modern" period, Felix engages with communications technology and literally passes through the transatlantic cable to his destination. Messmer, always keen to exploit a visual or textual pun, runs the cable under the Atlantic, so that Felix has to do battle with a swordfish. He later literally materializes from the name "Felix" on the telegraph ticker tape and arrives in Cape Town, which in seconds becomes "Ape Town" and the venue for a Charleston Dance Competition contested by some monkeys. This follows a sequence in which Felix is pursued by an ostrich, which becomes trapped in a hollow log—later a ubiquitous prop in many cartoon gags—and expulsion by an elephant with an ever-elongated trunk. Felix finally seeks the answer to the newspaper's question by looking at "the Family Tree," which seemingly offers the "rope of evolution" absent in Lawrence's view of the monkey in its tiered branches. The bottom branch houses a monkey; the one above an "Old Darkie" figure; the one above that, an Aunt Jemina mama doing her washing; and finally, in the top branch, the mother with a cradle full of black children. Clearly drawing upon the caricaturial sources from E. W. Kemble, Currier & Ives, and the Uncle Remus tales (Klein 1993, 191), the cartoon uses humorously intended racial tropes, but, it should be stressed, *not* in a racist way. This is confirmed by the fact that Felix asks the monkey if this "family tree" is related to the newspaper images he shows him of a "modern statesman" and "modern cake-eaters"—Caucasian *humans*—whereupon he laughs, dismissing Felix's question, "Are these your relatives?" with the dismissive rebuttal, "Ye Gods fellers—he says we're related to *these!!!*" A chase ensues back to Felix's home, and when the original man with the newspaper confronts him with the question "Do we come after monkeys?" Felix can truthfully answer, as the monkeys tumble form the cable wire, through Messmer's trademark visual puns, "The monkeys come after us!" Though the cartoon works toward its playful punch line, it is quite explicit in its contempt for modernity in the guise of contemporary white culture. Its position in giving black culture a voice, though mediated through the man/ape divide—and the questionable racial agenda this invokes—uses the animal narrative to play out a social debate in a way that enables a critique of the issues implied in the original question.

Interestingly, this kind of animal narrative, featuring the ape/human relationship, had considerable currency once *King Kong* emerged in 1933 and persists into the present day. Walter Lantz and Bill Nolan made *King Klunk* (Walter Lantz, USA, 1933) for Universal—the first of the major studios to establish a cartoon department in the light of Disney's success—in 1933, featuring Pooch the Pup, playing out the same journey to a prehistoric island, Klunk's love for Pooch's girlfriend, and the return to New York for the Empire State Building finale. Nolan was particularly attuned to topicality, having made the *Newslaffs* series since 1927 (Barrier 1999, 48–49). In Disney's *The Pet Store* (Walt Disney, USA, 1933), it is

Felix Doubles for Darwin directly explores the evolutionary relationship between man and ape, addressing the profound impact of Darwinian thought on popular culture and the modern world.

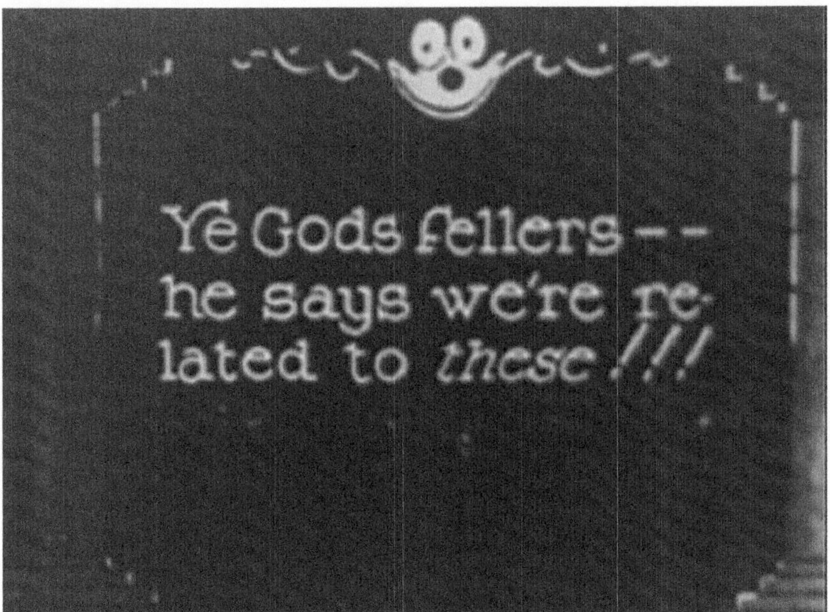

Felix Doubles for Darwin. In a satire on complacent race representation conflating black stereotypes with the representation of apes, and the pomposity of contemporary white politicians, black characters resist their supposed bond with modern white authority.

Minnie Mouse who becomes the object of a giant gorilla's affections, as he climbs atop a number of packing cases in an Empire State–like assent, and like *King Klunk,* prompts consideration of the ease with which animation can facilitate the representation of implied cross-species coupling. Though the 1930s Hollywood cartoon carries with it a high degree of innocence at one level, it should be remembered that though there is a sensitivity toward the notion that children were the main audience for cartoons, these cartoons were made by adults, with a full recognition of the presence of an adult audience in the viewing of cartoons. References to popular culture were inevitably used both to satisfy the writer/director/animator's desire to create narratives and gags and to reach an adult audience. It was they who knew the Kong narrative and, unconsciously, its romantic and sensual tendencies. It is almost certain, though, that such audiences did not make a correspondence between the erotic charge shared by Ann Darrow and King Kong and any vaguely implied sparks in the narrative featuring Minnie and the gorilla.

Contemporary readings—largely those initiated in the first instance by gay and lesbian critics embracing queer cinema and the performance of gender and sexuality in a variety of texts, but most clearly in cartoons that perpetually feature Bugs Bunny in drag—permit a more open interpretation. This allows the images used to carry a range of meanings. Bob Clampett was to use Kong imagery in *I Like Mountain Music* (Bob Clampett, USA, 1933) and *Goofy Groceries* (Bob Clampett, USA, 1940), while the Fleischer Brothers used the Kong template in *Terror on the Midway* (Dave Fleischer, USA, 1941), which features an encounter between Superman and a giant gorilla. This is particularly interesting because unlike the other cartoons that do not really engage with the animal nature of the creatures portrayed, the gorilla's imperative is about escape from a circus that ritually exploits the animals for entertainment, making elephants stand on their hind feet, parade in line, and so forth. As he breaks free from the circus tent, the other animals also break free from their cages, only to be rounded up and tethered by Superman, who later traps the gorilla in a trapeze net, before saving Lois Lane from a falling trapeze pole. Though the ape climbs toward this zenith, the cartoon resists the Kong cliché, and privileges Superman's seemingly humane resolution to the situation, where no animal is actually hurt. The ape here is treated only as "other"; it is not given a personality, merely an intuitive motive to flee the circus. Though in some senses threatening—he starts to pursue a small child, for example—this is not presented as a conscious act of conflict. This is a wild animal seeking escape, not an anthropomorphized adversary.

Though Kong appears in a cameo in *The Yellow Submarine* (George Dunning, UK, 1968), his most interesting appearance in a British cartoon is in Halas and Batchelor's *The Cultured Ape* (Halas & Batchelor, UK, 1960), where the assumed otherness or ignorance of the animal is subverted by making a jungle ape a virtuoso musician, who, like Kong, is captured and brought back to civilization. Ironically, civilization proves too uncouth for the cultured ape who finds his art and ability rejected by three strata of British society—the upper class, who are both jealous and resentful of him; the middle class, who merely prefer his efforts in the background to their chatter; and the working class, who prefer more popular, street music. It is perhaps only the British who could make a film that privileges its satire about class in England, and its view of art—"when the arts go out of fashion the artist must retire and wait"—in such an animal narrative. Though the cartoon is neither used for the purpose of creating gags nor develops a narrative that might engage with the surreal premise of its story to advance a metaphoric view of animals as different and special, it nevertheless uses the difference of the animal to forward a particular point of view. The rather arcane punch line that accompanies the ape's retreat back to the jungle suggests that the arts operate in a cyclic manner, and the distinctiveness of the ape's talents will one day be pertinent. This probably says more about John Halas's view of British art at the beginning of the 1960s than about any more universal or common perspective, and, crucially, it draws attention to the national, social, and cultural context in which animal narratives were made, and so must be addressed throughout. This is an important aspect of this discussion overall.

The Totem Pole

The polar opposite to the "other dimension" is totemism, which seeks to define the primordial relationships between animal and humankind more precisely. Usefully, from the perspective of this discussion, Russian theorist and filmmaker Sergei Eisenstein took up the idea of totemic thought in his unfinished papers discussing the work of the Walt Disney Studio between 1928 and 1941. Eisenstein, a fierce admirer of Disney's early "Silly Symphonies" and the features up until *Bambi,* suggests that "in Disney's works on the whole, animals substitute for people. The tendency is the same: a displacement, an upheaval, a unique protest against the metaphysical immobility of the once-and-forever given. It's interesting that the same kind of 'flight' into animal skin and the humanization of animals is apparently characteristic for many ages, and is especially sharply expressed as a lack of humaneness in systems of social government and philosophy" (Leyda 1988, 33). In this one statement alone, Eisenstein restates the plasmaticness of the animated form in the construction of animal characters, engages with the age-old use of animals in metaphoric guise, and notes that such work functions as a critique of American modernity, a theme common to the Felix cartoon cited earlier. More significant, he starts to consider Disney's "animism" as intrinsically related to the three stages of totemic thought: "The first stage: the unity of man and animal (the evolutionary stage). 'Factual' metempsychosis, and the belief in the migration of souls. The second stage: the unity of man and animal in totemistic belief. The third stage: the comparison of man with animal—the metaphoric series" (Leyda 1988, 49).

This provides a helpful context for viewing animal animation in three different ways—first in the spirit of seeing animal and human as intrinsically the same, bound up in an evolutionary temperament where both are characterized by their primal imperatives and do not operate as consciously segregated or separate creatures. The second model suggests the idea of viewing humankind as the physical, spiritual, and material mimics of animals, drawing upon a primal acknowledgment of animal prowess and power, and sharing what Jungian psychologists would argue is a "psychic identity" or a "mystical participation" (Jung 1964, 45), while the third model suggests a highly conscious, hierarchical interpretation of animals in the specific representation of human traits and mores.

Though Eisenstein's observations are prompted by the aesthetics and constituent tropes of the animal narratives in the "Silly

Symphonies," here I wish to consider a more explicit example of this formulation as it is played out in Disney's much later feature, *Brother Bear* (Aaron Blaise and Robert Walker, USA, 2004). The film works as an example of the interrelationship between the three totemic stages, and its self-consciousness about the representational agendas associated with animals may be seen as a departure from previous conceptions of animal-related narratives in the Disney canon. This is also explored later, but suffice it to say at this juncture that it is clear that the film is explicit in how it deals with the *Madagascar* Problem, namely, the way it approaches the complexity of animal discourse once the narrative moves beyond its readily attributable animal identities and explores a more unknowable terrain. Fundamentally, in this instance, the story defines its animal agenda not merely through the standard anthropomorphized orthodoxies of Disney characters, but through a mythic filter that legitimizes supernatural and psychological renderings of humankind and animals in a way that offers a perspective on both. Simply, instead of using animals to facilitate a narrative that operates as an Aesop-style moral fable tailored to the needs of the (principally) American popular audience, this film becomes a folktale about the relationship between humankind and animals *outside* modernity. It uses a narrative space to authenticate the possibility of what is arguably the paranormal or preternatural. This in turn allows for a more philosophic engagement with the animal politic addressed, and the role of the totemic structure used.

For example, as M. L. Von Franz has suggested of the role of the animal in the totemic model, "the 'inwardness' of each animal reaches far out into the world around it and 'psychifies' time and space. In ways that are still beyond our comprehension, our unconscious is similarly attuned to our surroundings—to our group, to society in general, and beyond these, to the space-time continuum and the whole of nature," adding, "Thus the Great Man of the Naskapi Indians does not merely reveal inner truths; he also gives hints about where and when to hunt. And so from dreams the Naskapi hunter evolves the words and melodies of the magical songs with which he attracts the animals" (Von Franz 1964, 208). Here, humankind and animal operate in the same psychic, psychosomatic, and material space, attuned to the vicissitudes of the relationship. It is this that *Brother Bear* explores. The narrative begins with images of Native American cave paintings, which inevitably recall the famed Lascaux animal tableaux, cited by Walt Disney himself in his *Disneyland* program entitled "The Art of the Animated Drawing" in the 1950s as the first example of humankind seeking to animate animal movement. The paintings, of course, were not only illustrative and were thought to possess magical qualities, and thus to kill an animal by ritually defacing the image was thought to aid the real execution of the creature. At the heart of such belief is the idea of the essential spirit in a living being, and that every man, woman, child, and animal possesses a spirit that can be liberated from corporeal form and exist forever on some universal plane. In *Brother Bear,* a shaman explains that the spirits who appear as lights in the sky are ancestors—both human and animal—who can still influence and affect the living environment, and it is into this conception of the world, where human and animal, body and spirit, living and dead, are omnipresent and eternal, that three Native American brothers are inducted.

Sitka, the eldest brother, and Denahi, the middle sibling, have already been given their totemic symbols to help guide them through life, and it is the youngest brother, Kenai, whose turn it is to begin his rite of passage to adulthood by engaging in the totemic ritual where he must recognize that "to become a man [his] actions must be guided by one thing—love," whereupon he is given the "bear of love" totem. Kenai is initially insulted by being given "a bear"—"they don't think, they don't feel," he argues—and in doing so establishes his intrinsic distance from any understanding of the animal realm. These creatures merely coexist in Kenai's world; they do not have an intrinsic relationship or bond with him in his mind. As an aside, it is worth noting that in such a character depiction, we are a long way from Snow White back in 1937, whose most empathetic and taken-for-granted bond was with her animal confidantes, who were literally her natural allies. Depicting Kenai's antipathy and disdain in this way also makes the first conflict between the brothers and a huge grizzly bear effectively about the primal fears of now familiar humans and the seeming difference, otherness, and threat of a predatory animal. In an extraordinary sequence, Sitka, the eldest brother, perishes; the bear survives; and

Denahi and Kenai are left traumatized, with Kenai throwing away his totem and swearing revenge, and Denahi, though distraught, knowing that "killing that bear is wrong." Sitka ascends to the sky as "the Eagle of Guidance," his spirit to become an important influence on Kenai as the tale unfolds. When Kenai finally enacts his vengeance on the bear, he is engulfed by animal spirits and Sitka presides over the ascent of the dead bear and Kenai's transformation into a small bear. This notion of transformation is entirely authenticated by the folkloric idea of shape-shifting and appears in many ancient tales, but it is also a literal, thematic, narrative, and aesthetic metamorphosis legitimized by the language of animation itself. Kenai literally and metaphorically changes, but this event is acceptable and sustainable not merely because animation enables such easy transition but because the story operates within the mythic infrastructure of the totemic world, and deliberately points up the presence, influence, and correspondent power of the animal within it. This is in many senses the fullest possible representation of "the other dimension."

From this point in the narrative Kenai, in becoming a small bear, sees the world from a bear's point of view, and while sadly this is also a justification for a Phil Collins song called "Look Through My Eyes" (!), it becomes a vehicle by which to challenge all the assumptions about the bear's place both within the animal kingdom and in relation to humankind. When Kenai first realizes he is a bear, for example, he can no longer talk to humans and so he attempts to express himself and communicate with them—as in the real world, of course—through sounds and cries. Only other animals can now hear him speak. Though the film creates this device to make its fundamental point about humankind needing to be more empathetic with animals and the natural order, the narrative thereafter, ironically, slips back into being a typical Disney text where animals talk and appropriate human characteristics. This is not to say that this makes the film any less successful, but in a similar way to *Madagascar,* this allows for a greater degree of irony in the comic construction of the story. When Kenai, for example, seeks to escape from a human trap he, as a bear, has been caught in, he points out to Koda, a young bear cub who is to become his friend and ally and who offers to aid his escape, that "this is a human trap and you're just a dumb little bear." Such irony is employed to more critical and incisive effect later, however, when Kenai and Koda are looking at some cave paintings that depict conflicts between animals and humankind, and Koda plaintively says, "Those monsters are really scary," adding, "especially those with sticks." Even at this juncture, Kenai still retains the idea that it is the bear who is the monster, and he is genuinely shocked by Koda's observation.

Indeed, his true revelation only comes when, in what may be viewed as a further example of critical irony, he is attacked by Denahi, his brother, and seemingly becomes instrumental in his death; ultimately he is forced to conclude that "he tried to kill us." Though the film then lulls the family audience with an interlude in which Kenai joins a family of bears at a salmon run—and Phil Collins once again has a chance to spoil the occasion with the "Family Time" song—this comic revelry, largely at the expense of Kenai's "difference" ("never hibernated, never sharpened his nails on bark"), is a prelude to the moment when he realizes he was responsible for killing Koda's mother in the incident where Sitka died. It is this which prompts Kenai into the key actions in becoming mature, as he knows he must tell Koda, who has long hoped to be reunited with his mother, that this will never happen, even though it will inevitably jeopardize their now strong friendship. Having done this, Kenai—like Alex in *Madagascar*—has "a dark night of the soul," but this is not overcome by any easy or comic resolution. Rather, it is at the heart of the film's implicit messages: first, about comprehending the intrinsic if sometimes deeply contradictory relationship between humankind, animals, and the wider eco-system; and second, concerning how this must be accepted at the material and corporeal level, but understood on more spiritual and philosophic terms.

The film's denouement reinforces this by staging another confrontation between Denahi, who has survived their previous conflict, and Kenai, who on the verge of defeat is saved by Koda. At this point, too, the spirit of Sitka intervenes. Rather than being "the other dimension," animals are reconciled with humankind by their equivalence in the spirit world. Denahi realizes that the bear he is trying to kill is his brother. Kenai, who by now has learned true empathy with animals, tries to make Denahi understand that killing a bear is unnecessary.

Koda is comforted by the spirit of his mother. Sitka—the "Eagle of Guidance"—orchestrates this confluence of the human/animal/spirit world as a moment of transcendent recognition, giving Kenai back his "Bear of Love" totem, prompting him to remain a bear and embrace his fraternal love for Koda. In this "story of a boy who became a man by becoming a bear," the mythic infrastructure has enabled a genuinely surprising ending in the sense that Kenai, in *not* returning to human form, renounces difference and opposition between humankind and animal and accepts the "psychic identity" or "mystical participation" with the animal, here made literal and authentic by the animated form, and achieves a model of assimilation that proves the essential sameness of living creatures in the primal order, now lost to the contemporary world. Phil Collins, once more, sings during the closing credits, but even he cannot undermine (and indeed, might even be further proof of) the idea of a crisis of modernity, where the animated narrative is constantly seeking the retrieval of the animal as part of the essential identity of humankind.

Wild Systems

Patrick D. Murphy has written of the male-centered emphasis of much Disney animation, the inherent sexism that is played out in relation to many Disney heroines, and, further, what he calls the "denial of *wild* nature" in most Disney texts (see Murphy 1995, 125–136). While there is much to address in these views, my interest here lies in Murphy's engagement with Gary Snyder's ecologically derived concept of "wild systems," and his suggestion that "the Disney ethos promotes escapism from the indeterminacy of 'wild systems' through the denial of process and difference" (Murphy 1995, 126). Inevitably, the animal is bound up with these wild systems, though it is peripheral to Murphy's main agenda, and the general premise is to prove (Walt) Disney's texts are inherently, socially, and culturally regressive and ideologically remiss. I have addressed this issue elsewhere (see Wells 2002a, 102–125) and merely wish to note that this perspective essentially casts Disney only as a reactionary conservative and deserves response. Such a view that has been challenged by Thomas Brode in recasting both Walt and his studio as progressive left-leaning liberals (see Brode 2004), but most pertinent here is that the coherence of such a politicized reading fails to take into account that these are *animated* films. One of the intrinsic qualities of animation is its illusionism and its resistance to modes of realism, especially those bound up with notions of documentary truth or social actuality. Critical readings of Disney chastise him and/ or the studio for producing stories that endlessly reprise oppressive acts of sexism, racism, cultural ignorance, and environmental insensitivity, and, perhaps worst of all, for propagating endemically old-fashioned American values. Supposedly, the natural world and the animals that inhabit it are wholly domesticated and service these perspectives.

In *One Hundred and One Dalmations,* for example, "the human female antagonist (Cruella Deville), with no interest in animals except for their fur, is identified more strongly with nonhuman nature—apparently predatory and rapacious—than the couple who care for the dogs. In contrast, the Dalmatians are depicted anthropomorphically, more in line with the civilized cultural norms that Cruella flouts. The animals are most noble when most nearly 'human,' while the human is most ignoble when most nearly 'inhuman'" (Murphy 1995,128). These dichotomies about what is human or nonhuman (implicitly animal) are naive and misrepresentative of the genuine contradiction, ambiguity, and unspeakableness in both the human condition, and that which we know of animals. Inevitably, Disney creates primitive archetypes of good and evil, but this does not mean that an audience does not empathize with both, or indeed, problematize the relationships in ways that embrace the more complex imperatives of the protagonists. What I wish to suggest here is that dichotomies never work in opposition; they only work in oscillation and tension. Consequently, Cruella is both primal and modern; Roger, the owner of the Dalmations, asexual and physically driven; and Pongo and Perdita, the parents of the pups, intuitive and calculating. Further, and in ways I have already stressed in relation to *Madagascar* and *Brother Bear,* the animated form inherently facilitates this flux of meaning and intention. It is this central idea which is at the heart of the critical formulation that I am developing in this discussion.

One might reinforce this view by addressing Murphy's remarks on *The Jungle Book* (Wolfgang Reitherman, USA, 1967). He advises: "One must studiously avoid the incoherence of inconsistent attribution of qualities here to suspend disbelief," railing, "The wolves can protect the boy from every other predator except the tiger? Tigers that do not feel hatred are no threat to humans? Panthers like people and are not threatened by hunters? Wolves, not to mention a North American bear, are major players in the jungles of India?" (Murphy 1995, 130). Simply, *animated* films can sustain the suspension of disbelief in despite of their apparent inconsistencies because of its illusionist and phenomenological status as a text. Audiences are not watching a wildlife documentary; they are viewing an animated fairytale that can play with generic orthodoxies and real world expectations.

Murphy ultimately concludes that *The Jungle Book* narrative "demonstrates a culture/nature split that universalizes all human habitation on the basis of the western alienated model" (1995, 126–130). But surely it is the critical model brought to the film that actually does this and not the text itself, which remains a playful engagement with the relationship between representing the animal and imposing a model of anthropormophism, at one and the same time preserving the wild system while playing out a human assumption about it. The film's essential incoherence in relation to real world orthodoxies and closure actually preserves the wild system—a chaotic, complex, natural order beyond human comprehension—while throwing into relief the methods by which humankind has sought to impose an identity on animals and the natural world. As Steve Baker suggests, "In today's world, animation, animatronics, and animal training (in *102 Dalmations* and elsewhere) help to conjure a spurious 'reality' of animal life and experience, while ordinary human knowledge of even domestic animal life becomes, it seems, more uncertain than ever" (Baker 2001, xvii–xviii). This particular condition, though, need not necessarily be a fixed one—nor indeed its reality be so spurious—and can actually facilitate more pertinent insights about both animals and humankind. Crucially, the outcome of this particular thematic flux, if the film is to be taken at face value, is that humankind must acknowledge difference, because it cannot fully apprehend or represent this alternative world. As Baker has commented, "The idea that animals are metaphorically indispensable to humankind has certain attractions, because it proposes a relation between humans and animals which is not necessarily an exploitative one, nor one which necessarily works by denigrating the animals" (Baker 2001, 81). This is an important factor in viewing animation as an expression of perspectives on animals.

One need only consider *The Jungle Book*'s signature tune, "I Wanna Be Like You," which deals with this irreconcilable notion of "difference," while simultaneously enjoying the assumed commonalities *and* distancing incongruities of a highly ambivalent culture/nature divide. Baloo the Bear's impersonation of an ape is a self-conscious recognition of the superficial tropes of identity, both in humans and animals; King Louis's desire to attain man's "red fire" and "walk like you, talk like you" is actually already being played out through his actions in the animation itself; Mowgli's enculturation in the jungle is about accepting the "Bare Necessities" of the seemingly predestined, natural imperatives of simply *being* an animal in an unconscious way, a sentiment that also chimes with the liberal, countercultural agenda of the late 1960s, of "turning on, tuning in, and dropping out," to become, ironically in this context, more human in some way.

Wild systems in animation are inevitably rendered through the tension between animalization and anthropomorphism. The fight between Shere Khan and Baloo is an exemplar of this, in the same way as the wildebeest stampede or the elephant graveyard works in *The Lion King* (Roger Allers and Rob Minhoff, USA, 1994), among many others. This necessarily leads to the view that a more detailed and inclusive methodology is required to accommodate both this flux of meaning and the previous tensions I have identified in the animal/human, nature/culture dialectic. The animated form almost inherently resists coherence as a textual currency, even if it speaks (particularly in feature-length films) to a conventional narratology. This enables the text to carry with it a diverse phenomenology and potentially subversive agendas, so in this particular case it is important to identify the degrees of animal and anthropomorphic within the discourse operating between and within nature and culture, or, to once again use Haraway's term, the "naturalcultural."

Bestial Ambivalence

The concept I have developed to accommodate this—and to answer the *Madagascar* Problem—is one I am terming "bestial ambivalence," and it is illustrated in the schemata in Figure 1.2. Simply, this schematic seeks to show how the animal is represented in the animated text, but it should be stressed that this operates as a set of oscillations within each text and does not remain static and fixed. This representational flux accommodates a raft of polar extremes: the irreconcilable difference of animals and its opposite, the sociocultural assimilation of animals; D. H. Lawrence's view of the distance between humankind and its animal ancestors—"the other dimension"—and its antithesis, Eisenstein's "totemic" relationships; the "wild systems" of the natural world and their appropriation within anthropomorphized human structures; and ultimately Nature itself and its supposed opposite, Culture. It is a conceptual tool that can be used in relation to specific animal characters or in relation to animal narratives in general. Though the rest of the discussion will use and advance the concept of bestial ambivalence, it is worthwhile offering a couple of short examples here to introduce the terms employed.

To look again at *The Jungle Book,* at the level of an animal character, for instance, one might choose Shere Khan, the tiger. The term "pure animal" is simply concerned with when the animal character is represented *only* through known animal traits and behaviors, previously exemplified in those described by Marcus Bullock earlier. This might also take into account the observations of animal behaviorists,

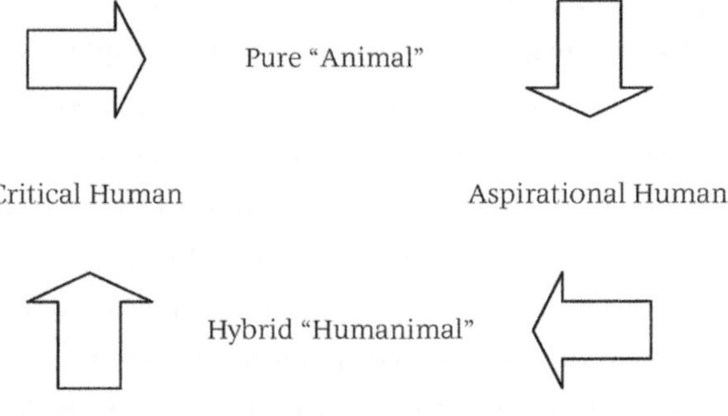

FIGURE 1.2. The Bestial Ambivalence Model

cognitive scientists, biologists, and so on. At the level of pure animal, Shere Khan the tiger stalks a deer and fights a bear for food and territory. In the "aspirational human" context, the tiger's character is used as a tool by which to demonstrate favorable human qualities and heroic motifs, and in this case would be measured by Shere Khan's ability to negotiate, behave with dignity, and exercise control. This is opposed by the "critical human" context in which the animal character is used to critique humankind, and as such Shere Khan's traits in this sense are measured by his more pronounced resentment of humankind's imposition on the natural order and in his aggressive pursuit of Mowgli. The final context—the hybrid "humanimality"—operates at the metaphoric and symbolic level, and seeks to show when a conceptual idea is shared by the parallel terms that have evolved to define and explain both the human and animal world. In this case, there is a parallel in the power and agency a tiger wields within the animal kingdom, and how power and elite culture is recognized in (Western/English) society. For Shere Khan, this is demonstrable in the juxtaposition of being an English aristocrat and holding a position of superiority in the assumed great chain of being within the animal kingdom.

Arguably, of course, this construction of the animal world may be viewed as a spurious invention and misleading, but the power, effect, and threat of the tiger in a range of circumstances is beyond dispute. One need only note the experience of Merian C. Cooper, the director of *King Kong,* on his earlier film *Chang,* when he requested of the villagers of Nan, in the former Siam, that they capture man-eating tigers for exhibition in the film.

> Muang [the villager's translator] had then translated the village chief's response. Man-eating tigers, he'd explained, were a great problem in Nan. They were supernatural creatures, called "spirit-horses" because demonic entities rode upon their backs. Such was the tiger they called "Mr Green," a man-eating beast ridden by a green spirit. The chief pointed to a young man sitting in the outer circle; his father had been killed and dragged into the jungle only a few weeks before. If they dared kill such spirit-possessed tigers, the wrath of the now horseless spirit

would kill and transform *them* into a damned tiger to ride. (Cotta
Vaz 2005, 142)

I quote this at incident at length because not merely does it confirm
the observable power and effect of the tiger, but shows how creatures
in all cultures become metaphorically charged with a range of narratives, identities, and sociocultural symbolism that creates a parallel
world to the literal one. A hungry tiger driven to kill and devour a
human being has become a supernatural, transcendent, yet culturally
integrated force. This parallelism is a hugely important, historically
and socially determined, characteristic of the animal/human interface,
and one readily used in animated film. To once again return to Temple
Grandin's perspective, drawn from the view that the autistic sensibility
may be aligned with animal consciousness, it is important to see that
such parallelism helps to specify the real nature of anthropomorphism
in the sense that she notes that "both the ethologists and the behaviorists were in total agreement that practically the worst thing that anyone
could possibly do was anthropomorphize an animal" (Grandin 2006,
14), but she nevertheless concludes that "it was important to think
about the animal's point of view" (15).

Grandin recounts a story in which a lion was given a pillow for his
additional comfort on a long trip but ended up eating it and dying. While
it is clear that the lion was given the pillow because it was a human
assumption that comfort could be facilitated for the lion by the imposition of something that would give a human comfort, Grandin merely
intervenes to say that by merely seeing this from the animal's point of
view would have prompted the use of leaves and grass for the lion to lie
on and not a pillow. In other words, the parallel assumption that the
lion would embrace more comfort is acceptable, but the way it is acted
upon and ultimately represented is key in the actual understanding of
the animal and its place in the naturalcultural. Looking at life from the
animal's point of view, of course, is not straightforward, but Grandin's
notion that the autistic gaze is one shared by animals, and my own infer-
ence that animators partially share this gaze, legitimizes the view that
anthropomorphism may be seen as a pertinent tool when it represents
an empathetic revelation of the animal's potential perspective or talent.

Any animated animal character is defined by a similar flux of meaning, and this is informed by varying degrees of emphasis and complexity. My argument here is that animation respects the intrinsic difference and otherness of the animal, and while it is self-evident that animators seek out the anthropomorphic relatedness I have described, the very phenomenology that is the condition of animation as a language also insists upon representing the distancing or alien aspects of the animal and nature as well as its familiarity. Thus, this calls into the discourse a range of perspectives that more purposefully discuss the animal or nature, rendering the issues within a radical or challenging light.

This might be immediately explored by looking at a particular animal narrative. The most pertinent in this respect is *Animal Farm* (Halas & Batchelor, UK, 1954), made by the Halas & Batchelor Studio in England, and based on the postwar fable by George Orwell. Joy Batchelor, the Watford-born graphic designer and animator and often unsung partner in the studio, recalled:

> To turn this satire into an animated film was to face the issue of dramatizing an animal story in which the characters must be as seriously portrayed as in a human story. No animal could be sentimentalized for the sake of the box office—the idea behind the story would not permit this. Once this story was selected, a new kind of cartoon film was to be made—a serious cartoon. A style of presentation in sound and image must be evolved to interpret this on the screen, and the essential incidents in the book planned out in dramatic shape and continuity. To effect this analysis, a breakdown chart was prepared, showing all the characters in their various relationships to the plot and to each other. It was obvious that certain animal and human characters, in which the book is naturally prolific (like Mollie, the vain and parasitic white pony), would have to recede into the background or be eliminated altogether, so that the animals and humans most concerned with developing the action and characterizing the clash of interests could be kept in the foreground. (Halas 1976, 77)

For *Animal Farm* to succeed in any way, the animation had to make the animals work successfully as believable characters, and for this to occur, the mode of caricature required was of a more realistic kind, and consequently, recalled the pure animal fully into animal animation for one of the first occasions in animation history. The idea of the pure animal was crucial in making *Animal Farm* a serious narrative that was properly differentiated from the traditional cartoon in which the animal was predominantly funny. As Steve Baker has remarked, many representational forms "seem to call on a common view that almost anything to do with animals is somehow funny, or at least likely to be funny. This funniness in animal representation—a release from the usual constraints of meaning—may range from the endearingly amusing to the surrealistic and bizarre, and it need have nothing whatsoever to do with the idea of an inherently warm-hearted response to the animal" (Baker 2001, 23). At one level, this kind of representation has been highly instrumental in determining alternative perspectives about the human condition, but at another has rendered the animal as an absent or purely abstracted

The animals confront Farmer Jones in the first move to overthrow the human oppressors, who abuse and exploit the farmyard animals—an illustration of one of the key political aspects of Orwell's novella. From Halas & Batchelor's adaptation of George Orwell's *Animal Farm*.

Napoleon caricatures the idioms and gestures of the political leader as the pigs begin their rule of Animal Farm, George Orwell's fable on the events of the Russian Revolution.

entity. It was the intention of Halas and Batchelor to recall the pure animal in order to move away from the discourses prompted by humor.

This was achieved in a number of ways but predominantly involved long nondialogue sequences that merely privileged animal movement, using the kind of empathetic anthropomorphism suggested by Grandin—or to return to Griffin and Burghardt's term, "critical anthropomorphism"—that revealed the "parallel" point of view of the animal. An animal anthem was constructed only from animal sounds. Scenes of brutality where animals kill other animals were included, and others in which primal expression by animals—most notably, Benjamin the Donkey's painful bray at the death of Boxer, the horse—is played out as the purest expression of emotion. It should be stressed that this kind of emotive expression, seen also in moments, for example, when Dumbo the elephant is estranged from his mother in *Dumbo* (Ben Sharpsteen et al., USA, 1941), or a dog whelps in pain as he slowly dies in *Dog* (Suzie Templeton, UK, 2001), are exemplars of genuine mourning and suffering actually experienced by animals. Masson and McCarthy have written: "When non-scientists speak of animal sadness, the most common evidence they give is the behavior of one of a pair when its mate dies, or the behavior of a pet when its owner dies or leaves. This kind of grief receives notice and respect, yet there are many other griefs that pass un-remarked—the cow separated from its calf or the dog deliberately abandoned. These are all the griefs humans never see: unheard cries in the forest, herds in the remote hills whose losses are unknown" (Masson and McCarthy 2007, 92).

These particular emotions are recognized and illustrated in animated films, however. Once again, of *Animal Farm*, the critic for *Cine Technician* stressed, "The theme is far from Disney, and the cruelties that occur from time to time are more realistic and shocking than any of the famous sadisms that have occurred in Disney films. The business of Napoleon bringing up puppies to be his own pack of killer dogs, the liquidators of those who oppose him is, for instance, bloodcurdling stuff. And the carting away of poor old Boxer is unrelieved agony" (Anon. 1955, 7). It should be stressed, too, that when Napoleon asks the animals to consider their future, they only have visions of a hurtling butcher's block and hanging carcasses in an abattoir; an image far from the Disney vocabulary. Crucially, though, the same critic identifies an important point when he notes, "The shock of straight and raw political satire is made more grotesque in the medium of the cartoon. The incongruities of recognizable horrors of some political realities of our times are emphasized and made more startling by the apparent innocence of the surrounding frame" (Anon. 1955, 7). Halas and Batchelor recognized that they were using the specific language of animation in a way that differed from the dominant model in the United States, and directing audiences to consider both how animation functioned as a vehicle for metaphysical enquiry and how animals lived and suffered—an ongoing preoccupation of Orwell himself. Batchelor noted "the scene with Benjamin and Boxer, where Boxer was hurt was also a very difficult one, because it was terribly emotional and [we] had only drawings to go by, no help from living actors. It had to be very carefully handled to avoid slipping over from tragedy to tragic-comedy" (Jenkins 1955, 70). Significantly, though, this was important not only because of the need to authenticate the narrative, but to enhance the seriousness of the message within the broader context of the Cold War. Like Orwell's original work, written in 1946, the film was exploited for a wider political need. It is on this issue that the film needs further address, just as it is in this respect that the concepts of aspirational human, critical human, and humanimality within the schemata of bestial ambivalence provide significant insights.

Halas and Batchelor made *The Shoemaker and the Hatter* (Halas & Batchelor, UK, 1949) to explain the Marshall Plan in 1949. Its writer,

Philip Stapp, had connections in the United States, and knew Louis De Rochemont, the producer of the "March of Time" newsreels at Paramount, from their shared time in the navy. De Rochemont ultimately produced *Animal Farm,* and it remains a strong likelihood that the film was actually funded by the CIA, which sought to make peacetime propaganda in the guise of entertainment to support the ideological currencies of Cold War politics. As Karl Cohen has written, "The CIA's Office of Policy Co-ordination, which directed covert government operations, had two members of the Psychological Warfare Workshop staff obtain the screen rights to the novel. . . . Mrs [Sonia] Orwell signed after [the CIA] agreed to arrange for her to meet her hero, Clark Gable" (Cohen 2003, 8). Through the highly regarded De Rochemont, those behind the production could approach a British animation company that would work much more cheaply than their American counterparts and without the complications of engaging with an increasingly politically active and allegedly left-wing animation industry in the United States. Though Halas and Batchelor had already considered making *Animal Farm* and begun preparatory treatments, it was the American funding, with its correspondent creative interventions, that ensured the project's completion, even though it went through some nine versions. The final film plays out a range of discourses, relating to Orwell's source material, Halas's own ideological convictions, and the American agenda. The aspirational human use of the animal implicitly extols the benefits of democracy, notions of dignity and mutual respect, the value of hard work and intellectual endeavor, and ultimately the sense of an English pastoral idyll, a highly specific and quasi-mythic version of the naturalcultural. The critical human perspective, at the political level, is particularly concerned with a rejection of the brutalities and exploitation of totalitarian regimes, as well as with debates about the treatment of animals and animal welfare. Finally, the humanimality in the film finds a direct parallel between the hierarchical construction of animals in the domesticated farmyard context and the political hierarchies inherent in the forms of government in revolutionary Russia—Orwell's original metaphor. The most controversial aspect was the change from Orwell's original ending; the film merely shows the continuing corruption of the pigs and the resolution of the animals in mounting another revolt. Though Halas always claimed that this was to create a more universal, humanitarian fable with an antitotalitarian position, enabling the audience to take some degree of relief and reassurance from the film, such an ending obviously suited CIA anticommunist objectives.

As Raymond Williams has remarked,

> In *Animal Farm* [Orwell's] strong and liberating intelligence transforms a bitter perception into an active and stimulating critique. Beyond the details of the local analogy, and paradoxically beyond the more fundamental despair, this lively awareness connects and informs. Even the last sad scene where the excluded animals look from man to pig and pig to man and cannot tell which is which, carries a feeling that is more than disillusion and defeat. Seeing that they are the same because they act the same, never mind the labels and formalities: that is a moment of gained consciousness, a potentially liberating discovery. In its small scale and within its limited terms, *Animal Farm* has a radical energy which goes far beyond its occasion and has its own kind of permanence. (Williams 1984, 74)

Halas and Batchelor's film does not merely offer a moment of "gained consciousness" about political agendas, but the intrinsic relationships between humankind and animal within the naturalcultural context I have argued is the determinant arena by which the continuities, contradictions, and contrasts of the animal (human and nonhuman) are revealed within modernity.

The strategic model of analysis I have constructed—bestial ambivalence—seeks to expose these ideas and issues while at the same time privileging the particularity of animation as a mode of expression that is especially pertinent in demonstrating and illustrating such core themes and principles. The model is both explicitly and implicitly employed throughout the rest of my discussion, and the following chapters seek to build upon its infrastructure by, in the first instance, showing how the animal story has evolved into the animated animal narrative; further, how animation has embraced a complex version of anthropomorphism; thereafter how it has determined its own philosophic, performative, and political stances and outlooks.

2

Of Mice and Men

What Do Animals Mean?

Lascaux and Beyond

The animal story has a rich tradition in art and literature. Animated film has embraced this tradition in a number of ways, both adapting narrative elements and design idioms. The animal story has proved attractive to animators and animation storytellers because it inevitably works as part of a surreal, supernatural, or revisionist reinvention of human experience, but perhaps even more importantly has reflected the ways in which social and cultural intervention in relation to animals has evolved and developed historically.

Describing what he argues are the special conditions by which animal painting evolved in England, for example, Basil Taylor notes:

These two hundred years [1750–1950] saw, besides the continuation of many existing sports, the emergence of fox-hunting and racing and, consequently, the systematic breeding of the thoroughbred, the hunter and the foxhound. They saw the foundation of modern biological and zoological study, the true beginnings of comparative anatomy and the scientific improvement of farm livestock in all its varieties. They saw a new enthusiasm for country life and an entirely new attitude to the animal creation in general. In no other country were conditions so appropriate for a school of animal painters and nowhere else were the demands met by such a vast and popular output. (Taylor 1955, 12)

This brief description alone demonstrates how creative expression and aesthetic outlooks became bound up with advances—though this might be a questionable term in some cases—in the engagement and development of animal cultures. Indeed, it might be argued that these become the very terms and conditions by which the naturalcultural emerged, essentially through the evolution of visual and textual narratives across converging disciplines, which defined the animal in the public imagination.

This, of course, all becomes part of Erica Fudge's holistic conception of animal history and crucially points up that "animals are present in most Western cultures for practical use, and it is in use—in the material relation with the animal—that representations must be grounded" (Fudge 2002, 7). In addressing the uses to which animals have been put and, significantly, how animal representation has functioned, Fudge believes that this properly enables the fullest recognition of the issues at stake in using and depicting animal forms and locates animals as sites of social inquiry and change. She suggests, "If it is to impact upon questions about the ways in which we treat animals today, if it is to add to debates about factory farming, cruel sports, fur farms, vivisection, and the numerous other abuses of animals in our cultures, then the history of animals cannot just tell us what has been, what humans thought in the past; it must intervene, make us think again about our past and, most importantly, about ourselves" (Fudge 2002, 15). Animated film has been a distinctive part of animal history by virtue of its consistent and enduring representation of animals in the modern era, and while some of its social and cultural relevance at the political level has been in many ways overlooked, it has nevertheless operated in the ways that I have already suggested as a sometimes reflective, sometimes literal, sometimes subversive intervention both in arts and animal cultures.

In an appealingly alliterative way, Desmond Morris has suggested a typology of ways in which humankind has defined animals, and the ways he believes they have been treated and used. He notes, "[Humankind] has viewed other species of animals in many lights. He has looked upon them as predators, prey, pests, partners and pets. He has exploited them economically, studied them scientifically, appreciated them aesthetically and exaggerated them symbolically. Above all, [humankind] has competed with them for living space, dominated them, and all too often exterminated them" (Morris 1977, 260). This brief overview usefully delineates a range of contexts in which implied real-world narratives become the stimuli for fictional treatment and/or visualization. It is easy to see potential dramatic conflict in the tensions between predatory beasts and those they prey upon, the impact of pests or vermin on the urban environment, the functional imperatives of animals in the service of humankind, and the seemingly emotional bonds played out with pets in the domestic arena. It is not hard to imagine, either, stories that engage with animal labor, interrogate animal form and physique, advance lyrical notions of animal beauty, or view the animal as an ideologically and philosophically charged sign. Arguably, these perspectives create a field map of animal themes which suggest that humankind in its reconciliation with the animal world—though some would argue this is violation—is recovering tacit knowledge that has become embedded in the natural order and moved beyond easy articulation or reclamation. Animal narratives in art, literature, and ultimately animation, then, represent a struggle to suggest and reengage with lost perspectives and primal knowledge. I address how the anthropomorphic instinct feeds into this in Chapter 3, but in this part of the discussion I wish merely to articulate some of the agendas that have characterized artistic and literary representations of animals in a spirit of defining core narratives, themes, and concepts that have been explored in animated film. I then seek to further advance the view that animation offers a particularly pertinent language by which a distinctive interrogation of the leading issues is possible.

To reiterate, Sergei Eisenstein remarked, "It's interesting that the same kind of 'flight' into an animal skin and the humanization of animals is apparently characteristic for many ages, and is especially sharply expressed as a lack of humaneness in systems of social government or philosophy" (Leyda 1988, 33). Eisenstein recognized that the animal story has played a particularly significant role in liberating humankind from its inhibitions and limitations in specific historically determined moments. He suggested that this also characterized a recognition of a lack of humanity in certain social systems or cultural outlooks. It might be argued that this also signals a desire to recover some notion of humanity through its intrinsic if sometimes problematic relationship to animals. Further, this represents the recovery of a deeper, less acknowledged regime of human/animal contact, in which a mutually exclusive bond and a locally defined call and response of necessity, need, and proximity, was consistently respected.

Archaeologist Steven Mithen has argued that "the earliest members of our genus were not great hunters of wild beasts, but largely sneaky scavengers, creeping in after the lions, hyenas and vultures had had their fill" (Mithen 2007, 120), noting, too, that even with the development of Neanderthal society, "it also appears that Neanderthals did not develop any relationships with animals beyond those of the predator/prey as had characterized human ancestors for the previous million years. There are no pictorial depiction of animals, no evidence that animals were used as symbols of power and authority, no trace of totemic thinking" (Mithen 2007, 120). While the Neanderthal was clearly a social creature with some technical and geographical intelligence, this was not yet predicated upon producing effective hunting technologies or blessed with any ready aesthetic leanings. In many senses, it was only when humankind was able to interact with animals more effectively at a number of levels that it was able to cultivate a more progressive model of intelligence. Early human cultures ultimately effected such a change as little as 100,000 years ago, when the first evidence of animal body parts being buried with human beings emerges, and seemingly, some notion of ritualistic or symbolic significance was bestowed upon the animal. The most persuasive evidence of this new relationship only really came about, however, when the first representational art was made by humankind, merely 30,000 years ago. Again Mithen offers a perspective: "Bison, horse and deer dominate this art, often painted in magnificent panoramas such as those on Altimira ceiling or in the caves at Lascaux or Chauvet. Dangerous animals were also depicted such as lions and hyenas, as were fish, birds and even on one occasion an insect. The quality of these paintings is astounding. They often demonstrate substantial technical skill and have considerable emotive power. The latter is especially the case when the paintings are seen by the light of a flickering candle within the otherwise dark and cold cave"

(Mithen 2007, 123). It is not a great imaginative leap to see within this scenario the first inklings of animated film as the light offers an illusion of the primary locomotion of the animal, now acknowledged by humankind as its co-partner in sharing the earth. Such work also suggests an implied interrogation of what part might be played by the animal in the evolving primitive cultures of human endeavor.

Walt Disney saw the cave paintings at Lascaux as a representation of the very beginnings of the animated form, in their attempted depiction of animal motion through the illustration of multiple crossing legs of running animals, and in the ways the paintings depict the day-to-day, naturalized encounters between humankind and beasts. Beyond the aesthetic and potentially social achievement of the paintings, though, there is clearly the possibility that the paintings themselves were a way in which humankind sought to record and preserve the ice age, and speak to its magical, mythical, and primal space. These everyday narratives and their socio-symbolic meanings were essentially lost with the complex developments of evolutionary change and the creation of social infrastructures. These changes, which alienated humanity from its place within the natural order and the intuitive understanding of animals, ultimately rendered animals as entities, which were only redefined by the physical, sensory, and intellectual vocabularies of modern human beings. So estranged had humankind become from the animal by the early twentieth century that the animal could only be reengaged as an objective "other" defined by technical means and a surviving unconscious imperative to reinstate some model of relationship. This became one of the most significant functions of the evolving practice of early cinema. For example, as Lippit argues, "What is remarkable in Muybridge's work, what immediately seizes the viewers attention, is the relentless and obsessive manner in which the themes of animal and motion are brought into contact—as if the figure of the animal had always been destined to serve as a symbol of movement itself" (Lippit 2000, 185).

Metamorphosis and Modernism

From the perspective of the development of the animated film, it is clear that the animal is the embodiment not merely of motion itself as the core characteristic of animation practice, but the carrier of notions of movement as the signifier of social change. Animated animals very quickly became an alternative iconography that challenged orthodox modes of representation within the confused unfolding of modern cultural life. The centrality of metamorphosis as one of the distinctive aspects of the unique vocabulary of animation itself was intrinsic to the ways in which change and evolution could be concisely represented and illustrated. This defined the animated film within the modern world as a key but largely unacknowledged model of modernist expression. But it is a form that drew readily on the mythic, surreal, and sometimes brutal excursions of the fairytale and animal literature to facilitate fluid, unusual, complex narratives that represented the new psychology of the modern age. Crucially, this meant that animation could embrace radical perspectives and challenge reactionary views of the animal by using storytelling forms, like the fairytale, that had essentially achieved this in previous occasions. As Marina Warner has noted, "Descartes had argued that animals had no souls, and in consequence no consciousness, but were like machines. Perrault vigorously defended animals' powers of imaginative understanding by quoting Isaiah's messianic prophecy (Isa 1:3) 'the ox knoweth his owner, and the ass his master's crib'" (Warner 1994, 146). Perrault, with other storytellers like the Brothers Grimm or Hans Christian Andersen, recognized the power and affect of using animal consciousness as a presiding language of challenging social orthodoxies or as a way of accessing more complex, contradictory, or unspeakable acts of human agency. As Warner again suggests,

> Fairytales feel out the rules: the forbidden door opens onto terra nova where different rules may apply. . . . Since the first medieval romances, with their fairies and monsters, the unreal settings and impossible situations have made possible the exploration of sexual experience and sexual fantasy. One of the chief tropes by which approaches to this forbidden territory are negotiated by animal metamorphosis: confronting or defining the outlawed and alien literally affects the figures in the stories; the beastly or less than human becomes an index of alienation, and often one's own otherness. (Warner 1994, 415–416)

Animal metamorphosis has been a crucial element of the animated film, and when not occurring as a radical motion itself—the transition of humankind to beetle in Caroline Leaf's *The Metamorphosis of Mr. Samsa* (Caroline Leaf, Canada, 1977), for example, or the process by which the Beast becomes a Prince again in Disney's *Beauty and the Beast* (Kirk Wise and Gary Trousdale, USA, 1989)—it occurs in a way that privileges cross-species engagement, cross-dressing, gender-shifting, and the performance of identity as a method by which unreal settings and impossible situations may be used as a vehicle to play with contemporary issues. These include interrogations of sex and sexuality, social status, notions of difference, and in the revelation of a more primal index of animality shared by humankind and animals. As Bugs Bunny becomes "Brunhilde" in *What's Opera, Doc?* (Chuck Jones, USA, 1957), he is simultaneously a cross-dressing rabbit, a parody of the tragic heroine, a Germanic girl, and a vehicle by which the orthodoxies of both cartoon and operatic narratives are subverted. Bugs is deliberately sexualized here and performs particular gendered tropes that leave the nature of his sexual identity in flux, oscillating between an over-determined masculinity, self-conscious drag-queen bravura, camp innuendo, and stereotypical extremes of feminine submission and desire.

The key question in this context becomes how the status of the animal affects this identity. Kevin Sandler has suggested that "gender imitation in animal characters does not copy that which is prior in humans since gender is already a fiction; it copies what is already assumed to exist in humans. Anthropomorphism can be viewed, then, as an imitation of an imitation of an imitation, a copy of a copy of a copy. By repeating this imitation, the animators create the illusion of a talking gendered animal while reproducing the illusion of gender itself. Anthropomorphism reiterates the schema of gendered bodies as fact, not fiction, by its imitative nature" (Sandler 1998, 159). This model essentially comments upon the way in which all animated characters become phenomenological creations, predicated on the flux of meaning caused by the relativity of representational possibility. Gender is not a fiction; it is a range of fictions with various degrees of social and cultural validity, embraced as a conviction and a reality in everyday experience. To suggest all is imitation is to evacuate animated forms of meaning altogether; further, in this case, and as I will discuss in the next chapter, animators do not merely imitate but interpret, and moreover, engage with the nature of the animal within this flux of meaning as well as using the core traits and tropes of gendered performance and identity. The animal is not absented through the imposition of these elements, and in some senses is foregrounded at moments when the primacy of the pure animal is required. Indeed, sometimes the notion of sexuality or gender is reinforced by an implied notion of animality, though this can imply that sex and sexuality is bound up with intuitive, instinctive, unconscious, transcendent practices, and operates beyond the aegis of performed identity. Key here is the idea that if gender is placed in flux by the animated form, it is further problematized by the shifting terms of bestial ambivalence, especially when a particular narrative seeks to play out a tension between animal culture and the shifting parameters of sexual desire and personal status. This occurs in Moscow-born Ladislaw Starewicz's *The Cameraman's Revenge* (Ladislaw Starewicz, Russia, 1911).

Starewicz's childhood interest in entomology was satisfied in adult life when he became director of the Natural History Museum in Kovno, Lithuania, and reflected in two early stop-motion animated shorts he made featuring animated insects, *The Grasshopper and the Ant* (Ladislaw Starewicz, Russia, 1911) and *The Cameraman's Revenge*. Starewicz originally made natural history shorts to explore aspects of insect behavior, but insects inevitably died under hot studio lights and so he turned to animated models. Such was the persuasiveness of Starewicz's animation, however, and the heightened paranoia in the West about the capabilities of creative and technical practitioners from Eastern Europe, that *The Times* reported that the insects were alive and trained by Russian scientists. Influenced by ballet master and stop-motion practitioner Alexander Shiriaev, who may have made the earliest Russian animated films between 1904 and 1908, and by *The Animated Matches* (Emile Cohl, France, 1908), a pioneering film by French auteur, Emile Cohl, Starewicz joined up with the Khanzonkow Film Production Company in 1911. Specializing in three-dimensional work, he combined the qualities of a fascination with the new cinematic apparatus and the idioms of the European folktale. Starewicz's use of insects gives the material a Kafkaesque tone, playing on the seeming otherness of insect forms to allude to human perversity and untrammelled desire. He saw in insects and animals characteristics that could be projected onto humankind, in a reverse practice of anthropomorphism that I address in my concluding chapter as ultimately an important characteristic of the animated animal film per se. *The Cameraman's Revenge* uses the perception of the insect and its seemingly alien characteristics as a signifier of inhuman properties, here existing in an unsentimental world characterized by the brutal indifference and claustrophobia of a surreal fairytale. Sal sends a Fly to spy on Bill, her husband, who is recorded on camera with his mistress. Sal also enjoys an affair with Clarence, a flamboyant artist. But Bill discovers Sal's dalliance, breaking a portrait by Clarence over her head. He too is undone, however, when the Fly, also a cinema projectionist, shows the film of Bill's betrayal to a public audience. A melodramatic masterpiece of love and deception, the film is considerably enhanced by its cinematic reflexivity, readily acknowledging the voyeuristic and intrusive capabilities of film itself.

Starewicz's influence can also be found in animated insects from Jiminy Cricket in Disney's *Pinocchio* (Hamilton Luske, Ben Sharpsteen, USA, 1940), the Fleischer brothers' *Mr. Bug Goes to Town* (Max Fleischer, USA, 1941), Lotte Reiniger's *The Grasshopper and the Ant* (Lotte Reiniger, Germany, 1954), Pixar's *A Bug's Life* (John Lasseter, USA, 1997), and *Pokemon* (Satoshi Tajiri, Japan, 1999–present), the latter coincidentally also inspired by creator Satoshi Tajiri's love of insects. Though the insect seems potentially different from the animal, the conditions played out through animation often render them similar, but tend to use the essential exoskeletal nature of many insects to pronounce a greater degree of difference or otherness in key characters, the idea that insects can be mobilized in greater numbers, or the notion that insects suffer from the greater challenges of scale and human indifference. In many ways, the insect represents a transitional phase between the human and the animal, a seemingly alien identity predicated on singularly pure states of existence, part-imperative, part-instinct, part-unknown abstraction, a state most powerfully captured and explored in *The Metamorphosis of Mr. Samsa* (Caroline Leaf, Canada, 1977). Caroline Leaf's perspective begins to suggest some core issues that are explored throughout my discussion, most notably the status and purpose of the animal, the particular investment by the animator in producing a specific outcome using the language of animation, and the overall relationship between humankind and animal in discovering afresh felt states of insight and emotional penetration. Leaf recalls:

> [*The Metamorphosis of Mr. Samsa*] was made at the same time as *The Street* and was made over a period of years, because I actually started it before I left Boston. I liked the Kafka story for its themes, particularly the issue about "appearance" and the idea that the interior state may be very different from what you see on the outside, which in this instance is a very tragic circumstance to be in. I liked the movement from the humane to the monstrous, and I liked the idea of metamorphosis, but narrative was my preoccupation. I felt that I was in some ways limited because in the novel there was so much more about the tension between the human and the consciousness of the beetle that I didn't get because I wasn't using language. On the other hand, the use of animation meant I could suggest other things, though, and the most important thing became the expression of "feeling" through story, and ultimately, how the film looks to achieve that. When I'm actually animating it becomes a visual problem frame by frame, and I almost forget what the narrative is about, yet at the same time I can say that I keep quite strictly to an overall narrative line—a controlling idea—that I have set myself to explore. I try not to vary too much because sometime an image looks interesting in itself, and I want to pull it this way and that, but I prevent myself because the character as I have expressed it visually might breakdown. I'd like an audience to be touched, to have sympathy and identification, and I try not to distract myself by being too self-conscious about having a point of view, and rather to create emotion through imagery. (quoted in Wells 2002a, 107–108)

Leaf's level of investment is important here as it signifies a particular empathy with not merely the subject, but the visualization of interior states apposite to and related within human and animal kind.

Her success in finding imagery that alludes to states of consciousness in living creatures is achieved by a certain ambiguity in the frame, half suggesting that what is being seen is being perceived by the animal or that the experience itself is uncertainly interrogated and represented as such. The relationship between the animator, the animal, and the animated image is explored further in the next chapter, but it is important to consider here that the movement Leaf describes as the shift from the humane to the monstrous is not the literal movement from human to animal, but the transition from a level of conscious control and understanding to one of pure alienation. This draws attention, however, to the possibility of animal consciousness, and its sheer difference from what is an intrinsically dissociated human world. As in the Kafka story, Leaf ultimately shows the disengagement of humanity through the living disembodiment of the creature. Humanity is merely reflected through the animal. The literal, metaphorical, and material notion of change is at the heart of this, and such metamorphoses become a literal representation of the condition of modern experience.

It is clear, too, that this principle condition of animation as metamorphosis—the ability for forms to transmute from one state to another—also enables it to demonstrate and illustrate simultaneously the oscillations and tensions I have explored between the other dimension and totemism, wild systems and anthropomorphism, and ultimately nature and culture in literally defining the naturalcultural. As Louise Krasniewicz has recognized, "These tales of metamorphosis are about power struggles, initiations, creation and re-birth, sex, love and war; in each case, transformation provides a way to connect separate worlds or states of being, to cross boundaries of space, time, and existence. Indeed, the depiction of humans who change into animals, animals who shape-shift into each other, or inanimate objects that morph into live ones are as old as human culture itself; some of the earliest human art, in the form of cave paintings that are thirty thousand years old, show man-beast combinations that suggest a metamorphosis in progress" (Krasniewicz 2000, 43).

Crucially, metamorphosis becomes the intrinsic condition of the concept of bestial ambivalence. At a more literal level, it also formally defines the states of pure animal in the guise of the *theriomorphic* image, and the hybrid humanimal in the *therianthropic* state. As Baker has pointed out, "A theriomorphic image would be one in which someone or something (in the words of the OED definition) was presented as 'having the form of a beast.' Therianthropic images, in contrast, would be those 'combining the form of a beast with that of a man.' . . . Where animal imagery is used to make statements about human identity, metonymic representations of selfhood will typically take theriomorphic form, whereas metaphoric representations of otherness will typically take therianthropic form" (Baker 2001, 108). Though these aspects of representation are quite common, they are not entirely proven in the case of animated film. The theriomorphic image in animation can wholly preserve the nature of the beast—the pure animal—while still invoking human characteristics, and the therianthropic image can be a conventional representation in animation, largely through the ways the design and execution of a character occurs. These constructions can be highly persuasive, though, when used as conscious devices, and a deliberate strategy in calling attention to the relatedness of seemingly separate social, cultural, personal, or phenomenological aspects of existence.

Wendy Tilby, co-creator of *When the Day Breaks* (Wendy Tilby and Amanda Forbes, Canada, 1999), which features therianthropic figures, suggests, "We are not merely a collection of physical parts such as limbs, cells and synapses, for it is our thoughts, our memories, our mothers—even our groceries—which truly define us. Our bodies are made up of bones and vessels and electrical currents like the buildings and pipes and wires which compose cities. But as with organisms, a city is not defined by its infrastructure but by its inhabitants or its 'life.' I was inspired in part by Socrates, who took for granted a kind of anatomical connection between individuals and their society—that our community is to each of us like a shared arm" (quoted in Pilling 2001, 58). This holistic approach, using an intrinsic interconnectedness in the physical and material aspects of existence, nevertheless required that the naturalized conditions of this everyday experience be in some way made strange without breaching the bonds implicit in the lived environment by making the world too surreal. Tilby and Forbes reconcile this by using the animal as the vehicle by which the ordinary is redefined and redetermined, while at the same time maintaining the relatedness and, indeed, the inherent life that the film wishes to reveal anew. Karen Mazurkewich notes how this was achieved:

> The two-photocopied and re-drawn protagonists actually take on animal form—the man's head becomes chicken-like, and Ruby's head resembles a pig. It's an eerie combination of human and animal. Tilby and Forbes have successfully straddled the gender issue, by turning their female into a pig. They found it difficult to design an interesting youthful character without adding prominent sex characteristics such as eyelashes or breasts. "It's hard to get just a person," says Tilby. . . . The women in earlier designs looked miserable. Tilby and Forbes found it difficult to shape a whole personality. So instead they turned their character into a pig to give it a little "joie de vivre." (Mazurkewich 1999, 194–195)

A chicken—a highly significant animal of seemingly pure abstraction in the animated bestiary, an idea I address in the next chapter—begins the day eating toast and planning a shopping trip to buy everyday items like fish, lemons, soup, and biscuits. Elsewhere, a pig peels potatoes and throws away some milk that has gone sour. The pig and the chicken bump into each other on the street before the chicken is knocked down by a car; his purchases roll across the road, and a lemon falls down a drain. Again Tilby notes, "That the characters were strangers was important . . . so I had them physically collide just prior to the accident to establish this and also to implicate the protagonist [the pig] in his [the chicken's] demise. Cause and effect. It suggests she might feel guilty for bumping into him, delaying, rattling or distracting him. A key image at this point was a life (physical and intangible) strewn out on the road—groceries, hat, glasses, bones, cells, teeth, family, memories, experiences. Another was of the lemon falling into the sewer grate, hinting at things lost, of infrastructure, of a hidden world beneath the street" (quoted in Pilling 2001, 59). A dog scavenges food while the pig rushes back to her apartment and makes tea, desperate to bring the world back to order. The therianthropic identity of the characters draws attention to the ways in which physical difference and separateness is negated and overcome by implicit psychological and emotional ties. This can be seen as a comforting connection or a confirmation of alienation, but is clearly a felt experience predicated on a sense of continuum from birth until death, cradle to grave, spirit to flesh. Though the film shows a cow doing the ironing, a dog on the phone, a goat shaving its beard, and animals traveling on the train, this seems as pertinent as the exposé of the city wiring, drains, light filaments, telegraph wires, and the lemon in the drain, simply because the animation has encouraged an understanding that everything is linked, bound by unseen energies, life forces, and primal bonds that vindicate the vicissitudes of life. At one and the same time, life seems fragile yet enduring, past yet perpetually present, conscious yet based on animality. To know the subterranean, the dark, the unknown, is to confirm the orthodox, the light, and the known as things to believe in. Here, the animal is the very lifeblood of existence. The chicken's soul departs; the pig's habitual ways continue; connected or disconnected the day breaks, passes, concludes; the world carries on.

The playful tensions between the theriomorphic and the therianthropic are further evidence of the way in which metamorphosis facilitates the terms and conditions of bestial ambivalence, and as I have suggested throughout, preserves a view that complex conditions of potentially radical representation are occurring even within texts one might otherwise have viewed as conservative or explicitly misrepresenting the natural order. Metamorphosis operates as a key lingua franca of this revelation. Of Disney's *Beauty and the Beast*, for example, Warner suggests,

> The new Disney Beast's nearest ancestor is the Minotaur, the hybrid offspring of Phaedra and the bull, and an ancient nightmare of perverted lust, and it is significant that Picasso adopted the Minotaur as his alter ego, as the embodiment of priapism, in the vigor of youth as well as the impotence of old age. But the real animal which the Disney Beast most resembles is the American Buffalo, and this tightens the Beast's connections to current perceptions of natural good—for the American Buffalo, like the

grizzly, represents the lost innocence of the plains before man
came to plunder. So the celluloid Beast's beastliness thrusts in
two contradictory directions; though he is condemned for his
"animal" rages, he also epitomizes the primordial virtues of the
wild. (Warner 1994, 315)

Recalling the mythic sources that animators frequently draw upon,
Warner locates a meaning in the Beast that plays out the very contradictions inherent in all depictions of the animated creature. At the
same time, this secures the significance of "the pure animal" in the discourse. Disney's Beast plays out primal urges that suggest the inarticulable conditions of animal existence beyond the profoundly superficial
trappings of bourgeois civilization epitomized in the castle he lives in
and the clothes he wears. While it might be comparatively easy to read
his yearning as merely the contemporary desire for love and companionship, and essentially the recovery of his humanity through his love
for Belle, there is also a greater longing about the release of an animality into more appropriate conditions and contexts. Beast's loneliness
is not merely a modern condition but a recognition of a profound loss
of what it is to be at one with a natural order rather than exposed by
the codes and conventions of an imposed and artificial one. The spell
that has been placed upon Beast is supposed to prompt an agency in
him by which he learns not only to love but to accept the terms and
parameters of civilized conduct and the diminished status of humankind. Love is the presiding answer to living in a contemporary world
otherwise characterized by violence, vanity, and venality, but further,
the only thing left that might operate as a trustworthy felt experience
evidencing a natural bond. Beast's trauma illustrates that there are
more powerful and pre-ordained bonds that have been sacrificed to
the estranged hierarchies of humankind as they compete within the
socialized infrastructure.

Beast's anger is actually a final resistance to this, and his castle is
a model of imprisonment and entrapment not unlike the imposition
of the cages at a zoo. He is debilitated by an oppressive culture and
made to submit to its conditions, largely through the idea that love will
reconcile alienation and replace the more complex, unfettered, and

uninhibited primal potencies of which his anger is merely one version. It is this which should be recognized as the true source of sentiment in many Disney narratives, and not the readily assumed idea that there is a backward-looking sense of nostalgia that underpins the established codes of resolution, or the fundamentalist moral closures or happy endings as they occur in many narratives. While it is true to say that Disney's deployment of moral archetypes of good and evil, and the victory of good over evil, may remain the presiding and memorable outcome of such Disney narratives, this is never unproblematic and, further, often uses the powerful resonance of animal cultures to challenge the contradictions at the heart of modern condition.

Isenberg has located this sense of "sentimentalization" across a number of literary and social forms, seeing some of them, too, as genuine antecedents of Disney's outlook:

> Sentimentalization of farm animals and pets was common in the nineteenth century, as an industrializing society romanticized its rural past, but an emotional regard for wild animals is a distinctly twentieth century (or, at least, a late-nineteenth century) phenomenon. It was first exemplified in the beginning of the century in the writings of Ernest Thompson Seton and Jack London; it was reformulated and informed by science and ethics by Aldo Leopold at mid-century; and it was encapsulated in legislation in the Endangered Species Act of 1973 and concerted efforts in the 1990s to reintroduce animals from the endangered list to their former habitats. (Isenberg 2002, 48–49)

Seton borrowed freely from the moral outlook of popular Victorian novels and the more sensationalist aspects of boys' adventure stories to present the frontier and the natural world as a continual struggle, not merely in the sometimes bloody confrontations between animals but with the moral trauma associated with the kill. This often prompted complex engagements with animal conscience, where, like Beast, a creature is torn between the new civilities of an increasingly impacting modern order and the desire to follow more natural, primal, and physically reconciliatory instincts and imperatives. In some senses, too, there is a struggle for the animals, and by extension, of course, contemporary humankind, with the acceptance of a Darwinian order. It is often the case that contemporary sentiment is used to disguise the extensive anxieties in dealing with "the survival of the fittest" as it shifts from a natural code to a social one. Isenberg suggests that there is a "moral ecology" in the heart of such narratives: "Moral ecology went beyond the mere sentiment of Seton. It assumed, like Seton and those that followed him, such as Felix Salten (the author of "Bambi: A Forest Life") and Walt Disney (the producer of the 1941 animated film version of *Bambi*), that wild animals inhabit a moral universe and that people would do well to emulate the innate morality—the natural law—of the wild. It goes beyond them in asserting that the order of nature constitutes a higher, morally and scientifically integrated order" (Isenberg 2002, 55). Sentimentalization in this context, then, is not a saccharine deployment of deliberately prompted and enforced emotion in support of a satisfying reconciliation, but an interrogative intervention that operates as a recognition of loss and a mark of social alienation from a more fitting order of existence. This moral ecology underpins the naturalcultural and becomes a constant model by which humankind seeks to find correspondence with the animal, assuming that one order has been lost to another, or that the animal is the prevailing trace of an order long lost to humankind, identifiable in particular moments or scenarios, but never fully recuperated.

Defending Disneyfication

Novelists like D. H. Lawrence and Ernest Hemingway saw this moral ecology in "the Other Dimension." Bullock has argued, "The animals are brought closer to the human world by their representation as spiritual beings, but their nobility and their distinction also keep them at a definite distance" (Bullock 2002, 108), continuing, "What [Lawrence and Hemingway] do achieve by foregrounding the vital experience of an encounter with another kind of being leads us to feel what it might mean to renounce the authority of the reigning social order altogether" (114). The logical extension of this view is that animals function as a meaning for freedom, and this is compounded and reinforced in animated films by the openness and versatility of the language of animation itself. It is also a point by which I can take issue with Steve Baker's view that "the animal is the sign of all that is taken not-very-seriously in contemporary culture; the sign of that which does not really matter. The animal may be other things besides this, but it is certainly one of its most frequent roles in representation. Terms such as stereotyping and trivialization are a little too imprecise to describe quite what is going on here: I propose instead to speak of it as the disnification of the animal" (Baker 2001, 174). While it is possible to see this idea in the light of seeking out the best definition for the most popular representations of animals in the contemporary era, and the common-sense ways that this has been absorbed into the culture, it does not do justice to the way in which Disney problematizes animal narratives. Further, as I show in the next chapter, it ignores the way in which Disney artists, like many others working in animation, engage with animals in a highly serious way in a spirit of representing animals on terms and conditions that both recognize the complexities and presence of animality and the ways this is best revealed through animation. If the animal is a mark of a particular kind of freedom, then animation helps to reveal the discourses by which the nature of the animal is somehow intrinsic to that notion of freedom rather than merely signifying this after the fact. The very proximity of animals to humankind materially, historically, and culturally serves to reinforce not merely the modern roles and functions that they have come to play, but the tradition that they embody. This is an insistent presence within the discourses made readily available through the empathetic realization of animals by animators and within the sympathetic langue of the animated form.

"Disneyfication," in the spirit that I view it—the problematization of sentiment within the flux of bestial ambivalence and the naturalcultural context—begins with the ways in which Disney's work (but also that of other animators and directors making animal animation) speaks to particular audiences. This is often a neglected aspect of thinking about the construction and execution of texts. Though Disney narratives, particularly in their feature length form, necessarily addressed a family audience and incorporated a flux of complex and mature incidents and themes, the main intention was to entertain and educate children; the latter education often played out through the experience of rites of passage rather than a didactic agenda, though clearly the moral parameters of many Disney films are, for the most part, fixed. The relationship between animals and children is at the heart of this and is readily supported by the long established view that children share a primal relationship with animals that has its roots in the evolutionary process briefly summarized above. Freud suggests, "There is a great deal of resemblance between the relations of children and of primitive men towards animals. Children show no trace of arrogance which urges adult civilized men to draw a hard and fast line between their own nature and that of all other animals. Children have no scruples over allowing animals to rank as their full equals. Uninhibited as they are in the avowal of their bodily needs, they no doubt feel themselves more akin to animals than to their elders, who may well be a puzzle to them" (Freud 1961, 13). Modern estrangement in adults, then, might be understood as not merely an alienation from nature, but from the ease of correspondence and understanding of animals that comes with the negation of hierarchy and the empathetic needs that forestall superficial questions of difference. Somewhat ironically, it is the modernist idioms in animation that permit an ontological equivalence in the depictions, representations, and elisions of children and animals and the recall of primal bonds and lost knowledge.

At a fairly straightforward level, this occurred, for example, in Richard Taylor's *Charley* public information films in the 1970s, when the relationship between a little boy and his cat was used to foreground health and safety issues for children, largely through placing the cat in jeopardy and appealing to the child's innate sense of care and attention for the animal, both within the narrative and in the audience. The relationship between the child and the animal was the core relationship in the child's life, and this device is often used in children's programming and films—William and Barksure in *William's Wish Wellingtons* (Hibbert Ralph, UK, 1999), Wallace and Gromit in *The Wrong Trousers* (Nick Park, UK, 1993), or the grieving boy and his pet dog in *Dog* (Suzie Templeton, UK, 2001), to name but three immediate examples. Desmond Morris cites a survey of 80,000 British children who were asked their favorite animal; the top ten were Chimpanzee, Monkey, Horse, Bushbaby, Giant

Panda, Bear, Elephant, Lion, Dog, and Giraffe, leading him to conclude, "The top ten animal loves all have humanoid features. They are not being chosen for their economic or aesthetic values, but for the ways in which they remind the children of people. They all have hair rather than feathers or scales. They also tend to have rounded outlines, flat faces, facial expressions, and a body posture that in some way or other is vertical, either because they are tall, or because they can sit up or stand on their hind legs. In addition they are often good at manipulating things—the primates with their hands, the panda with its front paws, and the elephant with its trunk" (Morris 1977, 263). While Morris's conclusion is persuasive, the aesthetic aspects of these attractions and preferences should not be ignored, as it is clear that the children's choices may be as much governed by what they know from the illustration in children's books and the conventions of the wildlife documentary as it is from a genuine and primal understanding drawn from their contact with and proximity to animals.

William's Wish Wellingtons. Barksure, William's trustworthy canine companion, is one of many animal companions to children, or lead characters in children's animation, calling upon a child's empathy and care for their pets.

Nick Park, here seen at the Bradford Animation Festival in the UK, holding his creations, Wallace and Gromit: Wallace, the well-meaning but slightly pompous inventor, and Gromit, his dog, "the brains of the outfit," who ultimately solves all the problems. This template of an animal who is abler and more competent than a human is often used in animated films. Photo by Paul Wells.

He further suggests, however, that "very small children are looking for big symbolic animals—presumably parent-substitutes—and the older children are seeking small symbolic animals—presumably child substitutes. It is not enough, therefore, for an animal to be merely humanoid—it must also represent a particular kind of humanoid" (Morris 1977, 263–265). This also seems a little too literal minded, and again predicates children's choices to be determined by familial needs and innate ideas about the fundamental human requirement to protect and be protected, to love and be loved. At some level, of course, this is likely to be part of the children/animal narrative and the discourse that arises out of the reception of animal stories, in all their forms by children, and perhaps adults alike. It is important, then, to once again consider what is distinctive about animated depictions of such animals, and in a more specific sense this seems to lie in the relationship between inherent primal connections between human-kind and animals and the ways in which animation can formally and self-consciously predicate its design and motion strategies to recall such connections. These essentially operate in two ways—as a model of empathy through juvenilization and interrogative awe, played out through spectacle.

In addressing the changing design of Mickey Mouse from his initial presence as a sharp-snouted, loose-limbed liminal figure in early shorts like *Steamboat Willie* (Walt Disney, USA, 1928) to the more rounded, prototypic, iconic Mickey that was in place by *The Band Concert* (Wilfred Jackson, USA, 1934), Stephen Jay Gould notes an increasing process of juvenilization that aligns the animal and the child: "Many animals, for reasons having nothing to do with the inspiration of affection in humans, possess some features also shared by human babies but not by human adults—large eyes and a bulging forehead with retreating chin, in particular. We are drawn to them, we cultivate them as pets, we stop and admire them in the wild—while we reject their small eyed, long-snouted relatives who might make more affectionate companions or objects of admiration" (Gould 1987, 504). This juvenilization becomes an important characteristic in the design of numerous animated creatures and not merely draws the child and the animal into the same unconscious, primal remit suggested by Freud, but also insists that aesthetic characteristics are important in the configuration of the relationship between the child and the animal within the diegetic and non-diegetic space. This alignment, while operating to some degree through aesthetic terms and conditions, nevertheless creates an enabling animated portal by which to access a more informed relationship about animals and animality than has perhaps been previously allowed. Animated animals are not just graphic and material conditions but the conduit for more complex archaic and arcane bonds drawn from a socio-biologically determined primordial order. This may seem an over-determined claim, but it allows for the idea that historicized, ideologically charged meanings may be intrinsically bound up with primordial socio-biological and psychosomatic affects, which are liberated through the model of bestial ambivalence at work in the fluid operations of animated film. It recognizes too that, inevitably, particular kinds of contemporary social understanding might be divorced from these more embedded and hidden primal agendas, or speak to them in ways that have shifted emphasis and intention. Apropos of this, Gould comments, for example,

> We cannot help regarding a camel as aloof and unfriendly because it mimics, quite unwittingly and for other reasons, the "gesture of haughty rejection" common to so many human cultures. In this gesture, we raise our heads, placing our nose above our eyes. We then half-close our eyes and blow out through our nose—the "harumph" of the stereo-typed underclass Englishman or his well-trained servant. "All this," [Konrad] Lorenz argues quite cogently, "symbolises resistance against all sensory modalities emanating from the disdained counterpart." But the poor camel cannot help carrying its nose above its elongate eyes, with mouth drawn down. As Lorenz reminds us, if you wish to know whether a camel will eat out of your hand and spit, look at its ears, not the rest of its face. (Gould 1987, 504)

This is a pertinent example of the ways a particular kind of anthropomorphic impulse has not necessarily been imposed on an animal, but merely assumed given its proximity to established human gestures. Indeed, there is a great deal of such approximation in animation, drawing upon apparent visual similarities in humankind and beasts. What the subsequent animation inevitably does is to provide what might be called a "supernormal" stimulus that invariably draws a greater degree of focus and attention to its real-world equivalents. This again speaks to points of access and empathy that show the simultaneous condition of pure animal, aspirant human, critical human, and humanimal embedded in the evolutionary and contemporary readings of the creature. This sense of the supernormal is especially important in foregrounding the highly particular relationship between children/adults and animals, and mediates between the multiple engagements that are prompted and recalled through the aesthetic and narrative premises of any one work. This also inevitably reveals the embedded historicized meanings of animals. Art critic Dave Hickey explains this on more accessible terms and conditions:

What we did not grasp was just exactly why the blazing spectacle of lawn-mowered cats, exploding puppies, talking ducks, and plummeting coyotes was so important to us. Today it's clear to me that I grew up in a generation of children whose first experience of adult responsibility involved the care of animals—dogs, cats, horses, parakeets—all of whom, we soon learned, were breathlessly vulnerable, if we didn't take care. Even if we did take care, we learned these creatures, whom we loved, might, in a moment, decline into inarticulate suffering and die—be gone forever. And we could do nothing about it. So the spectacle of ebullient, articulate, indestructible animals—of Donald Duck venting his grievances and Tom surviving the lawnmower—provided us a way of simultaneously acknowledging and alleviating this anxiety, since all of our laughter was premised on our new and terrible knowledge that the creatures given into our care dwelt in the perpetual shadow of silent suffering and extinction. (Hickey 1997, 48)

Hickey articulates how the supernormal representation of the animal in the cartoon stimulated a realization that there was a need to take responsibility for animals, and in some senses helped to both heighten a recognition of their mortality while also prompting the view that there needed to be an investment in their continuity and survival. Simultaneously, this is effectively a revelation of animal subjectivity, where the proximity, companionship, and taken-for-grantedness of the family pet or the favored zoo animal is suddenly redefined by understanding that the animal is "of itself," yet understood through the abstracted repository and repertoire of representational forms. The animated cartoon has served to render the animal in the present, but in its abstractedness begins to recall the ancient and primal knowledge about the animal that has been lost in the contemporary era.

On the contrary, however, there is sometimes the equal anxiety that the animal might be evacuated from such discourses. Poet Jo Shapcott has engaged with this issue in her poem "Tom and Jerry Visit England":

I dreamt of coming back to tell you how I marched
round the Tower of London, in a beefeater suit,
swished my axe at Jerry, belted after him

into the Bloody Tower, my back legs
circling like windmills in a gale
while ravens flapped round our heads.

. . .

I would be a concertina zig-zag by that time
with a bone china cup stuffed in my face
and a floral tea pot shoved on my head so hard
my brains would form a spout and a handle
when it cracked and dropped off.

I can't get this new voice to explain to you
the ecstacy in the body when you fling
yourself into such mayhem, open yourself
to any shape at all and able to throw out
stars of pain for everyone to see.

. . .

"Where's the mouse ?" I banged full face into a query—
and ended up with my front shaped
like a question mark for hours. That was scary:
I usually pop right back into myself in seconds.

. . .

Reader, it was my first tragic movie:
I couldn't find a mouse. (Shapcott 2000, 39–40)

While Hickey reads the excesses and exaggerations of the cartoon
as an exuberant model of survival and endurance, in effect excusing the
violence as merely part of its intrinsic artifice and illusionism, Shapcott
remains concerned about the ways in which cartoon conventions can
become more affecting and entertaining than the subjects they appear
to be representing. At the very best, Jerry has become only an idea of
an animal, at the very least has become absented altogether, not operating as a referent to an animal at all. In such determinations of the
animated form, the very arbitrariness of the body becomes part of the
broader vocabulary of metamorphosis stressed earlier—the imperative
to change and abstraction liberating the subject from its allotted and
seemingly inhibiting and fixed nature, materially, culturally, and representationally. While Shapcott's concern is a valid one at some levels,

and clearly functioning within a resonant poetic discourse, the ideas expressed actually speak to a long-held tradition that inevitably undermines the readings of more radical, surreal, or comic representational forms. This is the act of insisting upon a kind of literalness or realism as the core convention in the determination of truth. One need only ask the question, "How can a mouse drive a car, live in a big house and be the owner of a dog bigger than him?" (Ajanovic 2004, 51) to expose the cartoon, or any animated form, to allegations that it is not taking its animal subjects seriously, but this is to neglect how the animated form developed its codes and conventions and shifted the emphasis in its forms and subject matter. Midhat Ajanovic notes of Oswald the Rabbit, for example, "Already in Oswald's case, Disney made a huge step forward. The characters become 'aware' of their own bodies, contrary to Felix or Koko, who never ceased to be a mere spot of ink on paper. Oswald 'knows' that his body can bring him pleasure, as well as pain and suffering" (Ajanovic 2004, 49). Ajanovic is, in effect, signaling the early signs of Disney's personality animation, in which animals were given their subjectivity, even as they played out the exigencies of the form. This became apparent as the quality of the animation itself significantly improved and developed in the hands of such notable figures at Disney as Norm Ferguson, demonstrated in the "Silly Symphonies," which were effectively experimental films progressing the form itself.

In *Just Dogs* (Burt Gillett, USA, 1932), Pluto features in his first starring role in a tale set in a dog pound populated by a variety of dog breeds. The sense of verisimilitude in the representation, however, was significant because, as Michael Barrier has noted, "the animation in *Just Dogs* was not simply a more refined version of what Ferguson had already done. Ferguson's earlier animation although more lifelike than the animation that preceded it, did not invite direct comparison with real life; the animation in *Just Dogs* did" (Barrier 1999, 81). This had been anticipated as early as *The Chain Gang* (Burt Gillett, USA, 1931) when "the bloodhounds, in their single scene, snuffle along the ground, then sniff and howl into the camera; their jowls hang loosely, their nostrils wrinkle and flare, their movements echo those of real dogs. When the dogs appear, there is a sense, however faint and fleeting, of solid flesh on the screen otherwise occupied by phantoms" (Barrier 1999, 75).

Disney was moving closer to the revelation of the animal and progressing the form toward a hyperrealism, which, though diminishing some aspects of the freedoms of the animation language, began to ironically facilitate a way in which truly cinematic effects might be achieved.

This brings me to the second way in which the adult/child has been reconciled with the specificities of the animated form, and this is through spectacle. It is important to recognize that there has been a very particular kind of spectacle throughout the history of animation that effectively brings together the core issues addressed here—most pertinently, the recovery of primal knowledge through the animation of supernormal animal cultures, that simultaneously supports the real and the imaginary, the known and the projected, fairytale and fact. This is the spectacle of animated dinosaurs.

Walking with Beasts

During the late 1800s and early 1900s Winsor McCay, newspaper cartoonist and creator of comic strips "Tales of the Jungle Imps, by Felix Fiddle," "Little Nemo in Slumberland," and "Dreams of a Rarebit Fiend," also became a pioneer of the animated film in the United States. Though he had made earlier films like *Little Nemo* (Winsor McCay, USA, 1911) and *How a Mosquito Operates* (Winsor McCay, USA, 1912), it was with *Gertie the Dinosaur* (Winsor McCay, USA, 1914), that McCay gained full recognition, incorporating his animation within a vaudeville act, where, dressed as a ringmaster, McCay appears to interact with Gertie, cajoling her while she plays with a mammoth, and in a grand finale, appearing to enter into the cartoon world and ride off into the distance. McCay recognized that animation was best suited to the depiction of imaginary states and mythic creatures, but appreciated, too, that the enduring public fascination with the dinosaur enabled him to create a potentially popular imaginary character while tapping into the increasing interest in the work of the American Museum of Natural History, and particularly the paintings of prehistoric creatures by Charles R. Knight.

Stop-motion animation auteur Ray Harryhausen based his later models on Knight's work, and suggests that "his dinosaur and prehistoric animal paintings and sculptures had more than just a realistic

Gertie the Dinosaur. Winsor McCay's Gertie was animated film's first great personality and was featured in McCay's vaudeville stage act—essentially a combination of circus animal and domestic pet, but actually a living, breathing animal of strength and playfulness.

surface quality; they also possessed scientific reality and natural beauty. He was the first to reconstruct pre-historic life in a romantic form and the first to work in close collaboration with palaeontologists to attempt to achieve scientifically accurate anatomy. His long experience in drawing and painting live animals in zoos, together with his romantic and vivid imagination, helped to instill his pre-historic reconstructions with a 'charisma' only found in living creatures" (Harryhausen and Dalton 2003, 14). McCay's instincts as a newspaperman, artist, and performer enabled him to create this charisma in his animated dinosaur, and though the extensive detail that characterized Knight's work was not possible in animation at that time, McCay nevertheless created a plausible dinosaur whose weight, motion, and breathing suggested a real animal. McCay's eye for detail also ensured that Gertie's charisma was reflected in a playfulness appealing both to adults and children, yet characterized by the allure of being an animal. This was not a person in an animated animal's guise, but a subjective figure, not as scientific as Knight's paintings, yet as romanticized and consequently as close to a sense of a reconstruction of a past age as seemed possible. The key point of attraction here was a living, breathing, creature *in motion*, magically brought to life, but in many people's eyes, brought *back to life,* a long forgotten figment of an imagined yet somehow known primal order.

Popular interest in prehistory had also been stirred by the publication of Arthur Conan Doyle's "The Lost World" in 1912, which featured a South American expedition led by Professor George E. Challenger that discovers an unknown plateau inhabited by prehistoric creatures. Conan Doyle, always keen to blur the lines between fact and fiction, created a frontispiece for the book that apparently featured the expeditionary party, with himself bearded and disguised as the renowned Challenger. This was compounded further when First National Pictures made a film version of *The Lost World* (Harry Hoyt/Willis O'Brien, USA, 1925), which featured a brontosaurus—replacing the pterodactyl in the novel—rampaging through London. In advance of the film, in June 1922, Conan Doyle took some of Willis O'Brien's animated footage of dinosaurs to the Annual Banquet of the Society of American Magicians—who included notable figures such as famed escapologist Harry Houdini—and projected it without explanation of the source of the material, implicitly enhancing his own cause in Spiritualist thought and advancing notions that the past could be *re-animated*, even though, of course, he was fully aware of the illusionism he himself was practicing through this prank. The advances in animation—especially as practiced by Willis O'Brien—ultimately authenticated seemingly fantastic worlds, making them real in the public imagination. Interestingly, McCay had wanted to produce his animation of a dinosaur in order to prove that he was not working from photographic sources, and was imbued with the principle of motion through the empathetic relationship with the animator (see O'Sullivan 1990, 38). This merely authenticated Gertie's subjectivity further and supported the sense that creatures thought to merely be the stuff of fantasy were in some way part of the modern world.

The Lost World picked up on the modernist assimilation of Darwinian thought and the last days of the newspaper as *the* pioneering media of information and investigation before the advent of radio, film, and television. This readily contextualizes the discovery and presence of the dinosaurs further, as the story unfolds in the spirit of adventure story and travelogue, creating an authentic sense of an expedition taking place around 1908. Conan Doyle is careful to make sure that his expedition takes place within the space of a year and that the events, from the initial journey from Southampton to the point of access at low water on the Amazon to the projected "lost world" in southern Venezuela, is based on contemporary research and the outcomes of actual explorations and safaris. Once more, this seeks to support the illusionism of the piece in not revealing its artifice or fantastical elements. The combination of prehistoric creatures with real creatures, like monkeys and insects, equally supports the idea of an ontological equivalence in their presence, a view supported by the fact that Marcel Delgado, the creator of the dinosaur models for the film, drew directly on the work of Charles R. Knight and the sense of realism his paintings imbued in prehistoric creatures. It must be remembered again that these images effectively defined the dinosaur in the popular mind in the way that Steven Spielberg's *Jurassic Park* (Steven Spielberg, USA, 1993) might for contemporary audiences. As the brontosaurus marauds through London, destroying the city, engaging with panicked crowds, it is clear that animation has been able to transport the mythic animal into a modern context and idiom and ensured that the animal is addressed not through its familiarity, but its unfamiliarity; not its "heimlich," but its "unheimlich," as the seeming distinction between imagination and reality is erased.

The production designer for *Jurassic Park,* Rick Carter, suggests that this is still at the heart of making these kinds of representation function successfully:

> What we tried to do was find the animal in the dinosaur as opposed to the monster in the dinosaur. The idea was to not make them any less threatening, but rather to keep them from doing as much monster shtick. For our human characters, we wanted their situation to be more like they were being stalked by an animal that is a carnivore, as opposed to something that is psychopathic and just out to get them. That's one of the reasons we wanted to have herds of dinosaurs, to show that dinosaurs were just like any other life-form and that they lived out their lives in a somewhat naturalistic manner. (Shay and Duncan 1993, 14)

Crucially, the identity and presence of the dinosaur is authenticated by its animal functions and not an imposed generic typology; the motivation for the dinosaur in the first instance operates as the pursuit of food, and only sees humanity in the abstract. The threat here is not merely the imperative for the dinosaur to attack and kill, but in the otherness of the creature in terms of size, scale, and physical being, though as *Jurassic Park* also shows, this can be the prompt to awe and wonder in the observers, too. At one and the same time, the dinosaur film in general wishes to embrace the relatedness of the animal while foregrounding its difference, and this echoes the role and function of the animation itself—on the one hand a frame-by-frame illusionist craft allowing complete control over the artistic process and seamlessly absorbed within contemporary moving image practice per se, but on the other a different language of expression that privileges particular forms of representation outside the remit of traditional photographic processes of record.

As Ellen Poom, one of the senior animators on *Jurassic Park*, recalls, "With *Jurassic Park* we tried to use models to do the animation at the start but the movement turned out to be insufficiently fluid to be persuasive, so we did a test and built some dinosaurs that we could scan into the computer. We did some animation of T-Rex, and there was a strong sense that these were real animals moving around. . . . The animators studied a lot of live-action footage of animals running around—maybe feeding or hunting—just studying the movement to get some idea of the spirit and character of the animal. Also, they did some mime classes when they actually had to become a dinosaur and actually establish a character" (quoted in Wells 2006, 8). As I discuss further in the next chapter, this level of empathy is particularly significant in how the animator relates to the animal and how the animal is mediated through animation.

The doyen of the dinosaur film was Ray Harryhausen, who was profoundly influenced by Willis O'Brien and profoundly influential on the next generation of animators who ultimately worked on *Jurassic Park* and dinosaur films that followed it. Though Harryhausen created dinosaurs and related fantastic creatures for a range of fantasy features, including *One Million Years b.c.* (Don Chaffey, UK, 1966), *The Valley of Gwangi* (James O'Connelly, USA, 1969), and *Sinbad and the Eye of the Tiger* (Sam Wanamaker, US/UK, 1977), of most interest in this context is his work on Irwin Allen's *The Animal World* (Irwin Allen, USA, 1956), a feature-length documentary that showed the creation of the world, the era of the dinosaurs, and subsequent evolutionary development.

Harryhausen worked with mentor O'Brien on the dinosaur sequences, and though the film includes work that shows different types of dinosaurs and their habitat, the more realistic sequences featuring conflict and bloodshed were excised. Harryhausen recalls, "One of the deleted animation sequences was the fight between a stegosaurus and a ceratosaurus, ending in the former's death. We animated the ceratosaurus tearing the flesh from its victim with blood oozing from the torn body and the mouth of the carnivore. Irwin Allen had told me when I was animating to make the action strong, so I did. Echoing this graphic depiction of death, there were other sequences in the live action footage in which animals are seen tearing the flesh off other creatures. This was all too much for audiences at the previews, so all the scenes were cut, including my dinosaur dinner" (Harryhausen and Dalton 2003, 77). *The Animal World,* though it makes valid claims to the status of documentary, is nevertheless flawed by, first, the speculative nature of its depictions of dinosaurs, and, second, the limits placed upon it in not showing the less palatable aspects of animal life. This remains the case even in the contemporary era with works like *Walking with Dinosaurs* (Tim Haynes, UK, 1999), when the authenticity of the documentary enterprise is validated by the illusionism of the animated dinosaurs. This kind of work traverses the space between the necessary realism required to realize quasi-science fictional texts like *The Lost World* or *Jurassic Park* as plausible narratives, and the realism pertaining to producing nonfictional visual essays. Crucially, though, it is predicated on the same assumptions, using the representation of the pure animal as a *pre*-text to legitimize the introduction of more anthropomorphic tendencies that enable storytellers and documentarists alike, to empathize with, or comment upon, the relationship between animals and humankind.

This brief tracking of the dinosaur animation is a pertinent intervention in the understanding of the animal as it is played out through models of bestial ambivalence, the development of differing conceptions of the naturalcultural, and the interventions of animation technologies from McCay's hand-drawn Gertie to O'Brien and Harryhausen's 3D stop motion to Spielberg's computer-generated creatures. There are other examples, too, most notably, Disney's first fully computer generated feature, *Dinosaur* (Eric Leighton, Ralph Zondag, USA, 2000), which sought to use the most up-to-date research about possible dinosaur skin colorization and the potential evolutionary relationship between dinosaurs and birds (see Cotta Vaz 2000, 75), in order to properly evidence the animal. Interestingly, in Peter Jackson's version of *King Kong* (Peter Jackson, New Zealand, 2005), there was a return to Charles R. Knight's representations of dinosaurs in the use of crocodilian or reptilian scales in order to achieve a more archaic sense of the creature, and an investment in thinking about dinosaurs as perennially scarred survivors of perpetual struggles for territory and survival (see Wake 2005, 150–153). Arguably, this attention to detail not merely facilitates the most persuasive animation, but gets ever closer to a particular empathy that reveals the animal in itself. It is this concept I wish to pursue further in the following chapter.

3

"I Don't Care What You Say, I'm Cold"

Anthropomorphism, Practice, Narrative

The Anthropomorphic Instinct

I have suggested that it is vital to see how the animal discourse functions both from the point of view of those who make animated films and those who seek to offer particular models of criticism. As I have tried to demonstrate, the animated animal fits within a paradigm of bestial ambivalence, informed by the particular oscillations and cycles by which the elision of human and animal works within animated film and the varying competing scenarios within the naturalcultural divide. This begins to offer a view of the ways in which animals are represented from the point of view of critical and cultural interpretation, functioning as a created phenomena, as a symbolic paradigm to evaluate, and as supernormal stimuli by which to access a deeper, more primal mode of lost knowledge and experience. This chapter is specifically concerned with how animals are represented from the point of view of animators (e.g., scriptwriters, directors, filmmakers) as a practice phenomena and a creative paradigm.

Animals became the vehicle for a high degree of projection in the formative development of animation as an art form and in the evolution of animation as an aesthetic language, initially acknowledged only for its very execution rather than through the meanings and effects it may have produced. Indeed, arguably until 1943, when the first analyses of the Warner Bros. output emerged, animation only had one message, and it was "Disney." The Disney aesthetic became inextricably bound up with the definition of animation, a very particular realism, and an inner-directed Republican conservatism, engaging with the gothic threat to middle-American populist sentimentalities (see Wells 2002a). At the heart of the Disney aesthetic is a model of what became known as "hyperrealism," underpinned by Walt Disney's own conviction that animals had very real personalities, expressed through their bodies, which it was the responsibility of the animator to understand, embrace, and re-create:

> Often the entire body comes into play. Take a joyful dog. His tail wags, his torso wiggles, his ears flop. He may greet you by jumping on your lap or making a circuit of the room, not missing a chair or divan. He keeps barking, and that's a form of physical expression, too; its stretches his big mouth. But how does a human being react to stimulus? He's lost the sense of play he once had and he inhibits physical expression. He is a victim of a civilization whose ideal is the unbotherable, poker-faced man, and the attractive, unruffled woman. Even the gestures get to be calculated. They call it poise. The spontaneity of animals— you find it in small children, but it's gradually trained out of them. Then there's the matter of plastic masses, as our animators put it—mass of face, of torso, and so on. Animation needs these masses. They're the things that can be exaggerated a little and whirled about in such a way as to contribute the illusion of movement, you see, like a bloodhound's droopy ears and floppy gums or the puffy little cheeks and fat little torsos of chipmunks and squirrels. Look at Donald Duck. He's got a big mouth, big belligerent eyes, a twistable neck and a substantial backside that's highly flexible. The duck comes near being the animator's ideal subject. He's got plasticity plus. For contrast, think of the human being as the animator sees him. . . . The typical man of today has a slim face, torso and legs. No scope for animation, too stiff, too limited. (quoted in Schickel 1986/1968, 180–181)

Some important points emerge here. First is the recovery of animals as a vehicle by which the expression of human emotion may be not merely visualized, but recovered and explored. In this rare insight about the human condition, Disney cites the repressions of American culture, evidenced in the elitist gait of constructed poise, as a disengagement with the spontaneity and creativity of human emotional life; an emotional life he sees alive and well in animals. Essentially, because animals express emotive currencies purely through physical movement and abstract sound, Disney sees a direct parallel with the ways in which emotional life can be expressed through the particular conditions informing animation. Effectively, by aping animals physically, materially, and representationally, Disney can use these tropes to facilitate the animated form itself. Interestingly, Disney believed this was best expressed by the use of circular "masses," and the construction of a "squash 'n' stretch" model of movement that would remain responsive to the most anatomically correct design and movement cycle pertinent to each animal. For Sergei Eisenstein, the Russian formalist filmmaker and critic, however, this more hyperrealist approach was a less liberating aesthetic than the one created by Ub Iwerks in the "Silly Symphonies," but (perhaps surprisingly, given their political leanings) both shared the view that such plasmaticness—in Eisenstein's words, "a rejection of once-and-forever allotted form, freedom from ossification, the ability to assume any form" (Leyda 1988, 21)—was crucial to an understanding of animation as an aesthetic vocabulary that was ideologically charged and that challenged the prevailing oppressiveness of Depression-era America. Even more pertinent here are Eisenstein's remarks about the totemic currency of the language of animation explored earlier, and the ways it spoke to the evolutionary development of humankind's relationship to animals. This engaged at a number of levels with the core principle of anthropomorphism in animation, and as I have suggested in my analysis of *Brother Bear*, enabled a repositioning of the ways in which the imposition of human characteristics on animals might work if recontextualized in other mythic, supernatural, and primal orders. This usefully chimes with my own paradigm of bestial ambivalence because it simultaneously sees the animated animal as perpetually active in a range of discourses, and speaks to how anthropomorphism works within the broad parameters of animation.

As novelist and critic Howard Jacobson has noted,

> Anthropomorphism [is] attributing human emotions to the non-human. And much frowned upon by animal behaviorists, butchers, livestock-experts and fox hunters, it was. Today, at least as far as behaviorists are concerned, a little seasoning of anthropomorphism is allowable. Else, it is conceded, we consign animals to never feeling anything as we do, and therefore never feeling anything at all. But the concession favors us; the measure of all things is still consciousness as we understand it. (Jacobson 1997, 4)

But it is the very nature of this "consciousness" that must be taken into account in the sense that if there remains an imperative to use anthropomorphism as an interrogative tool, it must signal itself not as a homogenous tool of expression, but an inclusive and multiple engagement with the potential relationships that arise between humankind and animal. As Jacobson concedes, and Bullock confirms,

> we find it entirely commonplace to take the term "anthropomorphism" to name that familiar inclination to project human feelings into animal experiences. We do not have great difficulty in recognizing the temptation for what it is, when we find ourselves looking for a sensation or emotion we know in ourselves in order to interpret a posture or gesture in an animal. Anything that strikes us as "expressive" in the behavior of another creature makes us pick something in our human vocabulary of appearances to which we see a correspondence, and then let that "expression" speak to us as though we had made a reliable translation from one bodily form to another. (Bullock 2002, 112)

This is clearly the experience described by most animators, who seek the most empathetic correspondence to the animal form in their depiction of both anatomically viable movement and gestural suggestions of emotion. Arguably this is still, and only, a projection of human value and judgment, but it is surely the way in which humankind makes sense of all its relationships. The denial of expressiveness in animals, or indeed, other human beings, amounts to a decision that animals do not possess a voice, a language, a mode of communication through their bodies, and a fundamental rejection of the likeness that might characterize animal identity and animal cognition. Such a denial, particularly in creative idioms that seek out a particular empathy with the animal—absolutely intrinsic to much animation—is to suggest that both the animal and its representational tropes as well as points of sympathetic realization have no validity, and that there is no knowledge of the animal. This in itself is clearly untrue. To take but one example, it has been proven that "chickens . . . have a 'vocabulary' for conveying information about food. Apparently they name certain foods, or at least certain qualities of food, with special cackles" (Page 1999, 109), while "in recent years, researchers have learned that swarming honeybees also dance to indicate information about a possible new home, communication that is just as complex as the dance for food. It turns out that weaver ants have a system of head wags to direct their fellows to an odor trail which will lead to food sources, and a different set of gestures (when the entire body is jerked backwards and forwards) that indicate intruders in the nest" (Page 1999, 120).

Having discovered such behavioral models and communicative cues, animal researchers have effectively shown that to observe an animal or insect is to potentially prove that they might have alternative languages that are not embedded in the textual idioms possessed by humankind, but that nevertheless may be evidenced and apprehended in factual yet quasi-narrative terms. While it has often been denied that an animal can think if it cannot think without language, this is to disavow the alternative languages with which they might speak and the essential limitations in humankind in understanding such languages. Indeed, Lippit has gone as far as to suggest that "animals—and their capacity for instinctive, almost telepathic communication—put into question the primacy of human language and consciousness as optimal modes of communication" (Lippit 2000, 2). This potential lack in humanity can only be potentially resolved by allowing the possibility and potential of the animal to communicate through the metaphorical pragmatism of anthropomorphism, but crucially, one that is grounded in the highest degree of visual mobility that allows the simultaneity of discourses. Animated animal works clearly stand as a powerful refutation of the disavowal of the animal and invite such discourses, which are challenging in their embrace of multiplicity and its realization of animal presence in a world that, arguably, in itself is increasingly distanciated from the animal as a co-inhabitee or incumbent.

In this respect, Kevin Sandler has suggested that "anthropomorphism becomes then a convenient fiction, a default schema to deal with *uncertainty,* a default schema to deal with *quasi-predictability,"* and ultimately represents a "fear for the unknown and unclassifiable" (Sandler 1997, 48). As is clear from my own paradigm, however, I view anthropomorphism as a tool by which a variety of discourses are simultaneously called into the interpretation of the animal and operate as a way in which any potential anxiety about animal otherness and difference might be potentially reconciled. Further, and to echo the points raised earlier about resisting criticism that takes flight from the animal, this view of anthropomorphism refuses the idea of the unknown and unclassifiable: it affords the possibility that ideas such as Grandin's autistic gaze or Griffin's concept of "critical anthropomorphism" can be accommodated as a credible example of informed and evidence-based relationships to animals, and suggests that it is possible to bring other analytical disciplines concerned with animals to bear in the analysis. Even more important, as I noted earlier, it is my view that animators themselves have a very invested and powerful relationship with animals, which is evidenced through their observation and critical record of the animal in the animation itself. Related to this point, Jonathan Burt plausibly argues, "Although the animal on screen can be burdened with multiple metaphorical significances, giving it an ambiguous status that derives from what might be described as a kind of semantic overload, the animal is also a marked site where these symbolic associations collapse into each other. In other words, the animal image is a form of rupture in the field of representation" (Burt 2002, 11). Steve Baker also concurs with this point, noting "the visual image of the animal, however minimal or superficial the degree of its 'animality,' invariably works as a Derridean supplement to the narrative. It is apparently exterior to that narrative, but it disturbs the logic and consistency of the whole. It has the effect of bringing to light the disruptive potential of the story's animal content. It limits the extent to which the narrative can patrol and control its own boundaries" (Baker 2001, 139). While it is obvious that the animated animal carries multiple metaphorical significances, the nature of its symbolic associations remains for the most part clear if read within the paradigm of bestial ambivalence or the terms and conditions of its naturalcultural order, and rather than "rupturing" representational orthodoxies prompts a range of continuities in representation. Further, it properly enables a more precise representational approach that relates to other disciplines and cultural perspectives.

Talking the Talk, Drawing the Walk

The two most famous of Disney's "Nine Old Men," Frank Thomas and Ollie Johnson, writing in what has become the bible of Disney's full classical animation style, *Disney Animation: The Illusion of Life*, write, "As artists, we now have new responsibilities in addition to those of draftsmen and designer: we have added the disciplines of the actor and the theatre. Our tools of communication are the symbols that all men understand because they go back before man developed speech" (Thomas and Johnson 1981, 16). They then cite the work of noted scientist and animal researcher Jane Goodall about her work with chimpanzees, and the particular systems of nonverbal communication and gesture that characterize animal relationships, as intrinsic to their work in animation, noting that "most of these expressions of feelings and language symbols are well known to man, whether they are buried deep in his subconscious, or still actively used in his own communicative behavior" (Thomas and Johnson 1981, 18). Jonathan Burt warns, however, that "pre-industrial practical relations with animals . . . are by implication pre-imagistic and unmediated by forms of representation. This is the fiction of the direct encounter. Measured against this, standard animal imagery will inevitably be considered palliative (substitutive), empty (spectral), and excessive (mass-produced)" (Burt 2002, 26). Crucially, animation, with its intrinsic delineation of animals as phenomenological presences, speaks to this sense of emptiness in the potential image by insisting that its conscious artifice inevitably recalls the effect of the impacting, self-reflexive, self-configuring artist, who is not speaking without language but using the tools of pre-language. To go back to Bernard's evaluation of King Kong, he stresses that "Kong is, in a sense, pre-experience; he is *prior* to experience and the consciousness it implies. Articulation is the (deceiving) tool of civilisation" (Bernard 1976, 130). This model of articulation, deceiving or otherwise, characterizes the ways in which we have come to understand animals rather than feel their empathetic relationship. As Burt argues, "It is easy to lose sight of the historical perspective when concepts of the animal are associated with ideas of naturalness, emotional directness, and simplicity; terms that are themselves important cultural constructs" (Burt 2002, 21). Such cultural constructs are essentially the products of the way in which language is deployed and locked in to a social model, and it is clear that this shapes specific perspectives on the animal.

Science journalist George Page suggests that this is inevitably the consequence of losing touch with pre-experience (arguably everything from pre-humanity to modernity):

> Intimate connection with the natural world may be our most primal and important cultural heritage, but it's also true to say that today we can only dimly remember it. We have to work hard to stay in touch, through our pets to a degree, but mostly with words. We enshrine the natural world with popular idioms such as "Mother Earth" and "Mother Nature," although "Stepmother Earth" and "Stepmother Nature" might be more accurate at the end of this millennium. National parks, private gardens, municipal zoos, household pets and natural history films are the closest most of us can get to Mother Earth nowadays. (Page 1999, 13)

Interestingly, Page does not include the animated film as a site that invites reengagement with the animal, but even at this level of the metaphorical use of human/animal analogies in the English language, animated film has been particularly adept at using the clichéd idioms of everyday exchange to point up the differences both between rhetoric and reality; the limitations in meaning set against the visual affect; and the inhibitions of articulation through language. Bullock suggests that "in the realm of ordinary speech, animal life reflects a view of our own nature in two very different lines of metaphors. Some express a higher character symbolized by the beauty and power of these other beings;

some express the lower aspect of compulsions and crude appetites" (Bullock 2002, 108), but there are other idioms that work on a more literal or ironic basis that point up the playfulness in the language that has been used to align human and animal kind.

Warner Bros.' leading director Fred "Tex" Avery was especially engaged in exploring this terrain. *A Day at the Zoo* (Tex Avery, USA, 1939), for example, features "a wolf in his most natural setting," sitting beside a doorframe, literally visualizing the common phrase "a wolf at the door"; "a pack of camels" is illustrated by four dromedaries smoking, an image that recalls the popular brand of cigarettes; "a North American greyhound" becomes a literal depiction of a bus; and "two bucks," a visual pun on the idea of two dollars, using two deer, is followed by "and five cents," illustrated by five skunks, obviously alluding to their particular "scent." The cartoon suggests that "no zoo would be complete without a monkey cage," showing a monkey and a man staring at each other, clearly recognizing their similarity, to the point where at one stage they swap and the man becomes captive while the monkey looks on. Essentially this is a visual joke, but informed by an underlying recognition of humankind's evolutionary relationship to primates, and with the subtle implication that their intelligence is of an equivalent status. Indeed, this idea is extended to privilege animal intelligence when an old lady secretly seeks to feed one of the monkeys in violation of the sign "Don't feed the monkeys," to which the monkey says, "Hey sister, can't you read ?" There is a sense here of a sympathetic public recognition about an animal in captivity, and the ways in which a domestic model of sympathy and support, played out through the desire to treat the animal, meets the more authoritative view of the zoo in having knowledge of the animal, but there is also the monkey's distance from the woman. Jokes carry with them not merely the mechanism by which an amusing sense of incongruity or misdirection might take place, but an implied set of assumptions upon which the comic event is structured. These assumptions are rooted in the sensibility of the animator/director and predicated on engaging with common and recognizable tropes about the relationship between humankind and animals in the highly managed and inhibited cultural contexts in which this has been historically established. Jokes like these essentially reveal particular attitudes toward animals and crucially privilege the ways in which animation can visualize the space between the intention of the gag, the execution of the gag, and what might be termed its socio-comic outcome.

To take further examples, it is fairly easy to anticipate that when the cartoon takes in "a family of white rabbits" and notes that "of course, you all know how fast they multiply," the gag will not be a literal engagement with the notion of a rabbit's procreative activities, but a play on the term "multiply." The intention of the joke is to set up a foreknowledge of animal behavior, only to lead to an execution where the viewer sees the rabbits rapidly computing on a number of adding machines. The socio-comic outcome here is minimal, but when the cartoon addresses the "South African talking parrot," the narrator's inducement, "Polly want a cracker?" is met with the response, "Nah, give me a short beer"; not merely an urbane adult gag, but a socio-comic indictment of the ways in which humankind patronizes animals in their very desire to communicate with them. It is important to recognize that seemingly simple comic devices like visual puns can have these socio-comic implications because they are easy to dismiss as mere jokes, or commonly recognized acts of playfulness about language rather than its meaning. Animation insists upon the primacy of its multiple and mobile visual discourse, and such visual puns—essentially "spot gags"—operate with a sense of the momentary and ephemeral that can undermine their significance. Looked at as an accumulative phenomenon, however, they reveal core themes that properly engage with animal discourses.

Even in this instance, a running gag, featuring Egghead teasing a lion throughout the cartoon, concludes with the fact that the lion finally eats him. The socio-comic outcome is obvious; humankind and animal are not easily reconciled by the orderly spaces that might suggest they are; humankind and animals, for all their similarities, are intrinsically different, but part of a wider naturalcultural order that relativizes and rationalizes their true relationship. Though this is a comic punch line, it is predicated on a core reality about the tensions between wild animals and supposedly civilized man, and the point is no less relevant because it appears in a "funny" cartoon. In many senses, this kind of perspective vindicates the clichéd description of the cartoon as "anarchic," because it calls into question a range of cultural assumptions and certainties through the machinations and outcomes of the animated gag.

Avery's approach to creating gags was rarely rooted in character comedy or situation, but in the comic tensions between the textual and subtextual, the literal and the ambiguous, and the exploitation of the visual freedoms afforded through animation. His self-conscious play with the form effectively reinvented the cartoon, and while this has been freely recognized in relation to the ways his methods diverged from Disney's classicism and hyperrealist styling, it has been insufficiently acknowledged that this allowed for different kinds of ideological and social discourse to characterize the cartoon. Crucially in this context, this enables an address of animals and the natural order in a different way than had been legitimized—one might say naturalized—in the Disney idiom. Avery's work in this particular area is especially revealed by his series of travelogue/documentary parodies of which *A Day at the Zoo* is one, and which deliberately engage with the assumptions of the famed James Fitzpatrick, MGM-produced "Traveltalks" films that unveiled the world to American audiences for thirty years from the late 1920s to the mid-1950s. Beginning with *The Isle of Pingo-Pongo* (Tex Avery, USA, 1938), and including *Believe It, Or Else* (Tex Avery, USA, 1939), *Detouring America* (Tex Avery, USA, 1939), *Cross-Country Detours* (Tex Avery, USA, 1940), *Wacky Wildlife* (Tex Avery, USA, 1940), *Ceiling Hero* (Tex Avery, USA, 1940), and *Aviation Vacation* (Tex Avery, USA, 1941), the series was a ready engagement with animal cultures worldwide as they were represented and ultimately re-presented within the frame of modernity. As Chuck Jones has remarked, "He ridiculed every platitude implicit in these cliché-ridden 'educational' films: a lizard doing a striptease while shedding her skin; different sides of a split screen for grown-ups and children; and after a description with loving detail of the heating system and absolute cold impenetrability of the polar bear, the bear in question looks sadly at the audience: 'I don't care what you say, I'm cold'" (Jones 1990, 99).

Avery recognized that there was little understanding of other cultures in these films, and merely a set of conventions—"And as the sun sinks slowly in the west . . ."—that exposed the limited knowledge and experience of the West, but more significantly carried a bogus sense of authority that his jokes readily undermined. In order to further authenticate his parodic take on such social ignorance—and to focus this particularly on the tensions between humankind and the animal world—he initiated what became Paramount's "Speaking of Animals" series, which used live-action footage of animals, but animated their mouths so that they could articulate similar gags to those in his travelogue cartoons. Sadly, Warner Bros. did not want to undertake Avery's idea, and though he managed to persuade Jerry Fairbanks at Paramount to produce the series, he only worked on the first three ten-minute films, "Down on the Farm," "In a Pet Shop," and "In the Zoo," all made in 1941, before he left, citing an inability to come to a suitable financial package. These films were packed with Avery's trademark gags, but more to the point his accumulative vision of the deep presence of animals in the contemporary imagination and the ways in which the very relationship between humankind and animals was the essential subject of the American animated cartoon per se. Though Avery himself would not have summarized his work in this way, it accords with Lippit's idea that "the animal can be seen, in fact, as the figure of modern subjectivity. Neither a regressive or primitive figure, animal being founds the site of an excess, a place of being that exceeds the subject" (Lippit 2000, 26).

Avery embraced this excess through his joke-making and its socio-comic observations, but crucially because animation facilitated his vision. The intrinsic language of animation itself may be informed by a process of creation and animistic sympathy that both allows the representation of the animal and an engagement with its material and historic place and prompts a model of expression that engages audiences at a powerfully empathetic level. It was this, however different their styles and outlooks may have been, that animators as diverse as the Disney hyperrealists and the Warners' anarchists shared, and it was, and remains, the essential tool by which animators have a privileged and alternative address of animal cultures. As Thomas and Johnson at Disney argue, "It is capable of getting inside the head of its audiences, into their imaginations. The *audiences* [sic] will make our little cartoon character sad—actually far sadder than we could ever draw him—because in their minds that character is *real*. He lives in their imaginations" (Thomas and Johnson 1981, 19). In relation to the animal, it is my contention that both in the creation of animated forms and in their reception, there is a greater degree of not merely imaginative empathy, but a recollection of the primal and unconscious points of connection and relationship between humans and animals. The very process of visualizing, depicting, and choreographing the animal reengages a more potent anthropomorphic instinct than that which might simply substitute a human identity on to an arbitrary animal. Ironically, the very illusionism of the form insists that the animal has to be addressed beyond the mere act of photographic record, or the particular processes, for example, where real animals might participate in traditional live-action film narratives. The animator is not engaged with training animals for such purposes, nor creating specific conducive circumstances by which animal behavior or notions of animal acting might be caught on film. Rather, this is expressed in a felt experience of the animator, which relates the animality of the animal to the animality embedded in the modern human consciousness, and which is released through the creative act of animating, and the language of animation in itself.

Animators constantly address this relationship between their own felt sense of the animal and the representation of the animal itself in a range of wholly personified contexts and narratives. It is the very process of making animation itself, which embraces and defines the bestial ambivalence I have suggested is at its heart because it consistently uses its specific tools to embrace the animal. Metamorphosis is used to demonstrate the physical and emotional transitions of animal life. Condensation is used to invoke the maximum of suggestion in the minimum of imagery, moving beyond the literalness of the photographic image to illustrate the flux of animality as it is intensely felt, half-recalled, consciously observed, physically empathized with, or intellectually understood by the animator. To put it simply, it is clear that the world cannot be understood if we do not listen to our own knowledge and experience of it, through all the available ways in which it can be engaged with, and further, through the ways in which it is possible to make connections and relationships. It is my particular contention that artists, creative sensibilities, and, in this case, animators and animation provide a unique point of access by which this may be achieved and, significantly, in the recollection and reengagement with the animal. While some may argue that this is always compromised in some senses by the simultaneity of meaning I have suggested emerges from understanding the animal through the paradigm of bestial ambivalence, and often through the comic contexts the animal is presented within, it is clear that the respect for the animal remains intact. It is freely evidenced in the midst of character development, the suggestion of personality, and the contextualization of the animal in narratives offering points of powerful insight and empathy about animals.

There remains doubt about this, however. Steve Baker argues, and surely and essentially apropos of the influence of American animated cartoons, that many representational forms "seem to call on a common view that almost anything to do with animals is somehow funny, or at least likely to be funny. This funniness in animal representation—a release from the usual constraints of meaning—may range from the endearingly amusing to the surrealistic and bizarre, and it need have nothing whatsoever to do with the idea of an inherently warm-hearted response to the animal" (Baker 2001, 23). As I have often remarked in conversation about this issue, it is very often the case that people mistake seriousness for solemnity and forget that comic idioms can operate as a radical language of expression and revelation in themselves. Though there is an implied skepticism in Baker's position, depicting the animal as funny does not necessarily disrupt the integrity or conviction with which the intrinsic animality *of* the animal, or the social, cultural, historical, or primal connection *with* the animal might be apprehended. This might be understood through a brief diversion about ideas concerning how animal characters might be thought of in order to facilitate the maximum use of the vocabulary of expression available to animation. Veteran animation scriptwriter Stan Hayward has developed an approach to enable the writer to determine a vocabulary for an animal and object that can facilitate the development of narratives or jokes, which he calls a "Classification" technique (see Hayward 1977, 40), where he recalls the many ways in our childhood play in which we transposed or converted things by their functions and associations into something else, and how people adept at graphic

	Classification	Association
	A four-legged animal	Other four-legged animals, i.e., cows and sheep
A horse could be classified as. . . .	A mode of transport	Other modes of transport, i.e., cars and bicycles
	Something to sit on	Other things to sit on, i.e., chairs, stools, cushions
	Part of a cowboy's accessories	Other cowboy accessories, i.e., guns, lassos, spurs

FIGURE 3.1. The Creative Classification Process

or verbal puns are doing something similar. This begins by classifying what an animal, object, or environment is and what its associations could be. So, for instance, in this context, when addressing an animal like a horse, it is possible to think about it through the already established social definitions it has been known by and think of a related association to enable narrative development, metamorphoses, and so on (see figure 3.1). Having determined a view of the horse at the social and generic level, it is comparatively straightforward to transfer these concepts to an animated narrative for a range of effects. Such transfer is at the heart of many graphic puns where things are associated by similarities in what something looks like or through things that fulfill a similar function. Hayward describes this in a potential sequence from Hanna-Barbera's "Tom and Jerry" cartoons.

> Cat in the kitchen tries to catch mouse stealing food. He throws egg (missile) at the mouse. The mouse takes a frying pan (tennis racket) and hits egg back. The concept has transferred to a tennis match. The scene is now open for bread rolls, fruit, vegetables etc., to be used as tennis balls. There is also the parallel concept of a war, which could bring in using saucepans and kitchen utensils as tin hats and armour. This would then allow knives and forks to be used as spears. Eventually the kitchen furniture might be rearranged as a fortress. (Hayward 1977, 40)

So, even here, a particular kind of critical or pragmatic anthropomorphism is in place, where the writer is not merely considering the use of human characteristics in representing an animal, object, or environment, but the range of possibilities in constructing new notions of character out of known associations and story principles. This enables an audience not only to both enjoy and empathize with the familiarity of that character but to embrace a new concept that is wholly facilitated by the ability for animation to literally depict fresh classifications of creature and concept. The ultimate use of these reclassifications is twofold: first, and perhaps, ironically, creating situations and scenarios that return the narrative to a consideration of the animal itself—a key aspect of this discussion—and second, creating scenes like those above that might lend themselves to more overt notions of sociocultural critique. The creative enterprise of making the animated animal film requires this degree of possible empathy, as well as the ability to develop the discourse-in-flux epitomized in the bestial ambivalence model and the literal dynamics of creating the animal-in-the-making.

Pranking, Pronking, and Practice

Chuck Jones, the most self-conscious and literate of the Warner Bros. animators, carefully theorized his own approaches to this question, sometimes imposing strict limitations on his work in order to test the very limits of the animated vocabulary but also the ways by which he engaged with the animal. Jones is quite clear about the uses of animals:

> In animated cartoons, we do generally prefer animals to humans. First, if your story calls for human beings, use live action. It is cheaper, quicker, and more believable. If, as a director, I could train a live coyote and a live roadrunner to act, I would use them. I am an animator and an animation director; therefore, I look for characters that cannot be done in live action. That is what animation is all about; it is an extension beyond the ability of live-action motion pictures. Second, as said, it is easier to humanize animals than it is to humanize humans. (Jones 1990, 227)

In some senses, as I have suggested, this is a little comically disingenuous, as the animalization aspect of the Jones's work is an intrinsic part of the process. Like Disney's artists, Jones regularly visited zoos but also studied animals in their natural habitat to understand the anatomical factors that underpinned processes of physical movement and expression in animals. As contemporary animator Christopher Hart has suggested to aspiring animators, "It is important to keep a reference file on hand for drawing animals. If you don't you'll just be drawing cartoon animals based on your recollections of other cartoon animals, and your drawings will show a lack of mastery. The next time you go to the zoo, bring along a sketchbook, and add any sketches you make to your reference file. You'll get the best understanding of animal anatomy by comparing the joints of animals to similar joints in humans" (Hart 1997, 58). Jones, of course, was a master of these kinds of technical comparisons, but recognized too that other points of comparison between animal movement cycles and behavior and human conduct were a constant source of narrative and comic stimulus:

> All you have to do is to look at the pop-eyes, the nervous mouth, and the strained neck veins of a camel to realize that there is someone with a shirt two sizes too tight. A photograph in National Geographic showed a dried-up, ragged camel who had just spent many days in the desert without water. As soon as he reached the oasis, he swallowed nearly half of his body weight in water. Unlike most mammals, the camel feeds water straight into his cells, and in the next picture, taken a little later, he had filled out completely and looked ready for another walk in the desert. That is an idea an animator can use. (Jones 1996, 78)

Jones both animalizes and personifies here, but essentially he notes the intrinsic metamorphosis in the camel's normal behavior, which nevertheless carries with it a comic incongruity suitable for a visual gag in a cartoon. This process, while not necessarily carrying the totemic import of our primitive ancestors, nevertheless marks out a phenomenological space that speaks to the specificity and significance of animals in the process of creatively engaging with the understanding of the human condition. It is a process, though, that is thankfully free of the often patronizing evolutionary hierarchy imposed in live-action wildlife documentaries, which I explore below. As John Grant has noted, however, such a process is not free of issues:

> [Jones's] characters may not move like the animals they hypo-
> thetically are—no rabbit walks like Bugs Bunny—but neverthe-
> less they move with a convincing pseudo-realism: if there were
> a creature like Bugs, then that is the way he would move, and
> the viewer never for one moment thinks otherwise. (Sometimes
> this observation of how creatures move could lead him up blind
> alleys. For example, his character Pepe Le Pew often goes into a
> curious, stiff-legged bouncing mode of locomotion that seems
> artificial to the viewer and that many find profoundly irritating.
> In fact, this is a genuine—if occasional—gait of certain animals
> such as the springbok, called pronking; Jones uses it to indicate
> the anticipation of bliss. However, realism and "artistic realism"
> are not always consonant.) (Grant 2001, 129–130)

By invoking the model of bestial ambivalence here, it is possible to
reconcile this analysis. Once more, when looking at the pure animal,
Jones uses the particularity of pronking as specific to, and a clearly
defining aspect of, the animal, and uses the distinctiveness of this locomotion both to identify the animal and foreground his use of animation
to essentially record it. In relation to the hybrid humanimal, it is worthwhile picking up on Grant's point about the gait of Bugs Bunny, one
that characterizes the construction of many cartoon animals and 3D
animal models. As Hart remarks in relation to the technical execution
of this construction: "The raccoon [I have drawn] . . . retains an animal
leg joint configuration, but combines this with the upright posture of a
human. [This] approach is very popular in animated feature films, for
which animals are generally drawn more realistically than they are for
animated television shows. The posture allows the animal to resume a
stance on all fours, at any time, without breaking reality" (Hart 1997,
70–71). Crucially, by what is essentially a simple reversal of direction in
configuring animal leg-joints, the design and potential locomotion of
the animal can oscillate between a plausibly human configuration and
a pertinently animal state, but as both Grant and Hart stress, *without
breaking reality*. The reality in question becomes the way in which the
animal character can be quickly recontextualized. This humanimal
will adapt to the changing conditions of habitat in relation to its

established personality, for example, becoming more urbane in the city and more animal-like in the animal kingdom or the wild or a more obviously natural order. This in turn facilitates the further oscillation between the critical human and aspirational human models, in which, to return to Pepe Le Pew, plays out an engaging tension between sexual confidence and vanity, self-awareness and self-delusion, and investment and compulsion. As Jones has noted, Pepe is "so sure of his appeal to women that it never occurs to him that his attentions might be unwelcome or offensive" (Jones 1996, 222), but even here, Jones exploits the slippage between human and animal. He translates the unacceptability of "a human being with bad breath, underarm odors, or smelly feet" into the natural "scent" of an animal, which is the intrinsic way in which a real skunk attracts a female mate, and further, he contrives the potential female mate as a cat because a female skunk "as a member of the same species would not find his smell unpleasant" (Jones 1996, 223). In what he describes as an act of "sweet miscegenation" (Jones 1996, 224), Jones uses the ease with which animation can accommodate cross-species coupling to prompt a comic context of relentless pursuit, but also to reinforce his consistent adage that "it was unwise to make assumptions about any animal." Observation, memory, and knowledge of an animal was a prerequisite not merely to the successful execution of the drawing but the fundamental concepts that intrinsically related humans and animals.

Jones, like virtually all animators working with animal characters, has a strong grasp of animal anatomies and the various ways in which the action of carnivores and herbivores is affected by how they have physically evolved to facilitate their dietary needs and adapt to their material environments. This underpins their predictive behavior, of course, and in doing so enables animators to either follow the determinants of that behavior in a consistent and realistic way, or to extend this further into less realistic, more cartoon-like or fantastical conduct that violates physical laws and orthodox outcomes.

Figure 3.2, based on the observations of biology professor Stuart Sumida and Rhythm and Hues animation director Bill Weisenhofer, demonstrates how, by merely thinking of the tension between realistic and fantastical behavioral elements in the construction of creatures,

Creature	Behavior	Example
Real	Real	*Cats and Dogs*
Real	Fantastic	*Scooby Doo*
Fantastic	Real	*Monsters Inc.*
Fantastic	Fantastic	*Shrek*

FIGURE 3.2. Sumida's Creature Behavior Structure.

Source: Lecture, Animex International Festival of Animation and Computer Games, January 2006.

new types emerge. So, when looking at the cat in *Cats and Dogs* (Lawrence Guterman, USA, 2001), the cat—like most of the creatures in manipulated live-action animal movies like *Babe* (Chris Noonan, USA,1995), *Animal Farm* (John Stephenson, USA, 1999), or *Charlotte's Web* (Gary Winick, USA, 2006)—operates essentially through the digital interventions that augment realistic animal conduct and behavior, or intervene to present cartoon behavior *as if it were real*; in this case, most memorably, the cat's martial arts activities. *Scooby Doo* (Raja Gosnell, USA, 2002), however, while presenting its central character as a family dog, recognizably a Great Dane with doglike characteristics, nevertheless enables the dog to operate completely freely within the open codes and conventions of the animated form, and embrace fantastic, largely comic behavior. In Pixar's *Monsters Inc.* (Pete Docter, USA, 2001), however, there are no animals: the monsters, most particularly Sulley, who echoes the look and behavior of a bear, are essentially legitimized as realistic in directly embodying the realistic gait or behavior of an animal. Only in the lead character of Shrek or his Princess Bride in *Shrek* (Andrew Adamson, Vicky Jensen, USA, 2001) is the figure liberated to purely operate as an animated phenomena by being a fantastical character in a fantastical environment, though clearly the character is essentially human in construction. Donkey in *Shrek,* while constructed with the physical characteristics and movement of the animal, plays against the (stereo) typology of the donkey as ass by being a wisecracking, fast-talking quasi-commentator on the action.

While these categories offer a simple point of access to understand the operation of animals and related creatures, they also begin to dictate the ways in which animated animals are configured within narrative. In the real creature/real behavior model, the animal is more fully acknowledged in its animality, either through the kind of work of quasi-live-action films suggested above, or in more traditional animation that prioritizes the animal in the narrative—in the long form, something like Halas and Batchelor's *Animal Farm* or Disney's *Bambi* or *Spirit: Stallion of the Cimarron* (Kelly Asbury, USA, 2002), or in the short form, William Kentridge's *Tide Table* (William Kentridge, South Africa, 2003) or Suzie Templeton's *Dog* (Suzie Templeton, UK, 2001). Sumida stresses apropos of *Spirit* that "horses are actually really smart and very curious and they have a range of emotions and feelings that you would expect of any intelligent animal; they are honest in that they show what they are feeling and how they are going to react, so animators have to be aware of that when depicting their behavior" (personal communication, July 2007). This degree of honesty is taken to its emotional extreme in Templeton's film when a boy's grief for his dead mother is exacerbated by the further death of his dog, the latter (in a probable echo of the former) smothered by his father as a supposed act of mercy in the light of its suffering. The pain shared by the humans and animal here seeks out the pure animal feeling that operates as a measure for degrees of difference from other kinds of representational forms. In the real creature/fantastical behavior model, which is largely characterized by the animal cartoon as well as the more fairy-tale or abstract interpretations of the animal, the performances not only facilitate the gag but more surreal or poetic interpretations, too. The fantastical creature/real behavior model presents alternative creatures but supports them with the allusion to real animals. This is mainly achieved by giving such creatures conventional anatomical and behavioral structures of similar animals. The fantastical creature/fantastical behavior model, however, legitimizes characters who can fully and completely engage with the phenomenological freedoms of the animated langue.

These models are helpful in that they delineate the relationship between creatures and their assumed behavioral tendencies, which in turn points up how the presentation and performance of the animal in question should be played out. Sumida and Weisenhofer stressed the presence of these models in animated or quasi-animated features, but they also feature in the short form and are often placed into further

Suzie Templeton's *Dog*, in a challenging reworking of the conventional kinds of representation of animals in animation, shows a dog suffering and in pain in highly persuasive 3D stop-motion animation. Copyright © Royal College of Art 2001.

flux by the particular choices animators and animation directors wish to make in revealing the emotional life of the animal, and how far this should reflect human agendas or comment upon the conduct of human life. In Alex Weil's *One Rat Short* (Alex Weil, USA, 2006), Weil concentrates on authenticating the reality both of the rat itself and the threatening environment he comes to exist within. The computer-generated rat is persuasive as a realistic depiction of a living creature and, crucially, does not talk. In its pursuit of an illusive, shiny snack packet, which floats lyrically in the drafts and breezes of the underground train system, the rat is single-minded in its attempt to follow its scent and its shining presence in the assumption that he will attain food. This imperative in the animal becomes the objective in the acting and animation required, and once more properly aligns the pure animal with plausible conditions of expression and experience. To further dramatize the situation, however, the narrative that this objective drives must change and develop, and the rat, still in its undistracted

Dog. A young boy's emotional pain at the loss of his mother is played out through the further loss of his dog. The dog is apparently put down by his father to spare its suffering, but this also reflects the father's deep-rooted emotional anxieties and sense of failure. Copyright © Royal College of Art 2001.

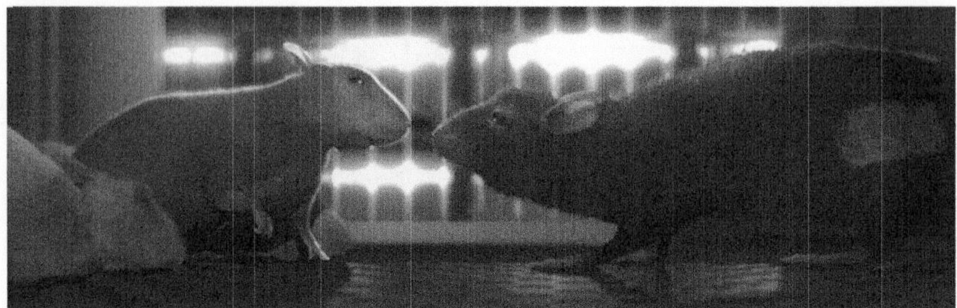

One Rat Short exemplifies the tensions between the metaphysical representation of the animal condition and the metaphoric implications of human attitudes to animals, and their subsequent treatment.

attention to the pursuit of the snack packet, finds itself in a futuristic animal experiments facility. This is an engaging narrative principle, in the sense that it potentially shifts the emphasis from understanding the rat as an arbitrary animal living by its instincts and surviving the vicissitudes of the external environment to an animal under threat, directly affected by the absent presence of humankind.

This shift is very important in that under these conditions the animal is fully revealed by virtue of the ways in which humankind seeks to entrap and treat the creature, particularly in a challenging sequence in which a machine grabs and syringes the rat. If an audience had understood the rat, and the other rats and mice in the facility, as mere vermin, these animals now seem subject to cruelty, which even if reconciled in the name of science is not foregrounded here as a necessary and compassionate process, but rather as an inhuman/inhumane act of distanciated brutality, wholly unconnected with any recognition of the animal as a feeling creature. Weil is careful to heighten the emotional tenets of the piece by including the rat's attraction to another rat, played out first through the male rat's observation of the female rat in the pincers of a machine transporting it to an experimental process, and later as they pick up each other's scent and rub their bodies together. In a clever narrative conceit, Weil shows that the rats in the facility are bar-coded in the same fashion as consumer products like the snack packet, and as the film reaches its denouement the machine misreads the barcode on the snack packet, which prompts an operational dysfunction and a possible opportunity for the rats to escape. The snack packet floats through the scene and beyond the facility doors, offering the imperative for the male and female rat to pursue it and attain their freedom. At this point, however, the rats are separated, the male on the outside, the female left in the facility, as the snack packet blows away and the film concludes.

The film invites a range of metaphorical interpretations. The snack packet seems to function as some unattainable hope or dream, but, significantly, its narrative function as the signifier of possible sustenance for the rat maintains the integrity of animal imperatives even in the light of the romantic scenario. The male rat's pursuit of the snack packet remains in place as its core objective from first to last in the face of both the threats from the internal and external environments and the attractions of the female rat. The pure animal remains at the heart of the narrative because Weil predicates the rat's actions on the instinctual needs of the creature rather than more conscious decisions. Ed Hooks, renowned teacher of acting for animators, has written extensively about the need for the animator to recognize such imperatives in the creation of characters, the development of narratives, and the maintenance of dramatic plausibility, arguing that "there are seven possible human emotions: surprise, disgust, anger, fear, happiness, sadness, and contempt" (Hooks 2005, 169), clearly recognizing that animals share these emotional states. It is the animator's empathetic engagement with these felt experiences in the animal that offer the potential to depict the most authentic idea of the pure animal. The emphasis on visualization in animation—aided by music, but often not compromised by words—enables emotional states to be illustrated and alluded to, rather than described or explained. When Hooks adds that "acting has almost nothing to do with words" (Hooks 2005, 172), he alludes to the profound affect of how physical, material, and gestural communication operates in the real world, and is made most readily available through the self-conscious ways in which the animator acts through and uses the purely visual premises of the animated form to foreground the felt experience. The pure animal in animation is the representation of felt experience and is readily exemplified in *One Rat Short*.

Hooks's analysis of *Tarzan* (Chris Buck, Kevin Lima, USA, 1999) looks at these issues in some detail from the actor/animator's perspective, identifying that action which is played out through close observation of physical and contextual reaction—largely the way in which animal behavior is understood—for the most part authenticates narrative intentions. In *Tarzan,* this is problematized to some extent by Tarzan's status as an ape man, and perhaps the most literal interpretation of the hybrid humanimal in my model of bestial ambivalence. On the one hand, Tarzan operates as a jungle creature, defined through his primal holler and his instinctive and sensual responses to other creatures and the environment, while on the other, he embraces human tendencies, most notably his ready adoption of language. This distinction is not as pronounced as it might have been. Following the initial action—in which Kala and Kerchak's infant gorilla is abducted by Sabor the tiger, Kala finds the infant Tarzan after his parents have been killed by the tiger, and Kala escapes from Sabor herself—the ape world is characterized by talking animals. At the narrative level, Kerchak, the male ape, wants to expel Tarzan, unwilling to adopt a creature from another species, but ultimately he accepts Kala's wishes. As Hooks notes, there are ongoing moments of recognition that Tarzan is different, but these are largely negotiated through touch—"Tarzan places his hands against Kala's. That is when it hits him that, without any doubt, he is of a different kind than his 'mother.' The self-realization and shift in emotion in that moment is just wonderful acting" (Hooks 2005, 164).

Moreover, there appear at this moment different kinds of consciousness, and this comes to inform later action sequences when Tarzan fights with Sabor, where Hooks suggests that "Tarzan is continually thinking and strategizing. Sabor is a lower intelligence animal and relies purely on instinct" (Hooks 2005, 165). Tarzan presents Sabor to Kerchak in an act of respect, subservience, and acceptance of his place in the jungle culture, a moment ruptured by a ringing gunshot and the onset of humanity into the narrative. There follows a very important moment in Tarzan's transition from dominantly animal to prototypically human, when he examines the spent bullet casing:

> He first smells the gunpowder and follows the scent. When he finds the casing, he does not immediately pick it up. He nudges it with his finger to see if it might move or something. It is only after

> he is satisfied that this is not a living thing that he picks it up.
> This makes perfect sense if you think about it. The closest thing
> to a bullet Tarzan has ever seen is probably a rock. He certainly
> has never seen man-made metal. Our minds work in a sequen-
> tial way, comparing what we see to other things we have seen in
> the past. It is impossible to understand the concept "furniture"
> until you first understand "table" and "chair." A bullet casing fits
> nowhere in Tarzan's frame of reference. (Hooks 2005, 165–166)

This idea of the particular frame of reference is helpful in understanding the shifts from pure animal to aspirational human to humanimal to
critical human, in the sense that within each context, Tarzan engages
with differing models of behavior and consciousness. This sequence
alone shows the pure animal in Tarzan when he is addressing the bullet
casing in the first instance as if it were in the first moments post-kill
that is, like Weil's rat, on the terms and conditions that best characterize his instinctive needs. Once the object moves beyond the remit
of his intuitive understanding, the frame of reference becomes one of
curiosity, the need to relocate the object in a way that gives him insight
as to what it is. This, both literally and psychologically, takes him closer
to humanity.

When Tarzan finally confronts Jane, he learns through mimesis
and embraces the possibilities of language, but for the first time, with
another human being. Their initial meeting is preceded by a long
sequence of Tarzan observing the human intruders on an expedition
to study gorillas: Clayton, the ostensible villain of the piece; the Professor, a bumbling, well-meaning oaf; and Jane, a woman, whom Tarzan
is immediately attracted to yet troubled by. These feelings ultimately
underpin Tarzan's central quandary, as he will have to seemingly
choose between Jane, representing his inclination to humanity, and
his adopted ape family. Tarzan, even while knowing his difference,
is unaware that he comes from human stock. Once more, language
becomes a significant issue at the moment when Tarzan learns some
English and is asked to guide the expedition to the gorillas, simultaneously becoming an aspirational human in demonstrating his conceptual understanding and emotional sophistication, and a critical human

in recognizing that he may be doing wrong in potentially betraying his ape family. Tarzan's imperative by this stage is, in effect, to secure Jane in his life and for her to stay in the jungle, and, clearly, little remains of the pure animal or humanimal apart from a recognition that his ape family might be in danger from Clayton. Though he touches his heart when he speaks of Kala as "his mother," Tarzan is actually caught between the ape and human worlds and has to engage with complex moral questions—particularly concerning the death of Clayton—and it is this which finally draws him away from the pure animal, though Hooks argues, "After Kerchak dies, Tarzan makes an almost imperceptible gesture. He gently chucks Kerchak under the chin. You will see animals do this kind of thing, but not humans. An animal will still try and rouse the dead, uncertain of the moment of death. A human knows right away what death means" (Hooks 2005, 173). In what is therefore a highly symbolic moment, Tarzan makes the transition from animal to human through the realization of mortality. This is a very important issue in discourses about the animal, and is addressed in the next chapter, but Tarzan's realization of death here is equally a moment of recognition that he must take Kerchak's place and reconcile his past with his future. This is further symbolized by Jane's staying with him in the jungle and the assertion of Tarzan's primal cry as the final statement in the film.

Hooks's work is highly enabling in understanding how the animator becomes an empathetic performer through animal characters and their narratives. At the heart of his analysis is not merely the recognition of the way in which physical performance tropes best represent animal behavior and culture, but the place of language in the anthropomorphic exchanges. Over and beyond the contexts in which animals speak as humans, even if they sustain anticipated animal behavior, the most important factor becomes when animals speak and when animals speak to humans. Again Hooks offers some apposite observations, but in relation to Pixar's *Ratatouille* (Brad Bird, USA, 2007):

> If you have the rat speak out loud English with any of the human characters, you will overly challenge the audience member's willingness to suspend his disbelief. Inter-species communication

is a fascinating challenge for animation. You can anthropomorphize inanimate things and animals all you want, but you have
to be very careful about how you have them interact with one
another, and especially with humans. In *The Lion King,* all of the
animals had human traits and personalities, but they related only
to one another. In *Finding Nemo,* the fish never directly communicate with that human dentist. In *Lady and the Tramp,* the animals
talk to one another, but not to the humans. In *Cars,* John Lasseter
solved the problem by not having human drivers for the cars.
(Hooks 2007, 1–2)

This is significant because by delimiting the animal world to itself, even when using language, some notion of the pure animal and the wild system, might be preserved, though, as we have seen, this is largely contradictory and prompts the *Madagascar* Problem rather than definitive animal narratives. Bird resolves his quandary by establishing successful nonverbal communication between Remy the rat and the Linguini, the ginger-haired boy, preserving the divide between the human and animal world. The other key human/rat relationship is actually imaginary. Remy's configuration of the French chef Auguste Gusteau is entirely fictional, another device to distanciate the human agenda from the rat world. Though operating differently, *Ratatouille*'s rat is similar to Weil's rat in preserving the absent presence of human intervention in order to better reveal the nature of the animal. It is an obvious remark to make, but the presence or absence of the human in relation to the animal makes a significant difference to the understanding of the animal, though this may be cultural, too.

Fred Patten, commenting on Japanese auteur Osamu Tezuka's inspiration for *Jungle Emperor,* later known in the United States as *Kimba, the White Lion* (Osamu Tezuka, Japan, 1965), notes: "Tezuka felt that if forest animals in *Bambi* had been as self-aware and mutually social as they were depicted, they would not have remained so fearful and remote from man. They would have recognized man as just another animal like themselves, and tried to communicate with him. This led to his own story in which the animals of Africa realize the advantages of civilization and try to take advantage of them and try to get man to recognize them as social equals" (Patten 2004, 152). Tezuka had a view of nature and culture that anticipates Haraway's concept of the naturalcultural in the sense that he believed that there was less difference between the natural world and civilization than established cultural thinking would allow. This is partly reconciled in the Japanese context through the filter of the co-presence of the spiritual world in the material environment, connecting past and present, primal lore with modern life. In recent years, *Kimba, the White Lion* has for the most part been discussed within the context of its apparent similarities to *The Lion King* and the dispute surrounding Disney's lack of acknowledgment of *The Jungle Emperor* as a source. Here, however, I wish to stress how the series reflects the investment in the animal and the natural world as a repository of particular values and a use of animation as a creative medium by which to express them.

Kimba's father, the great white lion Caesar, is killed by hunters, and Kimba, helped by his mother to escape back to Africa, is charged with leading the animal kingdom. "All must flee a beast with the brain, the jeep, and the gun" in order to preserve the balance of the natural world. As humans fell forests and capture animals for commercial exploitation, animals engage with a higher order intrinsic to a more ancient quasi-supernatural, supra-normal nature. Kimba's mother communicates with him through a configuration of stars; butterflies lead Kimba to the African shore; and animals embrace music as a way of knowing the abstraction of more positive and more closely related notions of human value and beauty. Moreover, Tezuka felt that as well as preserving this sense of animal identity through the principles of his storytelling, it was necessary to preserve the animal through the particularities of technique. "Why animals?" Tezuka writes in his preface to his technical manual, "Animals in Motion," for the Tezuka School of Animation, answering his own rhetorical question: "Because despite the amazing improvements in animation technology and the ever advancing capability of computer generated animation, one rarely sees impressive animation of animal movement," continuing, "This may be in part due to the fact that the appearance of animals, particularly in TV animation, has declined in recent years. Since that has become a trend of the times, we have tried to set this book apart by focusing on animals in the sincere hope that when animals do happen to appear, a life-like vitality will be added to their movement" (Tezuka 2003, 3).

Unlike American animation, which largely predicates its anatomical studies on the status of the animal as a carnivore or herbivore, and the concomitant movement this produces, Japanese animators essentially base their work on looking at animal skeletons—the plantigrades (e.g., bears, mice, monkeys), who place their foot on the ground when walking, from the toe to the heel; the digitigrades (e.g., dogs, baboons, lions) who walk on four toes while the heel stays up in the air; and the unguligrades (e.g., horses, cows, deer, impalas, or antelopes), who transport their bodies by hooves (see Tezuka 2003, 6). Assessing the movement of a horse, for example, the animators look at the walk, the trot, and the gallop, and examine cycles of motion, dominant legs, airborne moments, and height of leg, and look to details, for example, those concerning the representation of a foal: "The young horse, compared to the adult horse, is characterized by its legs being longer in relation to the rest of its body. The tail is also shorter" (Tezuka 2003, 31). In comparison, here is Christopher Hart's advice: "The young horse is often knock-kneed and long-limbed. The neck is not yet powerful, and the face can either be slender or slightly shortened, or both. The tail could be short or droopy, but not graceful, and the ears have grown faster than the rest of the body. He's a gangly fella, but cute" (Hart 1997, 62). The different imperatives are immediately noticeable. Tezuka seeks to preserve the pure animal in the design in the first instance, while Hart seeks out the humanimal immediately, casting anatomy for personality rather than its pertinence first and foremost to motion. Though a highly specific observation, this is part of a bigger recognition of the place and context of the animal in potential narratives, and, inevitably, this is related to storytelling needs and cultural context.

Nature and Narrative

Apropos of the Disney live-action wildlife film, Derek Bouse has argued:

> Upon consideration of a) the pre-Disney *pre-cinema* history of animal storytelling, b) the longstanding Disney practice of adapting

> for film pre-existing novels, tales, legends and myths, and c) the
> post-Disney development of the wildlife film as a *genre,* it seems
> tenable to conclude that the real nature of Disney's contribution
> (some would say his genius) involved translating into specifically
> filmic terms the type of animal story that had come to embody
> some of our most deeply held attitudes toward nature, and
> toward our own place in relation to it. (Bouse 1995, 20)

The relationship between nature and culture in the naturalcultural was explored earlier, addressing the various methods by which animals mediated ideas about both concepts, but I wish to engage here with how animals mediate the relationship between nature and narrative. Bouse's suggestion that Disney effectively established the genre of the cinematic animal story in this respect is therefore highly significant, especially as he goes on to define the classical paradigm of such a story. This is usually characterized by an initial establishing context of spring or a time of new birth or community ritual, which is normally followed by a rupture in this apparent calm and continuity: a lead character is orphaned, literally or symbolically, prompting a journey or quest that in turn operates as a rites of passage tale or avenging story. The character then finds new friends or an alternative community, and through adventures informed by trial, suffering, and overcoming major challenges, resolves any schisms in the response to a common plight and overcomes adversarial elements. Community is normally restored, and the main character in completing the journey is advanced spiritually and practically. This paradigm is recognizable, for example, from *Dumbo* (Ben Sharpsteen et al., USA, 1941) to *The Land Before Time* (Don Bluth, USA, 1988) to *Finding Nemo* (Andrew Stanton and Lee Unkrich, USA, 2003), but while the narrative is recognizable, it is clear that any revelation about nature or the animal that might emerge from these structural parameters is, in effect, an observation about human endurance in the face of life's inevitable vicissitudes.

The embedded knowledge of the animal in these narratives is often, both for the animators and the characters themselves, about overcoming physical difficulties—the size of Dumbo's ears; the limits of Apatosaurus; Littlefoot's strength and expression (producers Steven

Spielberg and George Lucas originally wanted no dialogue in the film); Nemo's damaged fin (and the limited expressive vocabulary of fish in general). Though these have some sources in actual animal behavior, they are aspects that service narrative imperatives and the storytelling mode of reconciliation and conclusion. What becomes important, then, is the struggle itself, and how characters relate to natural environments or adapt to alternative conditions. Dumbo becomes naturalized to the human world in succeeding as a circus performer; Littlefoot reaches his natural home in the Great Valley when reunited with his own kind; while Nemo is reconciled to the dangers of the sea, securing his father's trust that he can survive amid seemingly relentless predators. Indeed, *Finding Nemo,* with its opening scenes of a barracuda eating clownfish, sharks seeking food, and interventions by humankind, does most to balance the realism of context with the necessary progress of the characters. Crucially, then, although these brief observations point to the ways in which story structure and character speak to the natural-cultural tensions I have defined earlier, the bestial ambivalence model more pertinently shows "discourse-in-flux" or "animal-in-the-making," and illuminates how a text evolves to take into account these shifting determinacies. I wish to extend this further by suggesting that the bestial ambivalence model can, therefore, not merely be used as a tool to identify the nature of animal representation within a narrative, but can also be used to define a narrative per se. To conclude this section, then, I wish to identify four examples of animated animal films—the pure animal tale, the critical human story, the aspirational human narrative, and the humanimal scenario. All these were coincidentally produced for the "Stop, Look, Listen" children's educational series dealing with animals, produced by Channel Four in the UK for five- to seven-year-old children, and all were drawn from different parts of the world.

Biswas the Bull (Moving Still, UK, 1996), based on an Indian folktale, tells the story of a humpbacked bull who is born unaware of his species, identity, or place, and whose attempts to reconcile himself with water buffalo and elephants—often life-threatening and painful—render him alone until he recognizes the shadows of other humpbacked bulls and joins with them, sharing a primal bellow of relationship and continuity. There are clear echoes here of the classical narrative structure identified

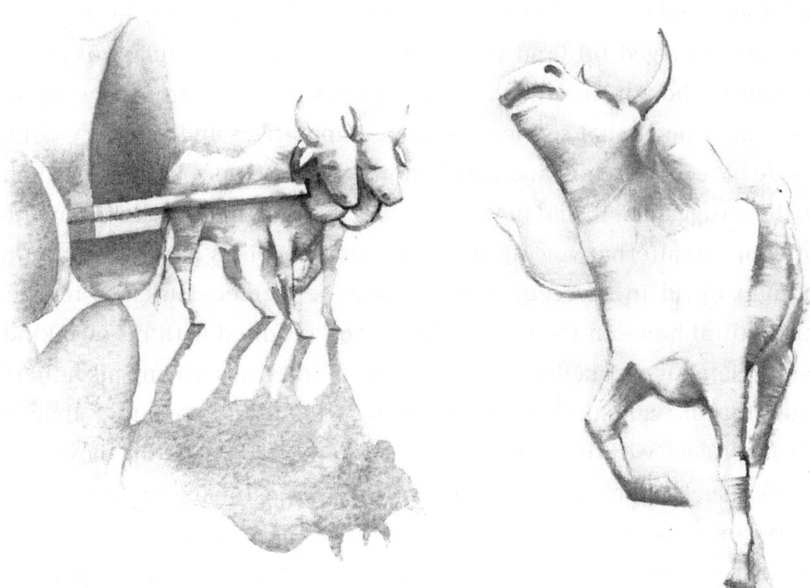

Biswas the Bull. Biswas's identity is affirmed, as in many cases of animal representation in animation, through the pure expression of animal cries and physical gestures. From *Animals*, created and directed by Tim Fernée.

above, but a major difference occurs in the way that the story is told and the animation is used. The film uses traditional voiceover storytelling technique, and though a first-person narrative is employed, the film resists the use of talking animals and privileges the animation to encompass the experience of animality—Biswas nearly drowning amid the marauding herd of water buffalo or being fearful as he observes the alien behavior of a basking elephant as he noisily evacuates water from his trunk. The final aspect remains the most important, though—the primal bellow shared by the bulls is the core signifier of the pure animal narrative in that it *only* focuses on the nature of the animal in the expression of itself. This is the core principle at the heart of this concept. It also chimes with notions of the sacredness of the animal in Asian cultures, and the sense of its respected bistance from humankind.

The tale of *The Wren, King of the Birds* (Moving Still, UK, 1996) from Ireland is an example of the aspirational human story, and though it once more uses first-person voiceover narration and privileges the animation to show the dynamics of bird flight, it does depict core

Biswas the Bull. Biswas is reunited with his kind and again confirms the specificity of his animal identity through his relationship with, and difference from, other animals. From *Animals*, created and directed by Tim Fernée.

characters with human expression and signals the importance of their point of view through recognizable human emotions. The story concerns the day when the birds decide to choose their king, and agree that whoever can fly the highest deserves the honor. The Golden Eagle is shown to be big, fierce, proud, and powerful, and assumes he will inevitably win. The owl starts the flight, and first hedge and tree birds give up, followed by swallows and larks, then geese, ducks, hawks, and seagulls, leaving the Golden Eagle soaring in the sky. Just as the Eagle believes he has won, the wren, who has concealed himself among the Eagle's feathers, flies out, flying higher than the now-terminally fatigued Eagle. The wren becomes "King of the Birds," "not for being the biggest of the birds . . . not for being the fiercest . . . nor for being the most beautiful of birds . . . but for being the cleverest." This kind of witty narrative is in some ways typically Irish in its invention, and operates as an aspirational human animal animation because its story premise is not about the processes of struggle and survival in the *securing* of identity, like Biswas, but a narrative concerned with showing

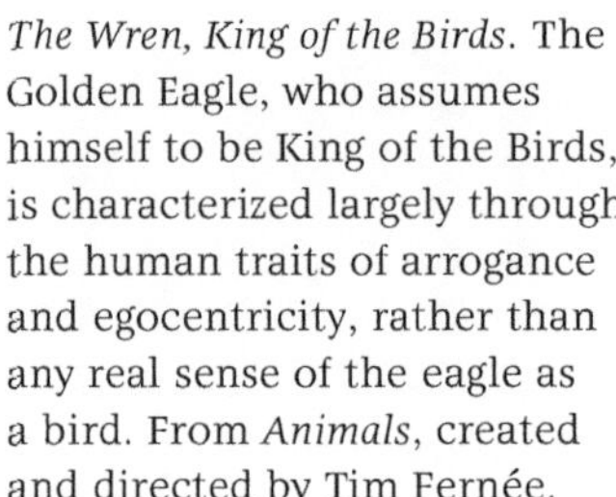

The Wren, King of the Birds. The Golden Eagle, who assumes himself to be King of the Birds, is characterized largely through the human traits of arrogance and egocentricity, rather than any real sense of the eagle as a bird. From *Animals*, created and directed by Tim Fernée.

the values in the *confirmation* of identity. Bird flight here is used more metaphorically, though its literal challenge to particular birds is accurate and doubles readily for a metonymic measure of aspiration and achievement. The story, if played out like an Aesop's Fable, would probably demonstrate pride before a fall, but more significant here are the presentation of value-laden ideals concerning how humankind sees its own worth—largely through physical size, strength, power, and beauty rather than through the intellect or imagination. The wren merely proves that wit and intelligence are ultimately more important, though it does value its own beauty, and the narrative itself plays out the idea that, although values are relative, true aspiration for humankind can only be achieved by challenging assumptions and advancing more pertinent models of progress.

Anancy the Spider (Moving Still, UK, 1996), a story from the Caribbean Islands, is a morality tale that operates entirely as a critical human model, because it is a tale told in the third person, advancing the narrative by talking about the uniformly unacceptable actions of "Great-grandfather, Anancy, the spider," and using the animation to facilitate the literal interpretation of impossible conceptual ideas. Here, though Anancy is seen to be clever, he is lazy, resting while others work, or worse, letting his son, Tikuma, mend his web. This sits

The Wren, King of the Birds. The Wren outwits the Golden Eagle by flying on his back, only emerging to fly higher when the Eagle is exhausted. Animals offer ready metaphoric narrative templates that reflect human hierarchies and social infrastructures. From *Animals*, created and directed by Tim Fernée.

uneasily, of course, with the common assumption of spiders as industrious creatures, taken to its logical extreme in a story like *Charlotte's Web* (Gary Winick, USA, 2006), where a spider signals levels of intelligence through not merely the construction of its web but by spelling words in it. Anancy, however, makes a distinction between manual craft, which he sees as beneath him, and his desire for wisdom. Others tell him to "get wise," meaning he should recognize his shortfalls, but Anancy sees this as a provocation to become cleverer, begging the god Jah to endow him with "all the wisdom in the world." Jah refuses and tells Anancy he must go into the world and find out for himself, and evaluate the difference between sense and nonsense. Here the animation plausibly illustrates Anancy's exchange with Jah and, further, Anancy's role as a news reporter as he interviews "the goodies and the baddies, the cops and the robbers, and of course, the spiders and the flies," as well as his gathering of papers, books, and films representing his great haul of wisdom. So proud is he of his achievement that he wishes to keep his wisdom to make him rich, and, fearful of those who would steal it, and mistrustful of even those closest to him, he decides to hide his wisdom in his wife's cooking pot. Again, the illusionist reality of the animated form authenticates this metaphorical principle.

Anancy the Spider. Anancy lazes in his web, contradicting the stereotyped representation of the spider as an earnest worker whose web is evidence of his craftsmanship and creativity. From *Animals*, created and directed by Tim Fernée.

Pursued by his son Tikuma as he attempts to hide the pot, Anancy is startled into dropping the pot and spilling the wisdom all over the world. The story concludes with the idea that this is why it is still possible to find wisdom anywhere, but it is necessary to "sort the sense from the nonsense"—something Anancy was clearly incapable of doing—and that such was Anancy's shame that he fled to the corner of the ceiling, "which is where he can be found to this day," playing on the typical depiction of spider webs in the corners of rooms. The animation here services the shifting registers of Anancy's prayer, his worldwide search, his embrace of material things, and his status as a spider, but the overwhelming focus of the story is a critique of human vanity, greed, and selfishness. This could not be more opposite than the conclusion of *Charlotte's Web*, which starts from the premise of focusing on "plain old animals who didn't question the order of things" through the dignifying

Anancy the Spider. Animation offers ready representation of symbolic and meta-phoric ideas—here Anancy's spillage of knowledge, represented in books, films, and so on. From *Animals*, created and directed by Tim Fernée.

actions of a spider in enabling the survival of a runt-pig, finally arriv-ing at the view that this occurred "all because someone stopped to see the grace, the beauty, and the ability of the humble creature"—clearly a more aspirational model.

The final example is *The Cat* (Moving Still, UK, 1996), a folktale from Egypt, which works as a humanimal example from the bestial ambivalence model because its narrative simultaneously signals the codependent relationship and common interfaces between the human and animal. This is a particularly pertinent tale because it speaks directly about the tension between nature and culture, here depicted as a metaphorical and historicized engagement between the wild and the call to domesticity. Here the animation privileges the physical action and expressiveness of the cat, while the voiceover, though told in the first person, signals that in the voice of the absent female householder, humanity is best signified through language. The cat claims itself to be the wildest of all animals, citing primal culture as a time and place in which nothing was known about humankind, until one by one, the dog, the horse, and the cow set off into the night, never to return, ultimately domesticated or exploited by humans.

The Cat. Resisting the traditional aspects of a cartoon cat, Tim Fernée captions the essence of the cat's aggression in its gestures, paws, and teeth. From *Animals*, created and directed by Tim Fernée.

When the cat decides to approach a woman at a household, she seeks to both enter the house "to sit by her warm fire and drink her delicious milk," but also to maintain her status as a wild animal. The woman dismisses the cat back into the countryside, but the cat, in the story's core narrative complication, suggests that if the woman could be tricked into saying three complimentary things about the cat, she would be allowed to enter the house, sit by the hearth, and have milk three times a day. The cat achieves this by comforting the woman's baby, stroking it under the chin with its tail when it cries, amusing it by bouncing and chasing a ball of wool, and catching a mouse loose in the household. The story concludes obliquely in some senses, the cat stressing, "And that is how I got my place by the fire. And when I feel like it, I go out at night to the wild places and walk by myself. As wild as ever I was." This works as a humanimal narrative because it half-uses the domestic definition of the cat, determined by humankind, essentially as an amusing diversion, a pet who can interact with human culture, and half-stresses the consciousness of the cat in maintaining its animality, the wild again signifying a more primal knowledge out-side the comprehension of humankind. This parallel focus stresses the

The Cat. The cat endears itself to domestic security while retaining its intuitive sense of the wild. From *Animals*, created and directed by Tim Fernée.

tensions in the *formation* and *construction* of the naturalcultural, and this is the core principle in the humanimal.

Journalist Richard Mabey has stressed that these kind of narrative or representational engagements enable humankind to remain "participants rather than spectators," able "to focus honestly on our relationships with nature, not imagine we can portray nature itself" (Mabey 2003, 4–6), but while it is clear that the former is true—participation being an active rather than passive requirement of the understanding of the abstraction of animation per se—I would argue that the use of the bestial ambivalence model in animation allows for both the depiction of relationships in the natural order and an evaluation and definition of nature and the animal itself. Animation as an art almost inherently offers pertinent comment on humankind's delusion that it manages and controls life anyway. At one level, it can offer anarchic, comic, cartoonal difference; at another, it can literally depict seemingly unimaginable states of consciousness or complex primal feelings. Further, it can visualize potentially impenetrable concepts and constructions. In all these areas of expression, the relationship between the beast and the text has been one of revelation about both—simultaneously, an insight about the animal and the creative artist as the embodiment of humanity. Animation is a ready vehicle to both illustrate and exemplify the relationship between animals and humankind through the necessity and consequences of change, sometimes denatured yet subversive, but most often most renatured and progressive, and it is this I explore in the following chapter.

4

Which Came First, the Chicken or the Egg?

Performance, Philosophy, Tradition

Phenomenological Performance

In a tour-de-force examination of the role of the animal in philosophic enquiry, Akira Muzuta Lippit moves seamlessly from Descartes's view of animals as unthinking machines to Leibniz's conception of animal as a composition of immortal, soul-like protean parts to Schopenhauer's view of consciousness being embedded across the whole animal world and thus shared by both humankind and beasts. He addresses Rousseau's notion of animals as sensually intelligent machines lacking in self-awareness, looking also to Kant's, Burke's, and Hegel's configuration of animals within language and through their articulation in a cry or sound, taking in Lyotard's notion that there is a sense of separateness in the "pure body" of the animal that accords with the human unconscious. He focuses on the Heideggerian denial of the ability for an animal to know the process or presence of its own death and the poverty of its existence in the human-formed world, but, equally, he details Nietzsche's joyful embrace of the ephemeral present in animal "becoming." Ultimately, Lippit suggests that "by tracking the animal across the philosophical spectrum, one discovers the systemic manner in which the figure of the animal comes to portray a serial logic: the animal is incapable of language; that lack prevents the animal from experiencing death; this in turn suspends the animal in a virtual, perpetual existence. The figure of the animal determines a radically antithetical counterpoint to human mortality, to the edifice of human-ism" (Lippit 2000, 73).

So, what then for the more literal-minded of us? How does this model of dense nuanced inquiry and intellectual engagement help to facilitate this particular discussion? I have already established that the concepts of bestial ambivalence and the naturalcultural speak to a range of open and dynamic discourses that are especially revealed by the working practices in, and execution of, the particular and unique language of expression available in animation. Consequently, I have also sought to illustrate that animation can accommodate the density of these discourses within its own models of a critical and pragmatic anthropomorphism, and its facility to invoke the particular terms of visualization that reveal the material and cultural presence of the animal. I want to further suggest, perhaps provocatively, that the facil-ity for animation to work as form which privileges phenomenological imagery—not quite human, not quite animal, not quite real, yet embed-ded in humanity, animality, and reality—enables it to stake a claim by which it can be seen to actually express, illustrate, and *perform* the terms and conditions of philosophical agendas. The following chapter will therefore explore the idea of animals within the frame of phenom-enological performance and philosophical inquiry.

John Halas of the British Halas & Batchelor studio insisted that animation was always a more complex medium than any common understanding of the American animated cartoon in some of its idi-oms might allow. He thus championed the animated film as a serious art form, arguing that it could support the expression of modern art through its ability to embrace any aesthetic application, but, more important, that it was an intrinsically metaphysical form (see Halas and Wells 2006). I have argued that the ways in which animation invokes and plays out the multiplicity of its discourses can work at a number of levels, but its particular ability to interrogate what I have elsewhere defined as a "primal" state (see Wells 2002a; Wells 2007) is particularly significant in the revelation of philosophical principles because it is predicated on the view that animation can readily depict interior psychological and emotional states—dream, memory, solip-sistic preoccupation, fantasy, heightened consciousness, feeling, and so on. This point of access not only reveals the conditions of sensibility and sentience but also has accord with the deep-rooted, archaic knowledge of animality. Crucially, within the animated space there is a high degree of performance that facilitates the particular impact of these spaces, self-consciously invoking the presence of acts of thought, conceptual preoccupation, and philosophic inquiry. As Claude Lévi-Strauss has suggested, "Animals are good to think" (see Lévi-Strauss 2007, 251–261), and provides a model by which ideas can be mobilized through performative idioms, embracing aesthetic choices, sociocultural constructs, and historical determinacy.

Within the context of this discussion, these ideas may be best understood through Boria Sax's idea of "animals as tradition," in which the respect for and preservation of animals is intrinsically bound up with the lore that has in some senses defined them, and provides the contextual platform by which a philosophy of animals might be readily determined (see Sax 2007, 270–277). Sax defines five key categories of animals as tradition—metamorphosed animals, divine animals, demonic animals, satiric animals, and political animals—and these provide ready signposts by which to address such animals within animated film. I explore these throughout this chapter but it is useful to preface this kind of discussion with a view of the way in which different human constituencies have been placed within such a model of tradition and helped to configure its lore. This is neatly summed up in Mark Baker's short film *Hill Farm* (Mark Baker, UK, 1988) in the figures of farmers, tourists, and hunters.

The film is essentially an engagement with three different views of how nature, embodied in the countryside, has become defined as the naturalcultural by those who occupy and exploit its space. The farmers have a strict and ritualistic routine that sees them feed their stock regularly, and they embrace a fully instrumental expectation of the animals in the production of food. When a cow drinks water, the farmer immediately milks the cow, almost as if one liquid has flowed through the cow and transmuted into another, and in both a shocking and highly amusing moment, the farmer's wife breaks a chicken's neck and immediately begins plucking it. There is no sense that the animals are anything but the stock of the farm, part of an economic chain that binds them into a purely functional role. These animals are being bred for consumption and inform the core labor of the farm workers. When a sheep strays beyond the confines of the farm, however, it is at the mercy of wild systems that are significantly different from the routines of farm life, and soon finds itself threatened by a huge bear. The film at no time treats the animals as if they are anything but living creatures absorbed within the particular existence of their context. The bear merely seeks food and sees the sheep as a potential meal, while the chickens and pigs on the farm are defined through their acquiescent conditioning at the hands of the farmers. When they are rounded up at night they are protected from the vicissitudes of the more abstract, ambiguous, and ambivalent predicament of the natural world.

Some tourists arrive, viewing the countryside purely as an aesthetic space, photographing the farm and distanciating themselves from its everyday imperatives and activities. Indeed, one of the tourists faints when he witnesses the farm wife break the neck of a chicken, and is self-evidently long removed from the more primal instinct that might enable a more ready identification with, and understanding of, the necessary actions of farm practice and the imminent challenges of nature. The farmer is a competent beekeeper and draws honey from a hive, and also performs manual tasks like bringing water from a hand-pumped well. The pump fails to work on one occasion, however, and this becomes a small crisis for the farm in the absence of more modern equipment. The third group of people involved in this countryside narrative are the huntsmen, whom Baker caricatures as highly provocative figures pursuing anything that moves, merely seeking pleasure from their apparent superiority to animals, persecuting geese and goading the bear.

The hunt's intrinsically English identity and qualities have been explored on a number of occasions, but particularly persuasive is Anthony Gross and Hector Hoppin's *Fox Hunt* (Anthony Gross and Hector Hoppin, UK, 1934), which, as David Curtis remarks, "uses fantasy to gently ridicule a cruel sport. Horses and riders meet outside a Palladian mansion and perform an acrobatic ballet with statues in the formal gardens. The fox quickly acquires a top hat from one of the riders, and leads the field on a chase across railway lines and along a newly built

Great West Road before escaping, leaving the hounds to scrap over his hat" (Curtis 1992, 134). Gross is particularly adept at using aesthetic ploys to redefine the chase, bringing a colorful lyricism to the absurdity of costumed and bedecked huntsmen as they are outwitted by the animals they exploit and pursue. Baker achieves the same thing by showing the huntsmen as utterly unthinking in their activities, shooting geese and humans alike. The hunt, like the tourists, operates in ways that merely show how distanced humankind has become from the common cycles of the natural world.

A storm breaks, causing damage to the farm. The farmers respond by repairing the damage and welcoming the return of the water to the pump, while the huntsmen shoot a chicken and recover a waterlogged gun and the campers leave. Baker is careful not to create a spectacular denouement but rather a sense of continuum, reinforcing the enduring lore embedded in the naturalcultural. This amounts to a recognition of the intrinsic difference in animals, the ways in which humankind has thereafter managed the relationship with animals in a spirit of exploitation, empathy, and excess, and finally, cultivated traditional rituals and processes that speak to an orthodoxy which naturalizes these models. These naturalized orthodoxies underpin Sax's categories.

Metamorphosed Animals

Steve Baker has argued, "In today's world, animation, animatronics, and animal training (in *102 Dalmations* and elsewhere) help to conjure a spurious 'reality' of animal life and experience, while ordinary human knowledge of even domestic animal life becomes, it seems, more uncertain than ever" (Baker 2001, xvii–xviii). I have a more optimistic view: while it is clear that there *seems* an increased distanciation between human and animal kind, not least in the prevailing use of the animal to service and fuel human existence, it remains unclear if there was ever a halcyon day when human and animal were bonded in a more satisfying or sympathetic way. It is often assumed—even within this discussion—that there is a kind of prehistory in which humans and animals were in some degree or context more in accord, and less involved in an implied call and response between empathy and exploitation. What if one were to propose that in the apparently synthetic creation of the animal world through animation, animatronics, and animal training, that rather than creating a spurious reality of animal life and experience, the opposite were true, and this creative endeavor offered the possibility of a much stronger understanding of the animal and relationships with it?

This, of course, has been the underpinning imperative of my argument throughout, and is most strongly suggested through the notion that animators have a particular sensibility that does indeed have a greater degree of empathy with the animal and, consequently, respect for the animal in the ideas and concepts that may be expressed through it. I suggested in the early part of my discussion that it may be the case that humans and animals may, under some circumstances, be able to think alike, noting Temple Grandin's view of "autism" as a model of purely and uninhibitedly "thinking visually," something she says animals do, and I suggest may be part of the animator's distinctive armory. I explore this further below, but at the heart of this is the notion of agency. In the real world, one of the major concerns of those invested in any aspect of animal conduct and experience is the level of agency recognized in and permitted to animals and, therefore, how much an animal has power to act. As Jonathan Burt points out, though, "Acting is both a form of agency and something done under the direction of someone else" (Burt 2002, 32). Simply, I want to take this view to some extent literally, looking at the way in which the animal works under the direction of the animator, but also to insist that this is related to a special condition in the animator, animation director, or affiliated artist working in animation. This is closely allied to the material and organic nature of the animal, and the deep-rooted ideas and concepts embodied in the animal. In this sense, the animator becomes the facilitator of the performance of such ideas and concepts, but through the specific kinds of visualization pertinent to the form.

Chuck Jones remains perhaps the most articulate animator in relation to this notion, effectively seeking to find the greatest degree of empathy with the animal while using the specific terms and conditions of animation to best reveal, while still exaggerating, these characteristics. Jones versed himself in the feedback mechanisms in animal neuroscience to trace the ways in which animal movement was in some senses unconscious, driven to consistently balance and correct itself under a variety of contextual and material circumstances. In one of his classic cartoons, *One Froggy Evening* (Chuck Jones, USA, 1955), Jones was clear that a traditional notion of an "anthropomorphic frog, like a man in a frog's costume, would never do," adding:

> The thing that had to be funny was that the man would believe that a real frog was singing. The audience had to believe that, too. So you had to think, well, how does a frog feel? I had to study frogs to make certain we had the real frog. He was built like a real frog, and he dripped like a real frog. You know they're really just a blob, with these goddam legs hanging down, and kind of odd. . . . This meant that you actually had two ways of moving: one was this nutty singer and the other was as a frog. (quoted in Furniss 2005, 77)

While delineating this essential differentiation between the "pure animal" (the overt "frogness" of the frog captured through its motion and configuration) and the "aspirational human" (the performer eager for success), Jones considered some research carried out by Princeton scholars, who sought to prove if frogs had a particular kind of "awareness" (see Furniss 2005, 77). Their essential findings were that frog consciousness merely complicated and sometimes inhibited the efficiency of the frog. Arguably, in relation to Jones's cartoon, this may be illustrated by the difference between the assertion of resistant frogness by the frog when called upon to perform by its would-be exploiter, the construction worker, and the real condition of the frog at its most complex and self-sufficient, here projected comically through its private performance skills. Jones's sensitivity to these intrinsic principles, while still facilitating the expectations and language of the cartoon, demonstrates a highly specific approach to visualization. It is in this that an aside directly engaging with Grandin's ideas is necessary.

Many people have come to associate autism with two distinct stereotypes—the disengaged, inarticulate, troubled child, and the specifically and extraordinarily gifted savant. These stereotypes effectively operate at the extremes of autistic behavior and bookend a continuum of autistic engagement with many degrees of variability. Animal scientist

Temple Grandin, following such notable figures as Hans Asperger and Oliver Sacks, has effectively redefined such a continuum by, first, properly articulating the nature of her own autistic sensibility and, second, suggesting that animals operate somewhere on this spectrum by virtue of their particular capacity to think in images. Grandin's intellectual pedigree is beyond question, and her work groundbreaking; Sacks, for example, has noted that "for Temple, clearly, there is a continuum of experience extending from the animal to the spiritual, from the bovine to the transcendent. Thinking in pictures, she feels, represents a mode of perception, of feeling and thought and being, which we may call 'primitive,' if we wish, but not 'pathological'" (Grandin 2006, xviii). As I have suggested, it is this idea of "thinking in pictures" that allies both the animal and the animator in a special creative relationship, which, in being grounded in a particular kind of empathy, speaks to the multiple discourses at the heart of bestial ambivalence, and through visualization releases primal knowledge, which may be at the heart of Grandin's notion of primitive thought.

Grandin herself says that "today, everyone is excited about the new virtual reality computer systems in which the user wears goggles and is fully immersed in video game action. To me, these systems are like crude cartoons. My imagination works like the computer graphics programmes that created the lifelike dinosaurs in *Jurassic Park*" (Grandin 2006, 5). Such a statement alone draws Grandin's model of thinking within the remit of the creative sensibility of the animator, who must necessarily progress work through the projection of imagined constructions through the available technological media that can embrace and record them. Animation, in this sense, works as a pro-filmic art, which defines itself as a model of associative, reflexive, and representational expression *before* its act of record. This in itself leads to one of the key defining characteristics of animation overall, which may also be linked to one of the specific conditions of the autistic mind identified by Grandin:

> My own thought patterns are similar to those described by A. R. Luria in *The Mind of a Mnemonist*. The book describes a man who worked as a newspaper reporter and could perform amazing feats of memory. Like me, the mnemonist had a visual image

for everything he had heard or read. Luria writes: "For when he heard or read a word, it was at once converted into a visual image corresponding with the object the word signified for him." The great inventor Nikola Tesla was also a visual thinker. When he designed electric turbines for power generation, he built each turbine in his head. He operated it in his imagination and corrected faults. He said it did not matter whether the turbine was tested in his thoughts or in his shop; the results would be the same. (Grandin 2006, 10)

Several important perspectives emerge from this assessment, most notably the way in which visualization services the mnemonic sensibility. This addresses the mental construction of materials and objects, which are conceived in a fashion that is thought to operate as a model of ontological equivalence with its potential physical or concrete outcome. These elements are absolutely crucial in the understanding of the distinctive language available in animation. Video artist Tim Sherman has advanced one of the most persuasive definitions of the animated form in this respect:

> Animation is the hard copy of memory, accessed while it is being rendered by hand, or by hands assisted by machine. In general, animation is memory that moves and evolves. . . . I am saying that animation—memory in the act of forming—alludes to something essential, yet unattainable: the imagination itself. . . . The romantics love the idea that the imagination can be witnessed as the life force of a pencil's line. . . . I love this idea myself. But unfortunately animation does not work this way. Animation is not the imagination revealed so directly, so wholly. Animation is the transparent act of manufacturing memory. This process of creating memory, as a kind of performance, is pushed or fuelled by the imagination, but the imagination remains hidden, unexposed. (Sherman 2005, 194)

Grandin's sensibility accords very readily with Sherman's definition of animation. Here animation functions both as a record of memory and an allusion to imagination itself. It chimes with the mnemonic quality of a sensibility visualizing something, and simultaneously reconciles the psychic construction of an imagined figure or object with its material presence. I wish to argue that the animator (animation director, etc.) in some senses shares this sensibility and executes a model of work in which the imagined becomes concrete in the phenomenological outcomes that follow in the animation itself. Crucially, in respect of this discussion, accepting Grandin's view of the animal as a nonhuman capable of perceiving the world like a human through a particular autistic frame, I wish to further argue that the animator has a specific empathy with the animal, possibly related to the autistic spectrum, demonstrated through the mnemonic tendency in animation as a form. As Sherman suggests, animation understood as a hard copy of memory prompts an act of psychic and metaphysical performance to recall the primal agenda or concept seeking expression and outlet. In this context, this process of visualization may be best illustrated by relating some of Grandin's views on her immersive empathy with animals—most particularly, cows—and an animated film by Alexander Petrov, called *The Cow* (Alexander Petrov, Russia, 1989).

Grandin has acknowledged, "The work I do is emotionally difficult for people, and I am often asked how I can care about animals and be involved in slaughtering them. . . . I tune in to what the actual sensations are like to the cattle rather than having the idea of death rile up my emotions. My goal is to reduce suffering and improve the way farm animals are treated" (Grandin 2006, 94). She adds:

When I put myself in a cow's place, I really have to be that cow and not a person in a cow costume. I use my visual thinking skills to simulate what an animal would see and hear in a given situation. I place myself inside its body and imagine what it experiences. . . . I have to follow the cattle's rules of behavior. I also have to imagine what experiencing the world through the cow's sensory system is like. . . . They live in a constant state of fear, worrying about a change in routine or becoming upset if objects in their environment are moved. This fear of change may be an activation of ancient anti-predator systems that are blocked or masked in most other people. (Grandin 2006, 168–169)

Though this is a somewhat lengthy exposition of Grandin's psychological makeup in regard to her approach to animals and animal welfare, it offers a powerful insight into the ways in which a dispassionate empathy is created, in order to embrace the particular truth of the animal sensibility and the modern fate of animals in many contexts.

This kind of sensibility is shared by many animators/artists in seeking to both explore their understanding of the animal and the discourses that are released when the actual conditions of animal existence are observed and acted upon. Using a painstaking painterly style reminiscent of Rembrandt, Alexander Petrov, like many Russian animators, including Yuri Norstein and Andrei Khrzhanovsky, and auteur filmmakers like Andrei Tarkovsky, seeks to sustain a similar empathy through a highly contemplative approach, which embraces and depicts memory, dream, and fluid states of consciousness in engaging with a young boy's relationship to a cow on a rural farm. This approach privileges a temporal focus that uses time as the core feature in measuring the specificity and affect of experience, simultaneously attempting to sensually locate the experience in an expressive idiom. It is this that defines the mode of animals as tradition in this case—not merely the metamorphosis of transition discussed in Chapter 2, but the sense of change, materially and metaphysically embedded in the animal figure and its culture.

Petrov tells the tale of a young boy and his affinity with mother cow and its growing calf. Their first point of empathy comes soon after the calf is born when the boy helps the calf drink milk by using his thumb as an artificial teat, encouraging him to imbibe from a pail. The boy's most intense bond, however, is with the cow, their feeling of connection seemingly an intrinsic aspect of the passing of time and the sense of undistracted investment in the organic changes that come with the seasons. When the calf is taken to market, though highly resistant to the boy's father, pulling away from its lead, the cow is clearly distressed at the absence of her son. The boy becomes aware of this and seeks to comfort the cow: "Cows don't cry; think something beautiful about your son." The cow then refuses to plow and becomes actively resistant to the needs of the farm, while the boy becomes increasingly invested in the cow at an emotional level: "Now I'll be your son." This is a powerful bond, predicated on an intuitive understanding of a shared animality;

one based on primal instincts and the essential recognition that the visceral connection of the mother/child relationship is shared across species, cultures, and time. The cow continues to resist, and one day breaks from her plow and escapes the farm. The farmer and his family search the nearby fields, calling out to the cow, but to no avail. This sequence, however, is crucial in reinforcing the different cultural investment in the cow as an intrinsic part of the running of the farm and the execution of its work. The cow is in some senses a personalized aspect of the process, not a merely mechanistic or operational factor in an industrialized model. It is a naturalized part of a lived experience, not to be judged by the sometimes indifferent standards of the western corporate production of animal products. In being an intrinsic part of a quasi-feudal farm-model of self-management and sustenance, the cow is embedded in the consciousness that underpins this premodern approach.

It is this consciousness that the boy understands, and in the absence of the cow imagines an almost sacred light flooding through the barn, and a baby—perhaps the boy himself—suckling the cow's udder. He fantasizes, too, that he can play with the cow, balancing on its horns. He is transported into the highest empathy with the animal, later stressing, after it has been discovered that the cow has been killed by a train, "Her milk, her son, her meat, her leather, her guts, and her bones, I'll never forget our cow." Crucially, the boy embraces the totality of the animal as a being, seeing her resources as a further model of connection rather than exploitation. Petrov depicts the killing of the cow in a way that presents the plow as if it were the train hitting the animal. This suggests that it was its role on the farm that truly killed the cow, implicitly recognizing that the sense of separation that the cow felt from her son proved to be the most powerful motive in its actions. By telling the story from the perspective of the boy, there is the clearest sense in which such emotions have been properly acknowledged in the animal and its place in this more archaic naturalcultural fully determined in all its senses. Petrov's film effectively works as a model of romantic realism in that pragmatic, everyday orthodoxies have been expressed through the filter of a more spiritual, more primal sensibility, at one and the same time discovering the animal while elevating it to a more equable position in a more primitive order. This is metamorphosis in time, space, and history, and not the socially engineered metamorphosis that is at the heart of the *Madagascar* Problem.

It is this kind of social engineering that is the subject of the humor in texts like *Madagascar* and which may be further exemplified in series like Dreamworks SKG's *Father of the Pride* (Various, USA, 2006). Sarmoti, father of Kate, and thorn-in-the-paw of Larry, his son-in-law, constantly chastises Larry with his tales of being a lion in the Serengeti: "You know, when I grew up in Africa, I didn't crack wise to my elders, but what would you know, you're zoo trash, you spent your youth in a zoo. I spent mine roaming the grasslands hunting wildebeest, surviving by my wits. All the time dreaming of a country called America, and its glittering crown jewel: Las Vegas." The ironies are obvious here, and the claims of the two cultures, readily if stereotypically, laid out; the raw conditions of the natural order set against the kitsch construction and control of the corporate order. Sarmoti's metamorphosis into a camp Vegas performer in the Siegfried and Roy magic spectacles is complete with the embellishment of a wig, hairspray, and a medal, and the source of constant play, where on the one hand he can keep a skin of a zebra—"this is my first kill; it is my last connection to Africa"—while on the other, embracing the identity and conventional behavior of a domestic cat—"I'm going to hit the litter box . . . hard." In one episode, Sarmoti reenacts the kill of the zebra as a ghost story to frighten and impress his grandson, but Kate, his daughter, is so angered by his intervention that she destroys the zebra skin ironically, if theatrically, once more recalling the original kill. Larry, watching Kate rip the zebra asunder, says, "Am I the only one who is turned on, right now?" answering his own question, once he realizes that Kate has not eroticized the moment, with "Yes." It is in this kind of action, though, even in a parodic sitcom, that tensions around the animal are being explored in the sense that the primal violence of the animal kill is often the subject of spectacle in features and documentaries, its shock value prompting various degrees of arousal in one form or another. Kate's reaction, though prompted by anger with her father, is nevertheless the ruthless unconscious action of the animal kill and not the cod-arousal of film-style violent action sequences. This play is a constant recognition of an order outside the predictable conventions of everyday human exchange, ironically facilitating animated spectacle by operating outside the equally predictable cinematic or televisual conventions that normally depict it. Though many of the incongruities in such narratives are inevitably the stuff of gags, it is important to remember that the very rupture that the gag offers in conventional storytelling is often the cleaving open of a meaningful space in the revelation and delineation of embedded and sometimes invisible or unstated narrative motives, or even alternative imperatives and perspectives.

If Sarmoti, Larry, and his clan are ultimately about the assimilation of the animal into the postmodern world, literally, materially, and metaphorically—"Larry, I want you to stay away from the edible neighbors"—and Petrov's cow is concerned with different models of a natural order that have equally assimilated but more readily acknowledged the significance of the animal, another model of metamorphosis may be found in its ultimate denial. Tang Cheng and Wu Qiang's *Bell on a Deer* (Tang Cheng and Wi Qiang, China, 1987) tells the story of a family of deer where a baby fawn is estranged from its mother and father following the brutal attack of an eagle. The injured fawn is found by a young girl called Mei who lives with her grandfather, who cautions, when the fawn refuses to take medicinal herbs and grasses from her, that "a fawn is a wild thing and belongs with its kind." The fawn's parents seek its scent in the forest and continue to pursue a trail in the hope of finding it. Mei continues to try and care for the injured fawn, encouraging it to play with her toys, giving it food, and training it to respond by placing a small bell around its neck. This gesture is an important one within the narrative and within the performative idiom that I suggest is at the heart of the philosophic principles within these narratives. Though couched within the terms and conditions of Mei's care, and the desire to build trust, the bell becomes a symbol for the fawn's socialization and intended conformism. The fawn's leg ultimately heals and he becomes part of the naturalized conditions of existence that Petrov features in *The Cow,* but in this context this merely points up the performed nature of the role the fawn plays within a human context and the true extent of the visceral emotional bond it shares with its own order.

The fawn is reminded of the connections with other animals as it cavorts with a monkey and a goat on a visit to market with Mei and her grandfather, but it is further domesticated by sharing Mei's chores. One day, however, in a clear demonstration of the way animation can facilitate the depiction of animal consciousness, the fawn relives the trauma of the attacking eagle and instinctively runs away. Mei hears the toy bell attached to the fawn and seeks to find it, but the cries of the deer are also heard by his father and mother, who are still seeking to find their child. The fawn sees his parents and wants to be with them, and though Mei is distraught at their parting, she realizes that her grandfather is right when he says "a deer must live the life it was made for." Mei gives the deer the toy bell, but, as the fawn departs with her parents, "the happy sound she loved completely disappeared." The fawn has been resocialized back into the natural order by the pleasures and pains of its own primal sensibility, rejecting the temporary metamorphosis of its status as a child's plaything and pet.

Though metamorphosis serves the radical shape-shifting and reconfigurations that can come with all animal/human interfaces in animated film—some of which are addressed later—the metamorphosis discussed here moves beyond metamorphosis as transformation, when something can literally become something else. It moves, too, beyond the idea of mutation, when something becomes a hybrid of two or more things; or propagation, when something splits, hatches, or doubles to create a number of changed elements or aspects. Here it becomes a model of *translation* in which a metaphysical insight is offered by revealing the relationship between former and current states and their oscillation. In many senses, this speaks to Sax's idea that even in despite of the totemic and tribal bonds humankind shared with animals, "for both men and women, the animal was that mystery in a partner that no intimacy could fully overcome" (Sax 2007, 273). This mystery is effectively the core principle of all metamorphoses in animated animal narratives.

Divine Animals

Animated film, as in all its manifestations, remains playful when addressing the divinity of animals, on the one hand respecting the place of the animal in religious systems and mythologies, while on

Run Wrake works against the implied innocence of the rabbit represented in a children's educational set, using the innocuous nature of the imagery to challenge psychological and ideological assumptions.

the other engaging with the philosophical tropes embedded in such traditions to invoke difference and sometimes disorder. One of the most interesting examples of an exploration of these principles is Run Wrake's *Rabbit* (Run Wrake, UK, 2006). Drawing upon the illustrative styling of the "Early Word" educational stickers used to help teach British children the alphabet during the 1950s and 1960s, Wrake also plays with some of the unusual characters included in the stamp set, simultaneously challenging some of the implied moral and behavioral expectations of the children during that era. For example, the film begins with a young girl staring at a rabbit gamboling across a field, and rather than imagining as the viewer might expect that the animal could be seen as a cute pet, she merely imagines the rabbit as a muff and pursues it with a kitchen knife. Though the rabbit escapes her, it is unceremoniously captured when her brother jumps down from a tree on top of it. The kill is carried home and sliced in half, releasing an idol. It was this that first attracted Wrake to the possibility of creating his story, finding the use of an idol as illustration for the letter "i"—somewhat unusual, and an undoubted legacy of Britain's delineation of the Oriental "other" during the period of Empire. It is clear, though, that Wrake wishes to explore this otherness through the notion of animality, as the release

Rabbit. The children release an idol from the brutalized body of the rabbit and, in assuming the primary power of their humanity over creatures, seriously underestimate the revenging aspects of the animal and of nature itself.

of the idol from the rabbit is not merely a provocation to magic but also a realization that the children's indifferent brutalization of the animal—later exacerbated through the killing of a sheep, a cow, and a horse—will inevitably have repercussions and consequences that will be revisited upon them.

The children quickly discover that the idol has attractive magical powers, able to turn passing flies and wasps into jewels, feathers, and ink. It is not long before the children realize that they can become king and queen if they create a plan by which they can secure more and more jewels. It is this that leads to the brutal killing of the animals, as they realize that flies will gather around and lay eggs in rotting animal flesh. Sure enough, the idol metamorphoses the flies, but only as long as he is fed rich plum jam, which soon runs out as the children's greed escalates. The children hit upon the idea of taking the feathers and ink to sell at the general shop where the shopkeeper is happy to purchase these items, imagining them as potentially lucrative pen and ink sets, giving them jam in return. Having already been once concerned that the idol had been eaten by their cat—an assumption that nearly prompts them to cut the cat in two with the ubiquitous kitchen knife— the children lock the idol indoors while they are away. The idol is angry at this treatment and lures a rabbit with a carrot to jump through the window so that he might escape. At first, he transforms the rabbit into a tiger to frighten the returning children, and is swallowed by the cat to make his escape. The children shoot the tiger, however, and watch it transform back into a rabbit, simultaneously returning all the jewels back to the constituent insects from which they were created, who in turn completely overwhelm and suffocate them. The rabbit then runs freely back across the field from which he came.

Wrake's morality play engages with the fairytale tropes of not seeking to exploit what you don't understand and the natural justice that seems to occur if you do, but, more significantly, he uses the power and divinity of the animal as the context in which this is addressed. In their abuse of the animal, the children fail to recognize its mutual presence in the highly stylized pastoral idyll that is the background and landscape for the "Early Word" series; an innocent and seemingly benevolent place also viewed in the "Ladybird" books depicting the period and equally rendered much more complex in Chris Shepherd's *Dad's Dead* (Chris Shepherd, UK, 2004). *Rabbit* is effectively a "revenge of nature" tale in which the sheer potency and longevity of the animal operates as a divine agent against the abuses and exploitation of the animal in the arbitrary cultures of everyday life. The idol is a symbol of the alienness of the animal; a recognition of its power in a more primal nature that overcomes the greed-ridden political economies of late capitalism, epitomized in the seemingly amoral children. Crucial to this perspective and understanding is a recognition of the ways in which the animal can transcend the limitations of death and operate at a level beyond the corporeal and finite.

This is reflected, for example, in Giannluigi Toccafondo's *La pista del maiale* (Giannluigi Toccafondo, Italy, 1992)—which translates roughly as *The Dance of the Pig*. As Chris Robinson has noted, this is

> a strange experimental piece that follows the last moments of a pig before it is slaughtered. Set in what appears to be a cold white room where pigs meet their fate, Toccofondo takes the haven of death and transforms it, momentarily, into a celebration and remembrance of the pig, and life. The blank white walls

come alive like cave paintings, a black and white drawing of the tail end of a pig appears. The animal is desperately trying to escape from the room. Stretching its body to a magnificent length, the pig manages to break free. The pig is alive, its color returns. All is well. Then there is darkness again. The color fades and the pig is being pulled back along the walls of the room. The images darken. The music heightens. Blackness sweeps through the frames. The walls begin to close in. In an instant the pig is gone. All that remains are its broken remains scattered on an anonymous table. It is the fate of pigs. It is the fate of us all. (Robinson 2005, 239)

This momentary release is both a transcendent vindication of the pig and an intrinsic statement both about the nature of the animal and the limits of the social world.

Toccafondo's film functions as a meditation on the oft-denied notion that an animal is not aware of its own death. This is an important perspective and worth dwelling on further. As George Page puts it, "Descartes's logic goes something like this: human beings have souls, as taught by Christian doctrine and as distinguished by consciousness; animals do not have souls because they cannot have souls, according to Christian doctrine; therefore animals cannot have consciousness either" (Page 1999, 7). The denial of consciousness is, of course, tantamount to the suggestion that an animal cannot be aware of its own mortality, nor can it imagine, anticipate, or fear death and thus cannot manage its circumstance in accordance with those parameters. Further, this in many ways accords the animal a particular kind of statelessness that leaves it without purpose or identity, or merely defines it only within the auspices of language itself. As part of Lippit's exploration of such philosophical engagements with the animal, he cites Henri Bergson's ideas about creative evolution, and the sense that rather than being in such a condition of statelessness, all living things are in a constant process of change, whereby the shift from state to state constitutes the intrinsic nature of lived experience and mobility: "Thus Bergson proposes an examination of the interval between states, the transition from state to state, and the movement that determines the character of each state as a way to address the broader question of being" (Lippit 2000, 84). Bergson suggests that the animal remains in liminal state between instinct and intelligence, which ultimately defines its consciousness. At one and the same time, this is a state in which a particular conceptual understanding can be achieved while unconscious, sensual, or intuitive participation in the physical and material world can also take place.

This perspective has much in accord with Grandin's notion of the autistic consciousness, in the human being and the animal, my own claims to the animator's proximity to this consciousness, and the ways in which this is played out through animation itself. Indeed, it is Bergson's interrogation of "the interval" between states that relates very powerfully to one of the key defining principles of animation. It has often been suggested that Norman McLaren's famous dictum, "What happens between each frame is more important than what happens on each frame" (Solomon 1987, 10), is one of the most significant statements in defining animation as a form, and perhaps ironically, though predicated on the traditional frame-by-frame construction of animated film, it remains even more pertinent in the digital era. It is important to properly address what McLaren is actually suggesting. Like Bergson, he is noting that the most significant aspect of the process is "the interval"—the space between instinct and intelligence, intuition, and conscious thought—that in animation results in the self-conscious aesthetic and technical decision made by the artist in the incremental manipulation and progression of the materials. Though this does not necessarily have to occur between "frames," it still occurs in the stage-by-stage accumulation of the development of animated motion and choreography in all forms of moving image practice, and ultimately defines what is *in* rather than *on* the frame space, however fluid and changeable.

This conflation of Bergson's ideas and McLaren's perspective defines "the interval" as the intrinsic state of the animal and a profound integer of creative (human) being. In McLaren's own work, it is a state recognized in the enigmatic figure of the chicken, a recurrent motif in a number of his films, including *Hen Hop* (Norman McLaren, Canada, 1942), where he describes a level of profound empathy with the creature, echoing Haraway's "in-the-making," Deleuze and Guattari's "becoming-animal," and Grandin's seeing like an animal: "When I was doing *Hen Hop* for instance, I felt that I was . . . doing that dance. I sort of got imbued with the spirit of henliness, I think. So, in a way, when you're animating a creature, if the creature is moving, you are that animal, you feel that motion" (quoted in McWilliams 1990). This is not dissimilar, of course, from the mantras of "abstract expressionism," the aesthetic styling perhaps most similar to McLaren's, best described by Jackson Pollock: "I don't paint Nature, I am Nature. . . . I work from the inside out, like Nature" (quoted in Collings 1999, 44).

This manifests itself further in the metamorphoses of another "chicken" film, *La Poulette grise* (Norman McLaren, Canada, 1947), in which McLaren meditates playfully on the "which came first, the chicken or the egg?" riddle by playing the creature out through a variety of contexts, but crucially as part of a cosmic visualization in which the chicken, the egg, the very abstraction of the animal is an embedded part of the universe. It is as much part of a constellation of stars and spectral atmospheres as the more homely barn or church, each place evoking a sense of the spiritual, which is merely reinforced by every aesthetic shift in McLaren's moving canvas. McLaren parallels the organic unfolding of his own synaesthetic creativity with the natural evolutionary cycles of birth, maturity, and flight into the ethereal unknown; an egg manifesting itself as a crescent moon, which in turn becomes a nest for the chicken, or a jewel in a flora sky, or a glowing celestial bracelet. The chicken becomes the embodiment of the divine animal, truly redolent of the powerful yet sometimes unknown or indescribable forces of the cosmos. If this is the closest manifestation of the experience of divinity in the animal, outside experience, then Chris Wedge's *Bunny* (Chris Wedge, USA, 1998) is a metaphysical excursion seeking to dramatize how this sense of the divine, the transcendent, and the otherness of immortality is known to the animal.

An aging rabbit, baking a cake in a kitchen, becomes aware of a moth that is rattling against a light bulb, attracted to its light but endlessly repulsed by its heat and materiality. He switches a light off, but the moth merely seeks out another, and becomes the object of a chase by the zimmer-framed "bunny." Finally, the rabbit finally swipes the moth into his baking mix, quickly stirring the creature into the batch, placing it in a dish, and putting it in the oven to bake. During the chase, the rabbit accidentally knocks a picture from the wall that shows the rabbit with his wife, whom we assume is deceased. So far, so "cartoonal" in some respects, but Wedge is careful to advance the metaphoric weight of the piece when the rabbit confronts the radiant white light that ultimately emanates from the oven as the dish cooks. This prompts a recall of the beginning of the film in which a blurry figure of a moth flies toward a celestial light source, and this in turn stirs the realization that the moth's continual confrontation with the bulb is a signifier of the fine line between life and death. It is a calling to a corporeal end, yet an attraction to some notion of everlasting continuity, too. When the rabbit confronts the celestial light in the oven, like the moth, he is at the point between living and dying, and at one level he is embracing his death. There are clear connotations of suicide here, which is perhaps the final consequence of missing his wife too much and having little to live for. At another level, he is responding to the promise of an everlasting life he can share with his wife. Through this deceptively simple device, Wedge has created an emotional life for the rabbit and shown its point of view. It will attain a divine state, suggesting all creatures have an afterlife and a sense of inclusion in a more sacred, ethereal, cosmic understanding of the universe, so defined in *La Poulette grise*. Once more, the self-evident sense of consciousness in creating the animation serves to depict consciousness as a state within the animation. The rabbit, like the hen, is not a visualization of nature; it is nature, and in being so accesses some of the more complex questions about being.

It is thus also a profound revelation of the quality of animation possessing and illustrating what might be regarded as the sacred idea of life in relation to death. Alan Cholodenko has consistently argued that this condition—one that moves beyond the scope of the animator and the material conditions of culture and political economy—is the most powerful credential of the animated form. An essential animus is enshrined in animation. The animatic—animation revealed in and of itself—and its attendant spectral tropes best reveal the purpose and affect of life "apprehended." Of Felix the Cat, Cholodenko notes,

The felicity of Felix is that, as a figure of metamorphosis, of plasmaticness, as Eisenstein called the "essence" of animation—that formless form that, giving all form, is itself never givable "as such"—as figure therefore of the animatic, he gives the lie to any attempt to fix, arrest, isolate and thereby render inanimate (such a figure of) animation in any particular creator/animator/author of him, in any determinate origin. Felix exemplifies and performs animation, the animatic, in the at once necessity and impossibility of defining, finalizing on, resolving, an origin, including of animation. In this sense, plasmatic-ness, the animatic, would be that nothing that enables and at the same time disenables everything, a nothing that would include not only the human animator's "self-figuration"—Donald Crafton's term for that distinctive feature of the animated film, the animator's "interjecting" himself as a kind of self-projection into the film—but, to recast Crafton's term, the animatic apparatus's "self-figuring" in film animation. (Cholodenko, personal correspondence, July 2007)

This state of annulment yet fulfillment, resistance yet resolution, identification and absence, aligned to the larger questions about the nature of existence itself, is ultimately the divinity of the animal in animated film.

Demonic Animals

Arguably, many animals in the animated film are demonized in a spirit of creating the typical anarchy in archetypal chase and conflict cartoons—someone has to be the enemy and if it is not Elmer Fudd, then Sylvester, Tom, and their ilk need to take on villainous trappings in their pursuit of their prey. On the one hand, this might be viewed as an exercise in merely using and exacerbating the primitive urges and imperatives of the hunter and hunted, well established in animal cultures, while on the other a convenient vehicle by which to facilitate cartoon chase gags. This is taken to its seemingly logical conclusion in propaganda films like *The Ducktators* (Norman McCabe, USA, 1942) when a "bad egg," born as an ugly duckling, grows up to be "ducktator," Adolf Hitler, and is joined by Mussolini and Hirohito; their storm-troopers lead the world to war only to be challenged by the archetypal dove of peace. The hunters become Axis oppressors, the hunted become the implied audience, and the animals are demonized through their association with oppressive, authoritarian, evil human beings. The same occurs in Halas and Batchelor's *Abu* series, including *Abu's Poisoned Well* (Halas & Batchelor, UK, 1943) where a snake resembles Hitler and a frog looks like Mussolini. Pairings of dog and cat, cat and mouse, and cat and bird are the natural combinations when thinking about animals who are seemingly pre-programmed to chase each other, though, so there may be some justification in the consistent presence of such animals in cartoons, but equally these presumptions may also be addressed and challenged. In *The Wild* (Steve Williams, USA, 2006)—very similar in narrative and outlook to *Madagascar*—the oppositional relationship between lion and wildebeest is explored. It may be pertinent to remember that Mufasa the lion was effectively killed as a consequence of a wildebeest stampede in *The Lion King,* and while the wildebeest is inevitably seen as the prey of the lion in the real world, there is a sense in which it remains a particular nemesis in the animated one.

Samson, an elder lion, constantly regales his son, Ryan, with his exaggerated recollections of his time on the savannah, repeated so often as to have become a matter of ritual and repetition where Ryan can readily anticipate what his father will say. Within these tales, the wildebeest is imagined as a constantly metamorphosing and monstrous adversary that is ultimately conquered through the deployment of Samson's primal roar, something Ryan is yet to know or cultivate. Once more such animated narratives have recourse to some notion of the pure animal as a key signifier of natural identity based upon predatory or primitive hierarchies to set against representations of the aspirational and critical human that are played out through the limitations of the civilized or post-modern beast. Ryan, of course, is troubled by the fact that he has yet to attain his roar and wants to go to the wild in order to discover it. This mythical "other" place has a geography of threat and a sense of demonic challenge imposed by the sheer unpredictability of the possible adversaries, and is a long way from the bizarre pastimes— curling (!)—undertaken by the animals at night. Crucially, though, this

Abu's Poisoned Well. Hitler is represented as the seductive yet repellent figure of the snake; another common trope of animal representation is to align reptiles with cold-hearted aggressors.

sporting culture becomes a way in which Samson further imposes a model of masculine expectation and asserts his status over and frustration with his son, which constantly recalls Ryan's apparent inadequacy in not yet possessing his roar. This central premise in the narrative is once more important in highlighting the seemingly consistent crisis in masculine identity expressed in Hollywood movies per se. It is also addressing a very particular set of concerns about the relationships between fathers and sons, issues of legacy and purpose and a sense of loss that must necessarily find a context in such narratives in order to be resolved. The parameters of the animal become this context by offering a ready metaphorical and metaphysical place by which the physical, mutable, and unconscious might be recalled to overcome the limitedly cerebral, fixed, and conscious practices of behavior and expectation in the chaos of postmodernity.

Ryan seeks to escape to the wild by secreting himself in some green transportation boxes labeled "Zoo to Africa," which unbeknownst to the animals are part of a rescue operation where animals threatened by an erupting volcano are being evacuated. Samson and his friends—Benny the squirrel ("I'm not a trash collector; I'm a recycler"), Nigel the koala ("I'm a vicious jungle animal from the streets of London"), and Bridget the giraffe ("I wasn't meant for the wild. I was made to nibble, and be elegant, and to appear in children's books under the letter 'g')—realize he has gone and try to find him. This is what actually prompts a process by which Samson's self-delusion is exposed. Chased by street dogs, Samson fails to react, prompting Bridget to ruefully wonder why lions are at the top of the food chain. The food chain as a structuring device for the delineation of nature also serves to delineate the demonic in the sense that those animals who are perceived as predatory or intrinsically threatening are inevitably those animals who are about to eat others. Playing with urban myth, the narrative sees Samson and his friends encounter crocodiles in the New York drainage system. Nigel pleads with them not to harm him, saying, "We're one big family, right?" This seeks to draw attention to two of the most common clichés of animal representation—the implied hierarchy imposed upon the animal kingdom by humankind, and an undifferentiated model by which animals are somehow all perceived as the same. It is in the potential overturning of this hierarchy in the food chain that finally provides the film with its central conflict, as the wildebeest is marked as genuinely demonic in its self-conscious intention to overthrow the lion: "For centuries we have watched our brethren perish at the claw of the lion. Today we put our paws down. No longer will we dwell at the bottom of the food chain." This necessitates that the wildebeest actually change their feeding orientation as ordained by their bizarre leader, Kazar—"I am Kazar. Leader. Prophet. Choreographer. And with your help, carnivore"—who insists that the wildebeest cannot ascend to the top of the food chain unless it consumes a lion.

It is useful again to recall *The Lion King,* where, David Ingram notes, "nature . . . is similarly an economy in which those at the top of the food chain (lions humanized as middle-class Americans) are justified in their right to consume a nature which is guaranteed to remain endlessly renewing and abundant, as long as their power and authority is not usurped by their undeserving enemies, suitably marked as inferiors in terms of class and identity" (Ingram 2000, 24). *The Wild* posits a more nihilistic view that though the lion may reside at the top of the food chain, this authority is made fragile by the constructed nature of the hierarchy, and the inability to properly facilitate the role that this hierarchy imposes. Without the qualities and capacities of a real lion—qualities here rendered inadequate by postmodern urban culture—Samson and Ryan become vulnerable to harm and usurpation. The film suggests, by implication, that the very fundamentals by which representational orthodoxies—politically and aesthetically—are understood are profoundly vulnerable if not supported by authenticity and integrity. It is in the rediscovery of this authenticity in a fundamental animality that the lions reassert their intrinsic identity but, significantly, not in the service of authority. To know, understand, and accept the essential lion, and to resist the artifice of the wildebeest ambitions, is to reinstate nature, untrammeled by the interventions of the naturalcultural. Animation becomes a key language and expressive method by which this flux, uncertainty, and uneasiness are exposed, even in the guise of mainstream narrative entertainments.

By the time Samson reaches the wild, he is diminished both in his inadequacy as a father and in his limitations as an animal. He mistakes Ryan's scent for that of a skunk and is forced to admit that he is a fake and cannot protect his companions. His chief torment, however, is a childhood trauma, which he revisits when he cannot protect Ryan from an attack by vultures. He relives the moments when his father forces him as a cub to confront a mechanized wildebeest as part of a circus act, and the fact that he is frightened and humiliated because he cannot summon his roar. He was not born in the wild and has no recourse to what this means, nor does he understand what he is being put through in the cause of entertainment. This whole scenario calls a range of discourses into the discussion, not least the ways in which animals have been exploited and diminished by the human predication to present and parade animals for visual spectacle. Particular to this context, though, is the demonization of the wildebeest as Samson's monstrous imaginary foe, willing to challenge the natural order by revoking the food chain. The wildebeest is also imagined as a machine, literally illustrating Descartes's model of the unfeeling, disconnected animal, driven by its own limited and inhuman(e) imperatives. Though in time-honored Hollywood fashion Samson searches his soul to redis-cover his inner true self and, in this case, its attendant roar, in order to vanquish the ambitious wildebeest in their ambition to move from predator to prey, the final outcome of the film points to a final exposé of the naturalcultural condition. Ryan says, "At least I saw the wild before it disappears," to which Samson, pointing to his heart, replies, "I can still see it. It's right here." Ryan clearly recognizes that the physical and material nature of animal habitats and wild systems is gradually disappearing, just at the moment when Samson discovers some sem-blance of his essential animality.

This in itself is a useful summation of the way animated narratives of this kind simultaneously acknowledge the absent presence of the animal using the terms and conditions of bestial ambivalence, and ulti-mately prioritize the phenomenological performance of the animation itself to reassert animal discourses. The demonic wildebeest in this case is presented as a constructed animal that diminishes the given limits of the pure animal. For all its concentration on the character identities of Samson and Ryan, they ultimately represent the preservation of the animalness of the lion and the struggle to maintain the pure animal in the face of forces that undermine, marginalize, or destroy it.

This idea is further explored in Bill Plympton's short film *Guard Dog* (Bill Plympton, USA, 2006), which demonizes various animals (and other life forms) from the perspective of a pet animal who fears that his master is constantly in danger. Inevitably, this creates the incongrui-ties by which Plympton can facilitate his gags, but more importantly invests animals with more affecting and destructive tendencies than might normally be observed. It also suggests a sharp divide between the domesticated context and an imagined wild system beyond the subur-ban threshold, but which nevertheless falls short of the wild. A domes-tic guard dog barks with excitement and anticipation of his walk and, having been tickled by his master, proceeds with him into the seeming minefield of the local park, where he first encounters a little girl skip-ping. He then imagines the girl giving the rope to his master who then skips his own head off, the rope literally slicing his neck clean through. He chases the girl away, but this is just the first of a range of imagined threats the dog foresees for his master.

A squirrel uses a park swing to knock off the man's head, adding insult to injury by torching its gaping mouth; a bird configures its nest as a ninja star and hurls it menacingly; a grasshopper leaps into the head of the man, spinning his eyes and poking them out from the inside; a mole pulls a bull into his newly dug trench and encourages the man to fall into it, literally metamorphosing into Ronald McDonald on his descent, to an inevitable mauling from the embittered bull; a butterfly slices the man into fragmentary pieces; and even a flower rises up to cover the man in pollen, causing the man to excessively sneeze himself inside out. Such is the state of the dog's heightened anxiety that his frenzied attempts to chase away these illusory adversaries result in him strangling his own master with his twisted lead. Disconsolately, he pulls his master home.

Arguably, these are merely more aggressive variations on Tex Avery gags using the excesses and freedoms of the form to privilege comedy violence in the context of seemingly innocuous situations, and executed by the least likely of characters. It is clear, however, that to demonize the more domesticated and localized animals like birds, squirrels, moles, and insects is to reduce the distance by which the potential chaos and at the very least the sheer difference of the wild system might be recognized and understood. The guard dog becomes the unconscious embodiment of the inherent fear that the animals in the behest and close environment of humankind might turn against it and enact some further revenge of nature. Ironically, the man's death is actually caused by the animal most committed to his service, and though this is obviously a neat black joke, it also demonstrates that for all the tummy tickling and social ritual of affection played out between humankind and pets, there is still the possibility that the ability for these living forms to actually communicate effectively might only be a remote possibility. It is this fact, in the face of humankind's deep-rooted desire to associate and embrace the animal, that offers a truly challenging perspective. The nonassimilation of the animal becomes a profoundly demonic idea.

Satiric Animals

Arguably, any number of animal figures service satiric perspectives in animation. Bugs Bunny is almost exclusively poking fun at one subject, topic, or another, and the Warner Bros. cartoon per se operates a vehicle by which anyone or anything might be mischievously challenged or undermined. This remains an insufficient way of seeing the presence and affect of the animal in such satire, however, and of seeing when the animal is itself the subject of the critical and analytical address that characterizes satire and informs its targets and outlook. Though Nick Park and Peter Lord at Aardman Animation are not immediately viewed as satirists, merely the purveyors of a light English whimsy, it is clear that their feature-length work, over and beyond its strengths in creating humor, plays out narratives that are sustained by their thematic concerns and philosophic investment. *Chicken Run* (Nick Park and Peter Lord, UK, 2000) is as much concerned by its ideas and its ethical stance as it is its jokes. The story is set on "Tweedy's Farm," a thinly veiled battery farm-cum-pie-making factory, played out as wartime concentration camp. As Brian Sibley has noted:

> One source of inspiration was the "Song of the Bird," a book that Nick Park was reading at the time. A collection of stories retold by Anthony de Mello from various traditions around the world, it contained a fable called "The Golden Eagle." In this short story—no more than six paragraphs long—a man finds an eagle's egg and places it in a chicken's nest. The egg hatches and the eagle grows up amongst the chickens, assuming that it is also a chicken. He one day sees a great golden eagle soaring through the sky above the yard where he lives, but never flies himself because he believes that he is a chicken—and chickens cannot fly. Eventually he dies, as he has lived, unaware of his true identity. (Sibley 2000, 47)

This gives a small insight into the ways that Lord and Park wished to respect the integrity of the animal at the heart of their story, privileging the idea of an animality that must be recognized as the distinctive aspect of the characters, even as they play out comic and metaphoric scenarios. It is an animality within the narrative, however, that is compromised by the exploitation of humankind, and somehow only half-known; something that mere survival is preserving, to be revealed only under more pertinent conditions—in this case, the escape to a Free

Range farm. Lord recalls, "We agonized over the question of whether chickens actually perceived themselves to be in prison or not" (quoted in Sibley 2000, 51), indicating that the issue of consciousness in the animal was a very important aspect of the decision-making process toward the construction of intelligent creatures. Like McLaren, Lord and Park use the ambiguous sense of proximity and distance in the chicken to properly evoke the sense of a related yet alien form, partly picking up on the real abilities of the creature—"When a cockerel sees an aerial predator such as a hawk, he issues a different alarm from the one issued after seeing a fox. Furthermore, a chicken who hears the 'hawk' alarm scurries for cover while looking up, while the receiver of the 'fox' alarm scans the immediate vicinity on the ground" (Page 1999, 109)—while also using the angular and awkward aesthetics of the birds for comic effect.

The heart of the film, then, is the tension between the chicken's assertion of their animality—their very lives—and the desire for humankind to cruelly kill and exploit the chicken for financial gain. This becomes an implicit critique of battery farms and to some extent industrial production methods, as well as an implicit plea for vegetarianism. Though dressed in the generic clothes of the prisoner-of-war film, the wartime romance, and the musical, and cleverly parodying the conventions of such narratives, *Chicken Run*'s essential satire is rooted in the politics of supply and demand within modern corporate culture. It is ironically made more affective and poignant by being played out in a nostalgic, seemingly old-fashioned style, and by its resistance to cartoon clichés. Even more ironic is that this serves as yet another example of the ways in which the seemingly innocent language of animation can carry with it subversive or challenging messages or ideas. Aardman Animation, in general, is particularly adept in creating a veneer of whimsy, innocuousness, and amusing distraction, while engaging in highly insightful observations about human foible and ignorance. Though this is rarely cruel, it is nevertheless revelatory, and sometimes operates specifically in regard to the relationship between humans and animals, particularly in the Nick Park–inspired television series, *Creature Comforts* (Richard Goleszowski, UK, 2003–present). Park's original Oscar-winning film, made in 1990, used real people speaking about

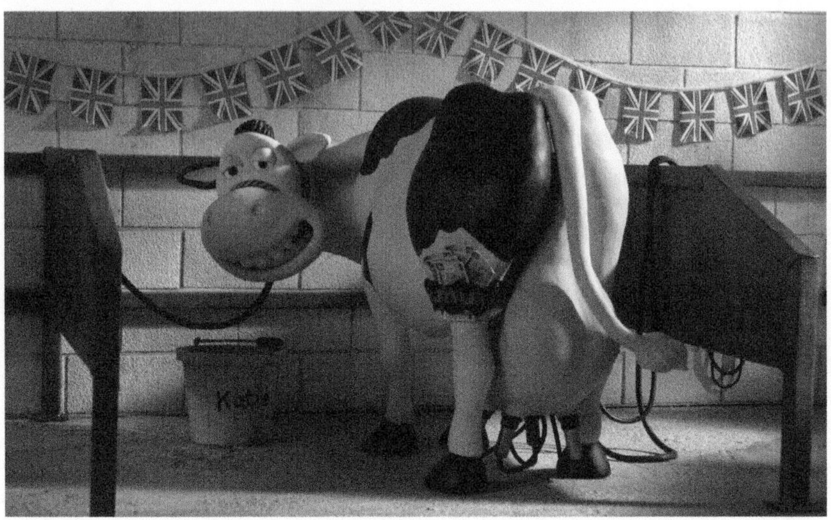

Creature Comforts wittily combines the voices of real people with animal representations, drawing attention to the foibles and complexities of both human and animal existence.

their attitudes toward zoos and their own living environments, and matched various comments and views to a range of animated animal characters. The series also uses this conceit but interviews participants on specific themes.

In the episode "What's It All About," two sheep stare at a chick, and using children's voices consider the age-old "Which came first, the chicken or the egg?" question once more, concluding, "It's confusing." Various creatures debate if humankind evolved from the sea or the land and then address evolution, one bemused cat noting, "What sort of idiot wants to prove he's from a monkey?" while a hamster insightfully suggests, "The difference between me and a monkey would be mainly, monkeys live in the jungle, and I live in Catford." Perhaps most revelatory is a bug who pontificates that "humans were created by this huge cosmic cow licking a stone, and as it licked this stone, humans rolled off." In "Being a Bird," street mongrels in a dumpster dream of what it would be like to be a soaring eagle or an albatross, while a cat and a dog enjoy birds singing in a bird bath, here represented through the voices of a doo-wop a capella group and rappers impersonating beat instruments. The central joke in the series in the incongruous placement of ill-informed or highly subjective human perspectives in the mouths of animals, who either perform the function of making the observation make sense or more often by exposing the difference between human and animal experience. Moreover, through this incongruity, the animation uses the ignorance, simple-mindedness, fantasies, and limits of human understanding as the stuff of humor. Though the satiric thrust of the programs is not barbed or aggressive, it nevertheless shows that the unselfconscious musings of ordinary British people harbor uninterrogated and assumed knowledge, petty prejudices and limited outlooks. The humor emerges from using the difference of the animal to expose the embedded nature of these perspectives.

The phenomenological performance in such an episode is to use the very essence of what a bird is, expressed through the animated characters, to contradict the assumptions played out through the human voices. When someone talks of the experience of taking off in an aircraft, this sits amusingly against the audience's knowledge of the bird's inherent ease in flying, while admissions of being scared of heights or having no sense of direction equally show the natural qualities of the bird in relation to those that must be learned or cultivated in humans. The limits of humanity—critical or aspirational—are shown through their disparity from the pure animal existing beyond the idea of what it is to be human, here fundamentally defined through language. *Creature Comforts* gently exposes the limits of humanity through the limits of its ability to articulate or express itself, and the construction of the animal as being.

It is this idea of the pure animal or of the animal as an essential being outside of human parameters that is readily used to make more highly charged critiques of human experience and conduct. Paul Fierlinger's *Still Life with Animated Dogs* (Paul Fierlinger, USA, 2000) uses Fierlinger's relationships with his dogs—his Scottish terrier, Roosevelt; his boxer, Ike; his Boston terrier, Johnson; and another terrier, Spinnaker—to reveal something of the political and cultural climate he himself lives through and endures, from Stalinist Prague in the 1950s to the changing terrain of the United States from the 1960s onward. Roosevelt, for example, is seen to be more effective in enduring the hardships of Czechoslovakian experience by subterfuge and caution—a quiet "civil disobedience"—rather than Fierlinger's more high-profile belligerence and resistance, and Ike, Fierlinger's constant companion by virtue of his falsely certified status as a "seeing-eye dog trainer," survived through restaurants providing him with choice foods because of his supposed role as a guide dog. Johnson and Spinnaker, too, provide major companionship for Fierlinger but, crucially, represent unspoken yet enduring bonds that survive shifting circumstances and implicitly make comment upon the oppressive conditions that have numbed the animality in humankind. This connection is only preserved by the sustained connections with animals such as pets. As Fierlinger notes, "[Dogs] require absolute commitment and faithfulness—good for keeping a person from depression—not just by their company but by keeping you so busy attending to them and watching out for them that one day the dog is dead, you're still alive and have received the gift of being a survivor. They make you feel important" (quoted in Robinson 2005, 87). The satiric function of Fierlinger's dogs, then, is to point up the increasingly absurd distanciation of humankind from its sense of self, from its intrinsic connection with organic and felt experience and its embedded complicity in the naturalcultural. Only the pure animal maintains a primal relationship with alternative knowledges and emotional life, and Fierlinger's animation captures the life his dogs endowed him with.

Political Animals

While my final chapter is engaged in looking at some of the political perspectives that characterize animal cultures and issues of representation, this section looks at the explicit ways in which animals have been used to express politically charged messages. Animals have been regularly used as national symbols, and they come to represent a set of characteristics pertinent to imagined communities and mythic constructions of nationhood. As Steve Baker points out, "The example of Mickey Mouse leaves little doubt that just about anything will do as a national animal symbol. The qualities deemed appropriate to such symbols evidently do not stop at dignity and steadfastness" (Baker 2001, 62). This seems a harsh assessment in the sense that Mickey's iconic presence as a "brand" has all but drained him of "mouse-ness," and whatever he has come to represent it is clearly much more connected to corporate rather than animal identity. It is important, though, not to dismiss this, as in particular historical periods the animal as a symbol in various modes of propaganda has taken on a high degree of potency. Consequently, in possessing bestial ambivalence within animated forms, such symbols allow the recall of animality at any time.

If one were but to take the animated interstices and intervals in Tony Richardson's *Charge of the Light Brigade* (Tony Richardson, UK, 1966), Richard Williams uses the national animal symbols of England (the lion), Russia (the bear), France (the cockerel), and Turkey (the turkey [!]), drawn from Victorian periodicals like the *Illustrated London News* and *Punch*, to show how myths are constructed through the graphic simplicities and directness of such symbols. Animals become the effective short-cuts by which power and ideology might be grasped and understood by a mass audience, without the complications of the actual political conduct and conflict included. This is the project of the rest of Richardson's film, and in juxtaposing the animated interludes with the live action narrative, he exposes the space between myth and reality, and simultaneously calls attention to the use of animality as an abstract form of primal potency. The essential spirit of the animal is used to underpin a notion of a natural force underpinning a nation's sense of its own intrinsic rightness. This embrace of the animal as some kind of vindication of a natural or naturalized agenda is a common theme, but it takes but little play with the alternative condition of animality to challenge these meanings and affects.

Joanna Quinn's *Britannia* (Joanna Quinn, UK, 1993), in reintroducing the pure animal of the British bulldog, uses the very unconsciousness of the animal as the distinguishing characteristic of thoughtless action, and then uses the metaphoric implications to critique Britain's material exploitation and imperialist abuse of its colonies and supposed partners. This comparative example shows how the animated form can place established and often fixed meanings into flux. Both examples use national animal symbols embedded in a particular historical context and, significantly, a specific ideologically charged caricaturial aesthetic normally associated with political cartooning, to revise the meaning

Britannia. Joanna Quinn's reworking of the British bulldog reinvokes the animal in a taken-for-granted national symbol.

not merely of the historical conditions and social outcomes but of the animal itself.

Such approaches see that the animal is intrinsic in the construction of meaning, not only in the ways that its carries received cultural associations, but through its own primal presence. This is taken further in Martin Pickles's *Crouching Ox, Crowing Rooster* (Martin Pickles, UK, 2005), where the film explores the possibility of a particular kind of animal sentience, and the recognition that the alternative natural order of which animals may be part represents a different kind of knowledge. This becomes an explicit rejection of Lippit's "edifice of humanism." Prefigured by an opening title that says, "There are so many things that animals know that we do not . . . ," the film, made for the World Society for the Protection of Animals and based upon supposedly true events that took place in China in 1975, creates a narrative based on the interior monologue of an ox, who in the course of his daily activities in the service of his farmer master becomes aware of something being wrong. A rooster shares this anxiety and promptly crows. Within a short time other animals start to behave unusually. The ox suddenly stops short in the road and refuses to move; his actions

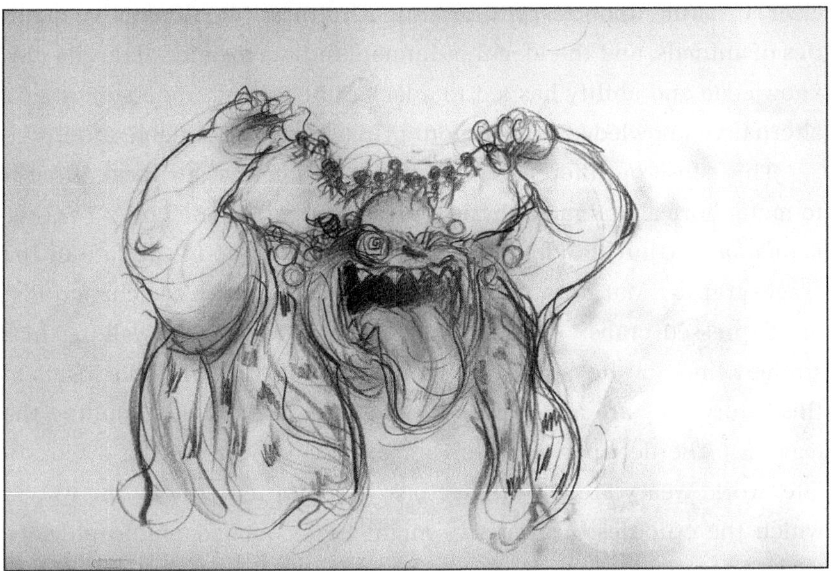

Britannia. Quinn's satiric caricature exposes the madness and brutality of colonial exploitation by using the nonhuman, pure animality of the dog to expose human complicity and vanity.

are a premonition that disaster is about to befall humankind and his fellow creatures. A little girl plays with her animal toys—an ironic statement about the simultaneous distance and proximity of animals, and a subtle point about power and control—when an earthquake strikes, and potential infrastructural devastation ensues. Though the animals have done much to communicate to the humans and prevented harm coming to many, some become trapped beneath the rubble unnoticed until once more, a pig becomes aware of a scent of a human under the debris and warns other people by snorting and acting in a way unfamiliar to the villagers.

In the original incident, it is claimed that over 90,000 people's lives were saved by the prompt evacuation of people following the unprecedented scale of unrelenting and unusual acts of many animals, which prompted officials to embrace the view that the animals were seeking to warn humankind about the impending earthquake. This leads to the assumption that the animals were merely demonstrating their highly empathetic bond with the natural environment. The film's message is clear, insisting upon respect for animal cultures, the distinctive qualities of animals, and the idea that humankind's arrogance about its own knowledge and ability has led to a lack of belief and understanding in alternative knowledge from a more primal and inarticulable order.

This sense of difference is often used, of course, to speak directly to metaphorical and metaphysical principles. Arthur de Pins's *The Crab Revolution* (Arthur de Pins, France, 2004) alights upon the fate of the "Pachygrapsus Marmoratus" crab, known colloquially as "chancroids" or "depressed crabs," because they are only capable of walking in a straight line and do not possess the ability to turn. To add insult to this injury they are also "the poor blighters the kids love pulling the legs off." The deadpan narrator, almost a caricature of the disconsolate, world-weary French intellectual, is comforted only by the way in which the cruelties of existence might be reconciled philosophically. He stresses: "Our fate is mapped out from birth depending on where we hatch," and de Pins shows various examples of crabs entrapped between "a rock and a hard place," as the narrator bemoans, "I don't even know where we are in the evolutionary scale." De Pins is essentially reflecting upon both the seeming inevitability of Darwinian selection but also the ways that this has been systemically adopted within ideological and cultural contexts. A crab, deformed by having his legs removed on one side, is thus destined only to turn in a circle, this new model of movement enabling him to ruminate on the world in a different way to his straight-striding colleagues. Consequently, he becomes a philosopher and argues that though walking in a straight line, backward or forward, may be viewed as debilitating, he suggests, "At least we are going somewhere," offering up an existential qualification to an otherwise limited activity. De Pins cleverly uses the intrinsic conditions of his creature characters to point up how humankind seeks to make sense of itself. Above the seemingly preordained circumstances of the crabs exists a human world indifferent to the existence of other animals, and with little care for the environment. An incident ensues where two trawlers collide—"a catastrophe only you humans could cause"—and the ships sink to the bottom of the sea, the crabs beneath them unable to turn away, facing unavoidable death. In such adverse circumstances, one crab does turn away, however, and escapes the sinking hold. Ironically, this act of deliberately turning away is not valued by other crabs, who perceive it as an unnecessary and undignified act of nonconformism. As the narrator asserts, in the crab world "old habits died hard," and in reality, it is better to accept that you cannot escape your destiny. The viewer learns also that the crab has achieved his turn by having the good fortune to land on the back of a buried flat fish who happened to swim away at the fatal moment. This seems to confirm that only chance and good fortune might liberate an individual from the restrictive conditions of existence.

This clever and amusing film privileges a certain model of highly determined animality as a fixed and unchanging mode of being, which is only affected by human intervention—children removing crab legs or sailors failing in their control of ships. Only through the imposition of metaphor is this condition made pertinent to human existence, as humankind seeks to find purpose and meaning. The nonhuman, complicit with the natural order, simply goes on, subject to knowledge of itself, unaffected by the seemingly singular human need to justify itself to itself. Lippit has argued, "Ultimately, the animal does not so much *exist as express*: in its cry and conceptualization, animal being is marked by expression rather than being-in-the-world" (Lippit 2000, 48), but in some senses, this kind of narrative reverses this view, insisting that it is the nonhuman, the animal, the creature that exists in the world, and it is humankind, in its desperate need to express, that seeks out the animal as a natural conduit for its most playful metaphors or complex metaphysical inquiry. In this light, this more accurately supports what Lippit has suggested when he argues, "Animal being forces humanity to acknowledge the finitude of world: that is, animals tear humanity away from the imagined totality of world" (Lippit 2000, 71). It is this which is ultimately at the heart of the concept of bestial ambivalence, in the sense that by calling into account the fluid and sometimes competing discourses of the human and the animal within the naturalcultural, there is an insistence that animality operates to disrupt the inhibiting limitations and arbitrary parameters of an imposed human order. At the same time, there is a recognition that this animality is an intrinsic part of the human condition that needs recovery and re-incorporation in the contemporary era. Animation becomes the most pertinent vehicle by which these discourses are revealed, but as is also clear from the analyses offered in this chapter and in the previous discussion, animation also recontextualizes the embedded tradition of the animal and places the complex perspectives about the human/animal divide into revelatory relief.

5

Creature Comforted

Animal Politics, Animated Memory

Political Carnivalesque

As I have developed my discussion, I have sought to establish the idea of bestial ambivalence as a model by which the flux of animal discourses can be discussed within an infrastructural model of the naturalcultural, stressing that animated animals may be viewed as supernormal stimuli recalling primal animal knowledge. Animated animals can also be understood as anthropomorphic phenomena foregrounding the acute sensibility of the animator in prompting visions of animality, and advancing a view of phenomenological performance in animal animation as a model of philosophic inquiry. My concluding chapter is an evaluation of the social and cultural outcomes that may be deduced from the representation of animals in animated films, looking at the core criticism that often challenges the idea that an intrinsically illusionist language like animation can endorse a positive and genuine view of the animal, or that views such a form of expression as merely using the animal in an exploitative way that refuses its identity. I seek to argue, however, that animation involving animals always points up issues of what I term "social embedding," exposing notions of consensus and the limits of democratic existence, and/or works as the vehicle for what I define as political carnivalesque, challenging parameters, boundaries, and social orthodoxies. The concept of bestial ambivalence once more effectively supports these positions.

Often one encounters the following argument: "In the long story of our relationship with animals, and our still evolving understanding of the animal mind, domestication marked the beginning of our estrangement" (Page 1999, 2). This seemingly contradictory statement seeks to mark out the view that with the advent of the pet and the creation of the zoo, as well as the mass-mediated representation of the animal in wildlife films and documentaries, the primal truth and fundamental identity of the animal and its relationship to humankind were lost. As I have argued, however, even though many species are under threat, and civilization systematically manages the animal, for good and ill, evacuating it from a primary position in modern cultures, there remains an inherent relationship with the animal that the animated film constantly reveals and promotes. This issue of estrangement has not merely been viewed as coming about through the assimilation of the animal and the repression or redetermination of animality, but through its very opposite. As Sam Keen has suggested,

> That we regularly use a whole repertoire of animal, reptile, and insect images to de-humanize our enemies shows us the extent to which modern technological societies are rooted in a metaphysic of war against nature. Once upon a time, snake, bear, dog, lion, wolf, were all considered totem animals, scared spirits, familial powers. Men and women took animal names, belonged to clans named in honor of wild things, admired the cunning of Coyote, the industry of Ant, the grace of hawk, the resurrecting spirit of Snake. Beasts were family, not enemies. Modernity began when we began to conceive of nature as a state of perpetual warfare, "red in tooth and claw," a struggle in which only the fittest survive. And in the state of nature, man was a raving wolf who could be civilized only by a social contract. . . . Our reason and our ability to make tools set us above animals, gave us the right to dominate. (Keen 1986, 134)

Like Page, Keen offers up a moment when a line was drawn between a time of supposedly harmonious and intuitive understanding and embrace of the animal and an enduring period in which humankind has recast the animal as "other," either as a naturalized phenomena absorbed within human culture or as a symbolic antagonist, operating as a conduit for Modernist ills and anxiety. While these divisions and their repercussions seem persuasive, it may be worthwhile to suggest that the ancient and totemic empathy, noted particularly by Keen, may also have been underpinned by a powerful sense of fear and alienation. Arguably, humankind has perpetually had to acknowledge its profound difference from the animal, and all of its actions—material and metaphoric—have been concerned with exercising particular kinds of power and influence over the animal, in order to create some sense of relatedness. Implicit in Keen's argument, too, is that Darwinian intervention has ensured that nature is perceived as a site of hierarchical practice and perpetual struggle in the name of continuity. This, too, is to simplify the evolutionary process and to reduce unconscious organic processes to the status of conscious conflict; a naturalized "fitness to purpose" to a system of chance and choices. Either perception of nature is surely as much of a metaphoric principle as the other, since the density, complexity, and variety in the operations of nature renders such specificity at least questionable. It is crucial that any preoccupation with the animal remains an ongoing and open engagement, and, rather than being estranged from animals, humankind is merely in the modern phase of creating its own metaphors by which to interrogate the perennial difficulty in knowing the animal. Further, humankind remains in a process of recovering the lost knowledge about the animal that has been embedded in past experience and taken for granted in everyday life.

The struggle to know the animal has been a long held and demanding task for humankind, and has not merely gone through a variety of historical phases but has been played out through the shifting dynamics of the nature and growth of human beings from childhood to senior citizenship and in the changes in social and cultural orders across nation and time. The preoccupation with the animal has been literally cradle to grave, and truly a matter of cross-disciplinary and interdisciplinary inquiry. Psychoanalyst of fairytales Bruno Bettelheim notes, for example, "An animal is either all devouring or all helpful. Every figure is essentially one-dimensional, enabling a child to comprehend its actions and reactions easily" (Bettelheim 1978, 74). This observation merely tells us that humankind has sometimes constructed the animal as a one-dimensional figure in order to clarify the identity of the animal in the child's experience or imaginary. It is ultimately a highly reductive statement but one that Bettelheim believes accords with the ways in which humankind must *necessarily* seek to assimilate the animal: "Only when animal nature has been befriended, recognized as important, and brought into accord with ego and superego does it lend its power to the total personality" (Bettelheim 1978, 78). Bettelheim is actually suggesting, then, that the animal is an inherent part of the human sensibility, and part of its intrinsic wholeness. Psychologically and emotionally, right from the earliest years, humankind uses a creative interpretation of the animal to clarify something in itself and achieve an embeddedness of the animal within the human personality. This recognizes both the relatedness of the animal to humankind, but also a method by which the necessity for the acknowledged difference in animals to be accommodated within the psycho-somatic parameters of the human condition. The animal is in essence embraced by creative and imaginative thought, continual models of which are offered by and to humankind through artistic and literary representation. Crucially, though, in the modern era, the animal has been profoundly defined and determined by the impact of the animated film. The animated film, in all its flux and openness, across its styles and techniques, through its phases and developments, constitutes the most significant modern interrogator of the meaning of the animal through its intrinsically metaphorical and metaphysical status as an expressive language.

The animated film, and the terms and conditions I have outlined within the concept of bestial ambivalence, ensures that the discourses about the animal remain in a constant circulation, perpetually interrogating the status and identity of the animal. The animated animal is measured thereafter against the changing views and knowledge of animal life as it emerges through both artistic and scientific sources, and those contexts that share a model of creative interpretation of creatures. The scientific desire to prove animal sentience, advance behavioral parallels, or enhance knowledge of the biological imperatives of animals, while often described in the technical language of prescribed disciplines, nevertheless shares the arts community's investment in the animal symbolic. Further, art and science share the social world's socioeconomic management of the animal, often using the critical anthropomorphism I have defined earlier. This is sometimes reflected in the degrees of intelligence seemingly characterizing animal behavior. As animal scientist George Page claims, "Almost all of us 'draw the line' somewhere between those creatures that we intuitively believe are endowed with consciousness, and those who aren't. . . . Most people draw the line for consciousness between the invertebrates and the vertebrates, and then draw another line for some sort of higher consciousness, if not exactly self-consciousness, just beneath the dolphins, primates, cats and dogs" (Page 1999, 42–43). This remains important because it becomes part of the implicit language by which the animal is measured in relation to its own particular circumstances and its specific bond with humankind.

Page further suggests, "All species have been shaped by the forces of evolution to meet their immediate needs. The more a given species needs to be conscious of, the more it is conscious of. Either that or it becomes extinct" (Page 1999, 100). This is a highly significant observation in that it empowers not merely the animal itself, but recognizes the level of consciousness in the animal that remains correspondent to the conditions of existence. This sense of adaptiveness is both an indicator of the ways in which animals relate to themselves, each other, and ultimately humankind, and become socialized creatures. As Page adds,

> The bottom line is that every creature's mind, or brain—including our own, of course—is exquisitely tuned by and tuned to the needs of its particular world. There is no contradiction between the fact that a pigeon can perform admirably on certain abstract categorization tests and the fact that it can peck away to no avail in a different kind of test. The bird who pecks in vain would never encounter these conditions in the real world, where pecking serves the bird very well indeed—and where, presumably, the bizarre talent that enables it to distinguish Monet's from Picasso's paintings also serves it well. (Page 1999, 99)

The "exquisite tuning" that defines both animals and humankind enables them to select contexts, privilege particular abilities and talents, avoid areas of weakness or inappropriateness, and play out the imperatives of survival and/or advancement on their own terms and conditions. Humankind and animals thus find themselves demonstrating similar kinds of generic outlook, while purposing their agendas—consciously or unconsciously—to speak to particular needs and outcomes. The interaction between humankind and animals becomes only one part of this. Crucially, humankind and animals, both as separate and related entities, are reflected in the ways animated film—represented by any number of examples in this discussion—depicts their common models of adaptation and the extent of their relativity. This casts animated animal characters and narratives, therefore, as the bearer of meanings that simultaneously address social issues while being represented in surreal or purely illusionist forms pertinent to the reversals, intrusions, revisions, and challenges of the carnivalesque.

The nature of the carnivalesque has been best defined and expressed by Mikhail Bakhtin's study of European folk culture through the work of Rabelais, and its examination of the ways in which the anarchic dynamics of carnival challenged the hierarchical oppressions of the Middle Ages, privileging the grotesque nature of bodily function as the key component in undermining the limits of social order (see Bakhtin 1984). Other critics have identified this model of subversion in many cultural activities, ceremonies, and events worldwide, surviving into the modern era, and view such practices as intrinsic to comic events; novelist Howard Jacobson adds, "In carnival, the masquerade is universal. No distinction between watchers and watched is recognized; everyone participates. And the logic of reversal is universal, too: what is holy is profaned, what is elevated is lowered, where there has been respect and awe there is now travesty, where modesty, lewdness. The crowned are uncrowned; fools become kings" (Jacobson 1997, 198). Jacobson is aware, though, that the parameters of the carnival have included a discourse about the role of the animal and animality as part of this culture of disruption and revisionism. Indeed, Jacobson's own thesis on comedy, even at its very beginning, insists, "If comedy, in all its changing shapes, has one overriding preoccupation, it is this: that we resemble beasts more closely than we resemble gods, and that we make great fools of ourselves the moment we forget it" (Jacobson 1997,

2). So the intrinsic view that there is an embedded alignment between animals and humankind, which I have suggested is shared by psychoanalysts, animal behaviorists, and literary and cultural critics, informs a highly particular currency of social pertinence in the redefinition of worlds. Jacobson credits animals with a high degree of insight in this regard, dismissing Arthur Koestler's contempt for domesticated animals and his grudging acceptance of the slight possibility that animals may have a playful consciousness:

> [The] slight implied by the idea of domestication—animals learning from us how to blow the whistle on their own instinctivity—meet the satiric contempt of which animals are capable. The parrot we teach to be a miniature airborne copy of ourselves is derisive not in our image, but derisive *of* it. The devilish eye, the rolling gait, the parodies of our voices, down to every wheedling nuance of our accent and pronunciation—what are these but satires on domestication itself? . . . as far as the comic is concerned, the balance of borrowing and imitation falls differently; it is not the animals who must check their satiric bona fides out with us, but we who continuously put ourselves to school with them. (Jacobson 1997, 3–4)

The animated animal film constantly becomes the school by which measure of the animal is played out as the barometer of human activity and foible: the status of the animal acknowledged as a center of a social universe, the benchmark by which humankind is seen, known, and understood. The social dynamic, the core stimulus for carnivalesque interrogation, is addressed through the animated animal film and thus becomes the epitome of the social carnivalesque, ensuring "that if the symbolic animal in film constantly points beyond itself to outside the frame of the screen then it cannot be characterized as dissolving into an empty or infinitely protean sign" (Burt 2002, 44).

A Universal Language

On Margarita Island in Venezuela, we were discussing the animals native to the area, and Doug [my husband] asked our guide if there were any deer. Our guide's English was good, but he didn't know the word "deer" and we couldn't get across to him what they were. I said, "You know, Bambi," and he immediately understood. A universal language, ay? (Lynne Perras, personal correspondence, December 2005)

The visual primacy of the animated text, and its dissemination (particularly in the case of Disney texts), within and beyond nations, has often determined that the animated animal has iconic status. Animal iconography has thus become charged not merely with the parameters of the social canivalesque, but also particular kinds of ideological pertinence. As early as 1930, "Douglas Fairbanks, Mickey Mouse's true alter ego, took a reel of Mickey Mouse shorts to the Polynesian islands as a means of breaking the ice with the natives. Ub [Iwerks]'s design of Mickey transcended language boundaries and cultural distinctions. In any land, under any name, Mickey was accepted lovingly. He was called Topolino in Italy, Micky Maus in Germany" (Iwerks and Kenworthy 2001, 72). This is not merely about the ways in which a graphic idiom can become a conduit for meaning imposed upon it, but the way it carries a common signifier of a shared animality—a sense of life shared by living creatures, ironically best expressed and foregrounded by the animated medium.

Crucial in this development was the way in which Mickey Mouse in particular came to transcend the aesthetic and cultural values that had already been imbued in the animated cartoon by the 1930s. The early cartoon was heavily influenced by comic strips—for example, Bud Fisher's "Mutt 'n' Jeff," George Herriman's "Krazy Kat," or R. F. Outcault's "Buster Brown," adapted as "Bobby Bumps"—featuring narrative vignettes that were essentially based on sight gags and amusing scenarios. This was even reflected in Disney's first "Laugh-O-Gram" cartoons of the 1920s, where "exaggerated character action . . . is illustrated by comic strip conventions such as eye dashes, speech bubbles, or more commonly, beads of sweat that explode from the heads of characters who are startled, angered, happy, or otherwise motivated. Stars and squiggles indicate pain. Speed lines represent movement. Exclamation points and ampersands indicate the unprintable being spoken" (Iwerks and Kenworthy 2001, 17). It was clear that such characters were fundamentally a mix of graphic marks—so much so that limbs could become alternative objects or props—and an idea that underpinned the jokes. Felix the Cat, discussed earlier, transcended the core conventions of the comic strip, largely through the quality of the physical comedy and the pertinence of the comic events within a social context. This can be traced to the strong influence of Charlie Chaplin on Otto Messmer, Felix's creator, who effectively used Chaplin's more motivated slapstick conventions to facilitate basic storytelling. Chaplin's idioms often pointed beyond their status as gags, and it was in films like *Felix Doubles for Darwin* that similar quasi-topical issues and social mores often addressed by Chaplin could be identified in the cartoon. Elsewhere, the purpose of the gag also spoke to the cultures of modernity but sought to be more revisionist.

Paul Terry, an established cartoonist in the burgeoning animation industry, making "Farmer Al Falfa" cartoons for Paramount following the First World War, consolidated his position with a series of films based on Aesop's Fables. Though Terry admitted that he had never heard of Aesop, he was nevertheless persuaded by writer Howard Estabrook that there was a range of morality tales that could be adapted which might prove popular with the American public. Leonard Maltin notes, "The fact that most of these fables depicted human foibles with animal characters was a perfect format for cartoons. Terry also learned that using animals in this way practically eliminated the possibility of offending anyone in the audience through ethnic stereotypes of human improprieties. This gave the series a good reputation with theatre owners" (Maltin 1987, 129). Terry recognized that this enabled the cartoon to carry a universality in its outlook, but ironically it is the punch line of these cartoons that is best remembered, since Terry substituted Aesop's more philosophical intentions with urban gags: "The fact they're ambiguous is the thing that made them funny. Aesop said 2600 years ago that 'the race to the altar is run in laps,' or 'Marriage is a good institution, but who wants to live in an institution?' If you put serious morals on, they wouldn't have gone at all, too heavy" (quoted in Maltin 1987, 129). Terry produced the "Aesop's Fables" for eight years, remarkably producing one cartoon a week, often using topical stories rather than Aesop's original tales. He rarely foregrounded the status of the animal as significant, even if, in narratives based on a principle like "one good turn deserves another," he used the device of a dog protecting a mouse from some cats because the mouse treated him well.

Further, like the comic strip–styled cartoons, these narratives did not progress the form, and it was not until Disney entered the animation industry and predicated his "Alice" comedies on the draftsmanship of Ub Iwerks that the form effectively extended. As Leslie Iwerks, Iwerks's granddaughter, and John Kenworthy remark about Iwerks's animation in *Alice in the Jungle* (Walt Disney/Ub Iwerks, USA, 1925), "In this film, he outdoes himself. A pair of juvenile elephants prance to an inviting swimming hole. A trunk of a young elephant boy turns into a suitcase trunk, which contains a pair of swimming trunks. One iteration of the trunk pun would have been funny, two rounds take it to the level of absolute corn" (Iwerks and Kenworthy 2001, 34), but this kind of gag, though taken up, refined, and developed later by auteurs like Tex Avery, was to change as character comedy advanced with figures like Oswald the Rabbit, who in many senses helped develop a kind of anarchic, romantic comedy that made greater demands of the medium but who also brought the animality back to the animal within the cartoon context. Russell Merritt notes that "now there are somatic consequences. When you tweak his nose, pull his ears, he hurts, He can cry. He can laugh. He can become a manic-depressive. You're getting away from the slapstick gags into more of these personality gags, and as you do that, some of Ub's quirky personality traits start coming to the surface. The sense of anarchy rules as it never had in the Alice cartoons" (quoted in Iwerks and Kenworthy 2001, 42–43). Two key points emerge from this that become intrinsic in the development of Mickey Mouse and inform the fundamental function of the animated animal I have discussed overall. The first is the recovery of animality at the heart of personality animation, and the second is the profound investment of the animator in creating a discourse in the characters that both reflects the animal and the sociocultural intentionality of the animator.

When Mickey plays out his barnyard antics in *Steamboat Willie,* he consolidates this template, and with it the determining discourse-influx that is represented here in the concept of bestial ambivalence. The supernormal status of the animal character—like all animated characters—persists over time, becoming a developmental phenomenon or phenomenology that adapts to its naturalcultural conditions while never sacrificing its traditional lore in relating both to reality and to representation. Given these conditions it is unsurprising that Mickey, like many other animated animals, retains his resonance and cultural conviction because his epistemological currency prevents him from becoming merely reduced to a brand, a style, or one singular metaphorical principle. Such a character can simultaneously represent the freedoms of the language of animation itself, the site of the animal and animality, and a range of critical discourses for and about humankind. Such universality speaks to both specificity and ambiguity, particularity and ambivalence, uniqueness and commonality.

It becomes clear, then, that the animal can specifically embody political discourses or merely reflect them, and it is this bestial ambivalence that has characterized some complex examples of propaganda and personal filmmaking throughout the history of animation. I wish to explore this briefly in three ways: first, in relation to a specific period of time; second, in relation to a particular context; and third, in relation to a particular issue.

First, a brief engagement with the status of the animal cartoon during a highly contentious period of change in the United States. Professor of ethnic studies Christopher Lehman has assessed the political discourses of animal cartoons during the era of the Vietnam War, identifying animation's enduring capacity to offer submerged metaphorical structures that offer pertinent comment on the social and cultural dynamics of a particular period and context. With such readings, care must be taken that animals are not evacuated of their own meanings, and not merely seen as phenomenological templates by which readings can be coincidentally attached. It is clear that the intrinsic relationship to animals that I have defined throughout my discussion, and embedded in this final chapter as an intrinsic quality in humankind, offers a route to other possible knowledge and perception in this respect, and also services an understanding of ideologically informed narratives. Particularly in the American context, but elsewhere, too, there remained a tendency for cartoons to link into and sustain trends and fads that emerged in popular culture. Consequently, in retrospect these cartoons become ready commentaries on the dominant traits and tropes, which characterize specific times and places, most notably in relation to entertainment figures, key events, and phases in generic or narrative developments in mediated forms. Lehman tracks American cartoons from the last vestiges of the theatrical cartoon period in the 1950s and early 1960s, still trading on the popularity of the stars from the Golden Era, through the emergence of the television cartoon. Some still regard the transition to television as the death of animation in the United States, and thus television animation remains undervalued and underevaluated, seemingly only recovering to some degree with the countercultural successes of *Fritz the Cat* (Ralph Bakshi, USA, 1972) and the *Sesame Street* series, which included animated educational sequences. Exploring one aspect of his discussion, Lehman notes, "Terrytoons found its greatest success of the Vietnam War by tapping into the growing popularity of rural imagery. The studio produced over one hundred *Deputy Dawg* episodes for television syndication. Focusing on a dim-witted canine police officer in charge of keeping animals out of a henhouse, the series spread to major cities in 1961" (Lehman 2006, 13). The relationship of the rural, and by implication the rule of nature to the role and function of animals in cultural exchange, should not be undervalued, as in this context the political agenda of the American South and its pro-segregation stance can be read against the narrative premise of the *Deputy Dawg*. Simply, the southern old guard is protecting the henhouse of America from the associated animality of Negro cultures, which in the real world are embodied in African American civil rights demonstrators protesting against those sustaining an antiintegrationist stance. Deputy Dawg's adversaries, Muskie Muskrat and Vincent Van Gopher, nevertheless steal eggs from the henhouse and the slow but inevitable change in everyday culture is quietly implied. The idea that the "other" within oppositional encounters is characterized by an untutored animality takes the discussion back, of course, to my introduction, and to King Kong.

Cynthia Erb stresses, "Much of King Kong's cultural use value issues from its status as popular dramatization of the ethnographic encounter, or of contact between First and Third Worlds. Within this narrative scheme, the character King Kong stands as a mediating figure caught between 'worlds.' King Kong's monstrous hybridity manages to absorb most of the binary structures characteristic of Western thought—East/West, black/white, female/male, primitive/modern" (Erb 1998, 17). Erb's claims to Kong's hybridity sits well within the discourse of bestial ambivalence I have stressed, and further prompts an engagement with the conduct of the naturalcultural through the primacy of debates about nationhood, race, gender, and identity within the changing premises of modernity. From cinematic giants like Kong to TV characters like Deputy Dawg, the supernormal nature of the status of the character as an animated animal invites a recognition of the social meaning of the animal within its context (Asia, the American South) and the carnivalesque of how the freedoms of expression in animation play out pertinent and related issues and ideas. Being caught between worlds allows examination of all worlds informing the representation. Sometimes, though, this remains incoherent and unsatisfactory in its outcome.

Again, Lehman notes,

[Friz] Freleng also demonstrated in *D'Fightin' Ones* [Friz Freleng, USA, 1961] that he could not intelligently discuss race via animation. He had the perfect opportunity to use animal figures to satirize race relations while drawing from the race-themed feature film, *The Defiant Ones* (1958). Instead of a black man and a white man handcuffed together, the director cleverly pairs a white dog with the black cat, Sylvester. Freleng could have made the stereotypical cat-mouse hatred a context for exploring black-white tensions. However, any discussion by the cat and dog of their animosity toward one another does not extend beyond a terse "I hate you." As the civil rights movement conducted sit-ins and freedom rides to force the issue of segregation into the U.S. media, Freleng retreated from the issue by using old slapstick gags. (Lehman 2006, 16).

Though many chase cartoons predicated on character conflict can be read successfully as engaging metaphors of reflection and critique in periods of unrest, through their default narrative premise of the dramatic tensions between known adversaries, it is clear that authorial intent and the use of the animal discourse at the heart of the piece must have greater purchase. Those animation directors who wish to move beyond the immediate metaphoric appropriateness into a signature style or comment usually dramatize the process of using the animal more directly. Significantly, for example, Chuck Jones noticeably reduced the scale of conflict in the "Tom and Jerry" cartoons of this period, privileging lyricism and reconciliation over violence, in a clear reflection of the rise of the peace and love countercultural perspectives. There was also a greater recognition of the living creature at the heart of conflicts; conflicts that were becoming increasingly brutal and unforgiving on both the national and international stage. The coincidence of the closure of Warner Bros. cartoons and the consequent demise of the insensitive and dogmatic Foghorn Leghorn, after appearing in cartoons for twenty-seven years, was equally fortuitous, as the maintenance of a bombastic southerner undermining those he thought to be inferior was increasingly anachronistic and unacceptable. The rooster, so often the arbiter of difference in many animated films, lacked the abstract qualities of its use by Park or McLaren here and was necessarily retired.

Crucially, when the animal was fully acknowledged in more auteur-led works like Ward Kimball's *It's Tough to Be a Bird* (Ward Kimball, USA, 1969) or Ralph Bakshi's *Fritz the Cat,* it carried with it a range of discourses once more pertinent to the bestial ambivalence model. Kimball's ramshackle bird is a far cry from Disney's signature style, and a countercultural icon of quasi-bohemian hippydom, complaining of the inhibitions, frustrations, and failings of being a bird in an open metaphor for the shifting parameters of social existence in a changing America. It deliberately uses the very difference of the bird as its chief agency. This idea is taken to its logical conclusion in *Fritz the Cat,* where Ralph Bakshi adapts Robert Crumb's underground comic as a full-length animated feature made specifically for adults. With its explicit sexual content, a consequence of Fritz's exploitation of the liberal outlook of the radicals involved in the antiwar movement, the film uses animality as a gauge by which political outlook and intellectual engagement are a mere veneer for more venal and self-serving practices. The pure animal here is the embodiment of the pursuit of intuitive and instinctual needs; the humanimal, the epitome of liberation; the aspirational human, the pursuit of democratic idealism; and the critical human, the deep-rooted skepticism that radicalism has little integrity while reactionary stances remain corrupt and pointless. Bakshi's X-rated feature was in some senses groundbreaking in reinventing the full-length animated film by resisting the funny animal motifs associated with the American cartoon, and by foregrounding pressing political concerns by subverting the expectations of these iconographic representations. Bakshi helped to politicize animation by politicizing the animal, something done some years before in Halas and Batchelor's *Animal Farm* and a number of authored shorts, but which had particular resonance in the United States.

The political can be further addressed in relation to a particular context, and here I consider Hans Fischerkoesen's film *The Silly Goose* (Hans Fischerkoesen, Germany, 1944), an exemplar of Fischerkoesen's extraordinary output from 1933 onward and an important film made under the increasingly oppressive conditions of National Socialism and the conduct of war. William Moritz has written extensively about the ways in which Goebbels had insisted upon more indigenous, quality animation production to challenge the already established claims of the American animation industry as leaders in the field. He details how Fischerkoesen, an established filmmaker with strong credentials in the advertising arena, was essentially commandeered to move from Leipzig, where his studio was established, to Potsdam, in order to be nearer UFA's studios and the Nazi sphere of influence (see Moritz 1997, 231–234). Fischerkoesen's *Weather-Beaten Melody* (Hans Fischerkoesen, Germany, 1942) was the first film made under these conditions, including state-of-the-art multiplane camera and optical effects, but its real claims lie in its auteurial resistance to the excesses of Nazi ideology, through the deliberate use of ambivalent animal characters and action. Moritz comments,

> The very idea of ambiguity was anaethema for the Nazis, who could only hope to maintain their fascist program by enforcing strict, unbending codes of behavior and absolute, inviolable "ideas and truths." Precisely because of its technical brilliance, *Weather-Beaten Melody* could contain quite a bit of forbidden material . . . from beneath the charming surface of this cartoon emerges a

subversive message: women, far from filling the unnatural Nazi-designated stereotype of revolving around "children, church and kitchen," can escape into Nature to be self-reliant and adventurous, erotic and free—they can rediscover or revitalize a suppressed world of forbidden joy that is found in music and friendship between diverse creatures; creatures who could be brown or white, a frog or a caterpillar, or even a pair of ladybug beetles who might be a same sex couple . . . the entire community of animals depicted in *Weather-Beaten Melody* are peaceful, friendly, fun-loving, imaginative and altruistic. (Moritz 1997, 235–236)

Compared to the animals in American animated cartoons, this offered a very different picture; one grounded once more in a view of nature as an active principle characterized by creatures embraced and embodying life in its most positive, intuitive, and uninhibited sense. Rather than representing overt ideas, the creatures are exemplified through the purity in their pure animal status, and implicitly challenge the perverse Apollonian order of Nazi ideas with a Dionysian reassertion of lived experience. Fischerkoesen's use of animus per se in the role of the animals, as a mode of resistance to the political machinations that would manipulate and repress it, was also a vindication of the animated form in its depiction. Unlike a Paul Terry, who abandoned the moral imperative of his Aesop's Fables, Fischerkoesen reintroduces a parable-like quality to service his implied political stance. This remains especially important when set against how animal imagery was used elsewhere by the Nazis. As Sam Keen points out, "The lower down in the animal phyla the images descend, the greater sanction is given to the soldier to become a mere exterminator of pests. The anti-semitic propaganda that reduced the jew to a louse or rat was an integral part of the creation of the extermination camps" (Keen 1986, 61). This is readily evidenced in the vehement anti–Mickey Mouse propaganda written in Nazi journals as early as 1931: "Mickey Mouse is the shabbiest, most miserable ideal ever invented. Mickey Mouse is a stultification device sent over with the Young-Plan capital. Healthy instinct informs every decent girl and upright boy that the vile and dirty vermin, which import bacteria into the animal kingdom, cannot be made into an animal type. . . . Down with the Jewish bamboozlement of the people, kick out the vermin, down with Mickey Mouse, and erect swastikas!" (quoted in Leslie 2002, 80).

In the face of such a principle, Fischerkoesen's humanitarian perspective is all the more extraordinary, and was developed further in *The Silly Goose*. Keen suggests that a logical extension of the reductionist strategies that demean the human by casting particular animals as the lowest form of life by comparison entitles oppressive ideologies to cast nature as an unacceptable other, and charge the self-righteous and empowered to monitor and marshal it: "If the enemy can be relegated to the domain of nature, it follows from the logic of our supernatural metaphysic, that he is a means, an *it*, a bit of raw material with which we are morally entitled to do anything we desire. Indeed, as the bearers of reason we have a moral obligation to tame the bestial powers and put matter to good use" (Keen 1986, 135). Fischerkoesen, rather than accepting this evacuation of the animal of its unfettered nature, or its reduction to an impersonal subject, insists upon the recovery of both the folkloric principles and tradition explored in the last chapter, and the insinuation of how the animal can transcend its oppression.

The Silly Goose features an imprisoned goose traveling on a wooden cart, which passes, among other things drawn from the exotica of urban city life, an exotic parrot and a fox stole. In three images, Fischerkoesen shows animal entrapment, brutality, and exploitation, but ironically these sights prove appealing to the goose, as she returns to the seeming drudgery of farm culture, where her siblings are being schooled in their essential function of laying eggs and participating in barnyard life. The goose's newfound influence is epitomized as she vainly contrives to create a sophisticated urbanite costume composed of a veil from a spider web, a straw hat, a caterpillar-as-stole, high heels made from corks, pig-hair eyelashes, and makeup made up from pollen. This new look attracts disdain and contempt in her fellow animals, but proves attractive to a gander, whom the goose rejects in favor of a woodland seduction by a fox. Up to this point, the cartoon has the essence of romantic melodrama, but its portents change as the goose enters the fox's lair.

The lair is peopled by slave animals. A weasel turns a spit; a cat works a treadmill while playing a skeleton-bone xylophone; and most challenging of all, a pen full of geese await slaughter. The goose escapes, and her fellow farm animals help to drive the fox away and liberate the geese. Suitably chastised, the goose warns her own chicks not to behave improperly. Fischerkoesen employs the ambiguities in the text to suggest that all moral parameters are open to being ignored or exploited, showing that the goose's attraction to urban glamour is in some ways understandable even if it is based on unacceptable practices. Further, the very desire to imitate such glamour and acquire its affiliated status is in some ways an inevitability of the attraction, and the very reason why those in power create such symbols of power and quality. To be seduced by the thing itself is to be seduced by the idea. Only when the goose is penalized, not for her vanity but for her foolishness, is the allure of power recognized for the brutalities and inhumanity it has been secured through. The fox becomes an ambiguous hero: on the one hand, charming and attractive, on the other, someone who ritualizes atrocity. This latter point is crucial because it uses the pure animal agenda of the real-world appetite of fox for goose, but advances the notion of critical human by the fox's ritualistic process toward death for his victims, which has clear echoes of the practices of the concentration camps. Animals here are seen to be abused and exploited, and though this may extol rural peasant culture at one level through Goebbel's "blood and soil" policy, it effectively exposes the inhumanity at the heart of human experience. Fischerkoesen's parable makes astute political comment through his embrace of the animal and his despair for humankind. *Weather-Beaten Melody* and *The Silly Goose* show the animal as the bearer of life itself under these conditions, and animation as the only language capable of being the bearer of the message.

This kind of political perspective may also be viewed in more contemporary contexts and in relation to a specific issue. Jonathan Burt has warned that "ethical questions arise most severely at the point at which the line between the fictitious and the real animal is most difficult to draw" (Burt 2002, 12). I have argued throughout this discussion, however, that animators and animation directors demonstrate a particular empathy and affiliation with their animal subjects that has constantly recognized this ethical responsibility. Animators use representational forms to consciously engage with personal and social issues that do not *absent* the animal from the discourse, but use it readily as part of a strategy of discourse-in-flux, or animal in-the-making. This places the animator within a larger political picture, which puts the representation of the animal in connection with bigger debates, mainly concerning animal welfare.

Animal welfare in this sense is not just a sentimental idea or a reconnection with nature but an attitude and an activity in the ongoing shifts and tensions of modernity, underpinned by the interrogative and interpretive remarks I have made in the application of the bestial ambivalence model. In this sense, then, in the first instance, I would like to address an animated film that wasn't broadcast. Aardman Animation, as part of its *Creature Comforts* series, wished to make an episode called "Lab Animals": "It was about people's attitudes to laboratory animals—some of them have strong attitudes, but a lot of people are fairly indifferent or don't know the reality and are not prepared to put themselves on the line, so it never really worked," recalls production manager Gareth Owen, to which animator Toby Farrow adds, "I thought it was very poignant because you've got animals in this awful situation and they're either unaware of it, or railing against it. We worked on it a long time and were very careful to make it clear that the animals weren't passive, that they were angry about their position or simply unknowing about what was to happen. For example, we had a pig innocently saying, 'I'm sure animals don't mind being cut up.' It's the dramatic irony." Finally, director Richard Goleszowski notes, "We had a smoking beagle, and two dogs pinned to the board covered in electrodes all complaining about animal testing and how unfair it was. It's funny out of context, but as soon as you make an episode it becomes very miserable and depressing" (all quoted in Lane 2003, 174). The production team ultimately felt that this might not be suitable for a family audience in a tea-time schedule and did not sit well against the tenor of the rest of the series, so they withdrew the episode. This merely raised the issue of a suitable context in which the program could be seen, as the work and the points that were made were important. A DVD release is therefore under consideration, directed to adults. In once sense, then, the prevailing innocence of the animated medium in the public imagination can be counterproductive, but this makes the form no less capable of dramatizing complex

I Am Not an Animal. The collaged construction of hybrid humanimals readily draws attention to issues of exploitation, adaptation, and resistance in social questions about the treatment of animals. Copyright © Baby Cow Animation/BBC.

animal-related issues. The Aardman example merely demonstrates a level of responsibility about how the episode might be received and how its issues might properly be addressed.

In Baby Cow Animation's *I Am Not an Animal* (Baby Cow Animation, UK, 2004), this issue is treated at the satirical level by combining the idea of laboratory testing with the established convention of talking animated animals. Project S is being conducted by scientist Mike Simmons at Vivi-Sec UK, seeking to create "Batch 4," a group of talking animals, who might eventually take their place in the real environment. The animals live in luxury, though this is only computer generated, but they demonstrate intrinsically human characteristics and tastes. The animals include a horse named Philip Masterson-Bowie, a dog called Winona Matthews, a monkey named Hugh Gape, a mouse dubbed Clare Franchetti, a bird, Mark Andrews, and a cat called Kieron. The animals' goal is one day to go to a special place called London, where they might use their skills; a "special place" where they can exploit their vocal and intellectual talents. The head of Vivi-Sec UK, Mr. Bronson, has other ideas, however, as he wishes the animals to be put down. Ironically, the animals escape through the intervention of animal activists, who find great difficulty in believing that the animals can converse, and when condemned to live in freedom cannot cope with the human environment. Though much of the comedy comes from the incongruity of the talking animal within the context in which it participates, this is actually dissipated by the familiarity of the convention in animated films. Further, any satiric import in the piece is undermined by not alluding to some of the real conditions of animal testing, or to some of the sources that inspired this kind of narrative, most notably Martin Rosen's *Watership Down* (Martin Rosen, UK, 1978) and in particular *Plague Dogs* (Martin Rosen, UK, 1982), the latter featuring lab dogs Snitter and Rowf, pursued by the authorities in the belief that they have anthrax. While clearly *Plague Dogs* is an anti-vivisectionist tract, *I Am Not an Animal* does not engage with concerns for animals, merely satirizing middle-class attitudes in outlook and expectation. *Watership Down* leavens its naturalism with some playful interludes that echo its natural idyll, but *Plague Dogs* sustains its realism to both distanciate itself from the limitations of the talking animal story, ironically exemplified in *I Am Not an Animal,* and to enhance its political comment. Here, sadly, for animals, there is only struggle and futility, but once more, this is actually foregrounded by the illusionist artifice in drawing these issues to the attention of the popular audience by challenging its expectations of animation and animal narratives.

In an avowedly independent work like Simon Pummell's *Butcher's Hook* (Simon Pummell, UK, 1995), this is more obvious. Using state-of-the-art animation and compositing techniques, Pummell suggests an apparently pristine and clinical environment in which a taxidermist is ultimately assaulted and transformed by dead animals. The film's title, "Butcher's Hook," is cockney rhyming slang for "look," and this is the real clue to the film's intentions in the sense that Pummell wishes the audience to both engage with aesthetics and pay attention to the everyday barbarism and cruelty made invisible by social and artistic conventions. Rabbits, puppies, kittens, and reptiles are held in preserving fluid; a skeleton of a snake writhes and circulates; a naked taxidermist

Butcher's Hook. The taxidermist amidst his seemingly oppressive world of antiseptic bell jars and cages, signs of imprisonment for both animal and humankind. Courtesy Simon Pummell, Koninck Projects for Channel Four.

haunts his laboratory—images that all at once eroticize and alienate, demonstrating the intrinsic relationship between animal and humankind, life and death, morality and perversity. Pummell constantly uses eye motifs and fluid canvases, problematizing what the audience thinks it is seeing. The imagery authenticates the animal yet makes it strange. This is informed by the implied sense of dead animals breaching cages and bell jars, and the emergence of the taxidermist himself as a skeletal, reptilian form, now a hybridized subject of his own experimentation and his own mortal complacency. The laboratory is ultimately overwhelmed by organic tree growth, and the piece ends privileging its ambiguity, rooted in the very essence of animation itself. Pummell gives life to his materials; his materials are those which articulate the arbitrariness of life and death; and his subject is the inherent animality that is the animus of experience and the fuel of creative expression in the animated form. *Butcher's Hook* both demonstrates and exposes the myth of control, using animation to prompt questions of what is seen and why. The ethical imperative to know and embrace the animal is at the heart of this painterly scrutiny, operating as a deep critique of social complicity and indifference.

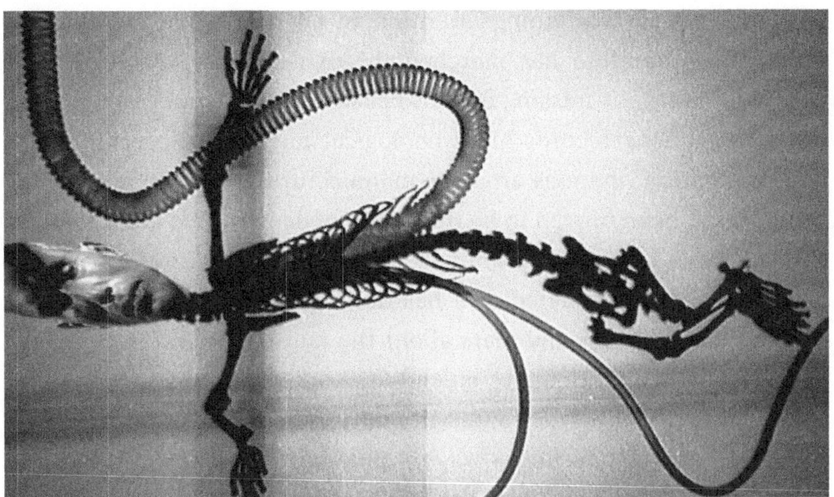

Butcher's Hook. The taxidermist becomes a hybridized humanimal, but one reflecting death, the questionable impact of progressive technology, and the ambiguous status of postmodern form and identity. Courtesy Simon Pummell, Koninck Projects for Channel Four.

Manufacturing Records

In concluding this discussion, I wish to stress that animation as a form has always been sensitive to the terms and conditions of representing animals, and while inevitably sometimes using animal figures for differentiation of character, it has largely engaged with animals on a basis of respect and significant purpose. What is clear, though, is that animals move beyond being ready vehicles for narrative clarity or comic excess and become ideologically and culturally charged phenomena in animated film commenting both on the status of animals *and* humans. Animation, in its intrinsic artifice of representational phenomenology and hyper-illusionism, has always been predicated on the idea of "seeing ourselves looking," and it is through the animal that humankind has embraced and endorsed both the idea of inclusiveness (the co-existence of human and human, human and animal, animal and animal) and the revelation of human endeavor and foible, animal cultures, and the art of animation itself.

For video artist Tim Sherman, "Animation is a complex category of meta-media phenomena, a manner of creative behavior quite capable of attracting and sustaining attention in all manner of media environments. Animation has marched through cinema, television, and now video, without missing a beat, because it is the concrete process of manufacturing records of psychological memory" (Sherman 2005, 195). Animation, then, as an art is manufacturing records, and in this instance has been proven to be the bearer of deep-rooted and profound psychological memories of animals and their relationship to humankind. In this the animated film has done great service in alleviating some of the anxieties and fears about the naturalcultural in the modern era. Sam Keen articulates much of this when he suggests, "In so far as our claim to dignity is rooted in our ability to transcend nature, it becomes necessary to find a way to deny our animality. We bathe to remove smell, dress to cover the body, create cities in which we are hermetically sealed against any intrusion of weather. Then we place animals in controlled environments—zoos—where we can watch them from a safe distance. All the while we destroy natural environments, using resources to turn matter into cultural artifacts" (Keen 1986, 135). As I have sought to demonstrate, though, the animated animal film is a stand against this, recovering animaility through primal knowledges, opening up related discourses that insist upon an address of the philosophic and historical impact of the animal on humankind, and foregrounding sociocultural and political issues that affect the animal. While no art form can significantly change the world and its seemingly relentless pursuit of its own end, the animated animal film has sought to rethink and re-create humanity and the animal, our view of nature, and our institutions. It suggests that humankind is properly facilitated by understanding the animal as an embedded part of itself, and a key element in the very recognition of life itself. In many senses, this has become one of animated film's roles in preserving animus in the seemingly alienatory conditions of late modernity.

Gianluigi Toccafondo's *The Tango* (Gianluigi Toccafondo, Italy, 1991) seeks to reveal the very impetus of such a life force as he moves from the refinement and control of a dance featuring Fred Astaire and Ginger Rogers to the fluid abstractions of fauvist expression, mutating human beings into animals but in a spirit revealing the energy and dynamism of physical expression and life known and, more importantly, felt. Perhaps surprisingly, in many senses, this also informs the more paradigmatic television narratives of Klasky Csupo's *The Wild Thornberrys* (Klasky Csupo, USA, 1997–2004), who live a constant safari, living with, and through, animal experience across the world; young Eliza Thornberry, blessed with the gift of communicating with animals and knowing their felt experience, too. There are a number of exchanges in the series where Eliza recognizes situations in which animals are under threat, only to realize that through their own instincts and means of communication they too manage their environment, and resist or avoid the abstract threats that may undermine their existence. Though the series self-consciously references the wildlife documentary and couples like Hans and Lotte Hass, Armand and Michaela Dennis, and Alan and Joan Root, it also points up that the act of photographic record or scientific observation is sometimes an insufficient gauge of animal experience. Eliza's intuitive understanding of animal sounds, gestures, and movements is as much part of this experiential exchange as the ability to biologically determine animal nature.

A final point might be made by briefly considering the work of two animators whose work spans the history of animation—a Russian, Ladislaw Starewicz, whose film *A Cameraman's Revenge* I have already considered, and a Japanese director, Hayao Miyazaki, who has become regarded as one of the form's greatest auteurs. Starewicz is an important figure because his work represents a continuum of the nineteenth-century tradition of the graphic illustration of animals as well as their relationship to humans in the works of Grandville, Daumier, La Fontaine, and Cruickshank. Further, in his own preoccupation with entomology and animal physiology, Starewicz had a particular empathy with insects and creatures that led him to create animation in a less sentimental or socially sensitive mode, preferring instead the brutalities and arbitrary actions of ancient folktales. These stories more readily reflected his own understanding of critical anthropomorphism as an amoral condition and the strategies for personification in animation as an intrinsic exposé of human contradiction. His use of "unattractive" creatures like rats in *Town Rat, Country Rat* (Ladislaw Starewicz, France, 1926) operates in a way that demands that the audience rationalize their repellence through a reading of their own less-than-appealing qualities. This use of the supernormal animal and the interpretation that might be available through the address of bestial ambivalence both asks for sympathy and identification but also once again insists upon an engagement with the Other Dimension, and a confrontation with both the alien in human identity and the alienation seemingly inherent in modern life. Starewicz's most famous work, *The Tale of the Fox* (Ladislaw Starewicz, France, 1930–1931), features a fox as trickster, sadistically humiliating a number of animal victims, including a lion king, in his rise to power. The amorality of the narrative recasts the animals in a great chain of being that is almost consciously Darwinian in outlook, and that has little relationship to the kind of circle of life reassurances offered by Disney's *The Lion King*. It asserts instead that the culture of the animal is sometimes without recourse to illusory oversocialized models of existence that are merely the misrepresentative veneer of modern civilization.

Hayao Miyazaki, working in the modern era, has a similar anxiety about the ways in which the social world constructs human identity, and throughout his work he constantly uses his narratives to privilege the presence of both the supernatural and organic regeneration of the natural order. His work seeks to redefine the dominant iconography of postwar Japan—the "mushroom cloud" of the Hiroshima and Nagasaki bombs; the high tech, postmodern urban cityscape; and the radical Americanized youth culture—by returning to a more traditional model of Japanese filmmaking in general, which uses the historically indeterminate multiplicity of narrative and design principles, mixing archaic symbolism, and a more meditative and contemplative engagement with philosophic inquiry. Miyazaki's work is of the stature of the masters Kurosawa, Ozu, Mizoguchi, and Oshima, because it is rooted in "Japanese-ness" and recalls the mythic parallel worlds of Gods, Demons, Animals, and Humankind. Consequently, this normalization means that humankind and animals naturally interact and know themselves through each other. In *My Neighbor Totoro* (Hayao Miyazaki, Japan, 1988), the forest spirits called Totoro protect and guide two young children in the cultivation of imagination and a spiritual belief in the regenerative wonders of the natural world. In *Pocco Rosso* (Hayao

Miyazaki, Japan, 1992), however, Marco the pilot carries with him great metaphoric weight as a creature disillusioned with humankind. Presented as a therianthropic character, a human-pig carries with him associations in Japan with middle-aged men disconnected from the hopes of youth and disillusioned by the increasing challenges of the modern environment. The "pig" becomes a hero, though, and in doing so asserts Miyazaki's critique about humankind's assumption of god-given superiority. Further, *Princess Mononoke* (Hayao Miyazaki, Japan, 1997) is a totemistic discourse on the power of nature and the presence of animal spirits in the process of change. Animal gods and human agents war for the land itself, and play out a complex morality play that engages with the differing and competing agendas of ideological rightness in the possession and culture of the environment. Fundamentally, though, this is a narrative about the realization that regeneration may not be possible; the eco-system they represent and use is not an endless resource and speaks more to loss and crisis than to hope and continuity. Antonia Levi also adds:

> Despite the historical and mythological references, [*Princess Mononoke's*] attitude toward humanity and nature is actually quite different from that of the ancient or even more recent Shinto. Animism is not environmentalism. Its reverence for nature is based on awe if not actually on fear. It holds out the hope that nature can be placated. Environmentalism, on the other hand, argues that humanity is capable of destroying nature, or at least altering it sufficiently so that the planet is no longer habitable. Environmentalism fears humanity, not nature.
> (Levi 2001, 41)

This is the fundamental knowledge that the animal world possesses; inherent in their understanding is the purity of the natural order from which they come, and which humankind can only ever partially understand. Miyazaki's film is perhaps the most pertinent expression of the unspeakable and the inarticulable that is in the possession of the animal, and it has been achieved through his use of the shifting discourses of bestial ambivalence not merely identifiable in the openness of the form, but in an open view of lived experience, too. As Chuck Jones has remarked, "Working against [both human and animal] stereotypes, animation directors and writers have attempted to explode human prejudices" (Jones 1990, 228), and in freeing both the animal and humankind from the prejudicial, animated animal films have ensured that the social carnivalesque operates as its presiding and provocative outcome. Richard Condie's *The Cat Came Back* (Richard Condie, Canada, 1988), loosely based on a 100-year-old folk song about a poor man who can't get rid of his cat no matter how hard he tries, is characterized by lyrical character animation and Warner Bros.–style physical gags, as a well as a campfire-style sing-a-long chorus that claims, "The Cat Came Back, They thought he was a goner, But the Cat Came Back." The animated film will always ensure that the animal will come back and endure.

BIBLIOGRAPHY

Ajanovic, Midhat. 2004. *Animation and Realism*. Zagreb: Croatian Film Clubs Association.

"All Animals Are Equal—but Some Are More Equal Than Others." *Cine Technician*, January 1955.

Allan, Robin. 1999. *Walt Disney and Europe*. Eastleigh: John Libbey.

Baker, Steve. 2001. *Picturing the Beast: Animals, Identity. and Representation*. Urbana: University of Illinois Press.

———. 2002. "What Does Becoming Animal Look Like?" In Rothfels 2002, 67–98.

Bakhtin, Mikhail. 1984. *Rabelais and His World*. Bloomington: Indiana University Press.

Barrier, Michael. 1999. *Hollywood Cartoons: American Animation in Its Golden Age*. Oxford: Oxford University Press.

Bekoff, Marc. 2007. "Wild Justice and Fair Play: Cooperation, Forgiveness, and Morality in Animals." In Kalof and Fitzgerald 2007, 72–90.

Berger, John. 1980. "Why Look at Animals?" In *About Looking*. New York: Pantheon Books.

Bernard, Kenneth. 1976. "King Kong: A Meditation." In *The Girl in the Hairy Paw: King Kong as Myth, Movie and Monster*, ed. Ronald Gottesman and Harry Geduld, 25–30. New York: Avon.

Bettelheim, Bruno. 1978. *The Uses of Enchantment: The Meanings and Importance of Fairytales*. London: Peregrine Books.

Bouse, Derek. 1995 "True Life Fantasies: Storytelling Traditions in Animated Features and Wildlife Films." *Animation Journal* 3, no. 2, 19–39.

Bradshaw, Peter. 2006. "Film Reviews: 'Barnyard.'" *Guardian*, November 20, 9.

Brode, Thomas. 2004. *From Walt to Woodstock*. Austin: University of Texas Press.

Bullock, Marcus. 2002. "Watching Eyes, Seeing Dreams, Knowing Lives." In Rothfels 2002, 99–118.

Burghardt, Gordon. M. 1997. "Amending Tinbergen: A Fifth Aim for Ethology." In Thomson, Mitchell, and Miles 1997, 254–276.

Burt, Jonathan. 2002. *Animals in Film*. London: Reaktion Books.

Carroll, Noel. 1990. *The Philosophy of Horror*. London: Routledge.

Cohen, Karl. 1997. *Forbidden Animation*. Jefferson, N.C.: McFarland and Co.

———. 2003. "The Cartoon That Came in from the Cold." *Guardian*, Mar. 7.

Collings, Matthew. 1999. *This Is Modern Art*. London: Weidenfeld and Nicolson.

Comley, Nancy L. et al., eds. 1987. *Fields of Writing*. New York: St. Martins Press.

Cotta Vaz, Mark. 2000. "Endangered Species." In *Cinefex 82* (July), ed. Don Shay, 68–93.

———. 2005. *Living Dangerously: The Adventures of Merian C. Cooper.* New York: Villard.

Crafton, Donald. 1993. *Before Mickey: The Animated Film 1998–1928.* Chicago: University of Chicago Press.

Curtis, David. 1992. "The Animated Films." In *Anthony Gross,* ed. Mary Gross and Peter Gross, 129–140. Aldershot: Scolar Press.

Deleuze, Giles, and Felix Guattari. 2004 *A Thousand Plateaus.* London: Continuum.

Erb, Cynthia. 1998. *Tracking King Kong: A Hollywood Icon in World Culture.* Detroit: Wayne State University Press.

French, Phillip. 2006. "Thoroughly Modern Marie" (Reviews). *Observer,* October 22, 17

Freud, Sigmund. 1961. "Totem and Taboo." In *The Standard Edition of the Complete Psychological Works of Sigmund Freud,* ed. and trans. James Strachey. 24 vols. London: Hogarth Press and the Institute of Psychoanalysis.

Fudge, Erica. 2002. "A Left-Handed Blow: Writing the History of Animals." In Rothfels 2002, 3–18.

Furniss, Maureen, ed. 2005. *Chuck Jones: Conversations.* Jackson: University Press of Mississippi.

Gehman, Chris, and Steve Reinke, eds. 2005. *The Sharpest Point: Animation at the End of Cinema.* Toronto: YYZ Books.

Goldner, Orville, and George E. Turner. 1975. *The Making of King Kong.* New York: Ballantine Books.

Gould, Steven J. 1987. "A Biological Homage to Mickey." In *Fields of Writing,* ed. Nancy L. Comley et al., 500–508. New York: St. Martins Press.

———. 1998. *Leonardo's Mountain of Clams and the Diet of Worms.* London: BCA.

Grandin, Temple. 2006. *Thinking in Pictures.* Foreword by Oliver Sacks. London: Bloomsbury.

Grandin, Temple, and Catherine Johnson. 2006. *Animals in Translation.* London: Bloomsbury.

Grant, John. 2001. *Masters of Animation.* London: Batsford.

Griffin, Donald. 1992. *Animal Minds.* Chicago: University of Chicago Press.

Haber, Karen. 2005. *Kong Unbound.* New York: Simon and Schuster.

Halas, John. 1976. *Visual Scripting.* New York: Hastings House.

Halas, Vivien, and Paul Wells. 2006. *Halas & Batchelor Cartoons: An Animated History.* London: Southbank Publishing.

Haraway, Donna. 2004. *The Haraway Reader.* New York: Routledge.

Harryhausen, Ray, and Tony Dalton. 2003. *Ray Harryhausen: An Animated Life.* London: Aurum Press.

Hart, Christopher. 1997. *How to Draw Animation.* New York: Watson Guptill.

Hayward, Stan. 1977. *Scriptwriting for Animation.* New York: Hastings House/Focal Press.

Hickey, Dave. 1997. "Pontormo's Rainbow." In *Air Guitar: Essays on Art and Democracy.* Los Angeles: Art Issues Press.

Hooks, Ed. 2005. *Acting in Animation: A Look at Twelve Films.* Portsmouth, N.H.: Heinemann.

———. 2007. "Acting for Animators" (newsletter). August. E-mail distribution.

Ingram, David. 2000 *Green Screen: Environmentalism and Hollywood Cinema.* Exeter: Exeter University Press.

Isenberg, Andrew. 2002. "The Moral Ecology of Wildlife." in Rothfels 2002, 48–64.

Iwerks, Leslie, and John Kenworthy. 2001. *The Hand Behind the Mouse.* New York: Disney Editions.

Jacobson, Howard. 1997. *Seriously Funny: From the Ridiculous to the Sublime*. London: Viking.

Jenkins, A. E. 1955. "A Film Technician's Notebook." *Cine Technician,* May.

Jones, Chuck. 1990. *Chuck Amuck*. London and Sydney: Simon and Schuster.

———. 1996. *Chuck Reducks*. New York: TimeWarner.

Jung, Carl G., ed. 1964. *Man and His Symbols*. London: Aldus Books.

Kalof, Linda, and Amy Fitzgerald, eds. 2007. *The Animals Reader*. Oxford: Berg.

Keen, Sam. 1986. *Faces of the Enemy*. San Francisco: Harper and Row.

Klein, Norman. 1993. *Seven Minutes*. London: Verso.

Krasniewicz, Linda. 2000. "Morphing, Magical Transformations, and Metamorphosis in Two Cultures." In *Meta-Morphing: Visual Transformation and the Culture of Quick Change,* ed. Vivian Sobchak, 41–58. Minneapolis and London: University of Minnesota Press.

Krauss, Rosalind. 2005. " 'The Rock': William Kentridge's Drawings for Projection." In Gehman and Reinke 2005, 96–125.

Lane, Andy. 2003. *Creating Creature Comforts*. Basingstoke and Oxford: Macmillan.

Lawrence, D. H. 1981/1950. "Corasmin and the Parrots." In *D. H. Lawrence: Selected Essays*. London: Penguin Books.

Lehman, Christopher P. 2006. *American Animated Cartoons of the Vietnam Era*. Jefferson, N.C.: McFarland and Co.

Lent, John A., ed. 2001. *Animation in Asia and the Pacific*. Eastleigh: John Libbey.

Leslie, Esther. 2002. *Hollywood Flatlands: Animation, Critical Theory and the Avant Garde*. London: Verso.

Levi, Antonia. 2001. "New Myths for the Millennium: Japanese Animation." in Lent 2001, 33–50.

Lévi-Strauss, Claude. 2007. "The Totemic Illusion." In Kalof and Fitzgerald 2007, 251–261.

Leyda, Jay, ed. 1988. *Eisenstein on Disney*. London: Methuen.

Lippit, Akira Mizuta. 2000. *Electric Animal: Towards a Rhetoric of Wildlife*. Minneapolis: University of Minnesota Press.

Mabey, Richard. 2003. "Nature's Voyeurs." *The Guardian Review,* Mar. 15, 4–5.

Maltin, Leonard. 1987. *Of Mice and Magic*. New York: Plume.

Masson, Jeffrey M., and Susan McCarthy. 2007. "Grief, Sadness, and the Bones of Elephants." In Kalof and Fitzgerald 2007, 91–103.

Mazurkewich, Karen. 1999. *Cartoon Capers: The Adventures of Canadian Animators*. Toronto: McArthur and Co.

McWilliams, Donald, dir. 1990. *Creative Process: Norman McLaren*. VHS. Ottawa: National Film Board of Canada.

Mithen, Steven. 2007. "The Hunter-Gatherer Prehistory of Human-Animal Interactions." In Kalof and Fitzgerald 2007, 117–128.

Moritz, William. 1988. "Some Observations on Non-Objective and Non-Linear Animation." In *Storytelling in Animation,* ed. John Canemaker, 21–31. Los Angeles: AFI.

———. 1997. "Resistance and Subversion in Animated Films of the Nazi Era: The Case of Hans Fischerkoesen." In Pilling 1997, 228–240.

Morris, Desmond. 1977. *Manwatching*. London: Triad Panther.

———. 1990. *The Animal Contract*. London: W. H. Allen.

Murphy, Patrick D. 1995. "The Whole Wide World Was Scrubbed Clean: The Androcentric Animation of Denatured Disney." In *Mouse to Mermaid: The Politics of Film, Gender, and Culture,* ed. Elisabeth Bell, Lynda Haas, and Laura Sells, 125–136. Bloomington: Indiana University Press.

Nussbaum, Martha. 2007. "The Moral Status of Animals." In Kalof and Fitzgerald 2007, 30–36.

O'Sullivan, Judith. 1990. *The Great American Comic Strip.* Boston: Little Brown.

Page, George. 1999. *The Singing Gorilla: Understanding Animal Intelligence.* London: Headline Books.

Patten, Fred. 2004. *Watching Anime, Reading Manga.* Berkeley: Stonebridge Press.

Pilling, Jayne. 1997. *A Reader in Animation Studies.* London and Sydney: John Libbey.

———, ed. 2001. *Animation: 2D and Beyond.* Crans-Pres-Celigny and Hove: Rotovision.

Robinson, Chris. 2005. *Unsung Heroes of Animation.* Eastleigh: John Libbey.

Rothfels, Nigel, ed. 2002. *Representing Animals.* Bloomington: Indiana University Press.

Rovin, Jeff. 1991. *The Illustrated Encyclopaedia of Cartoon Animals.* New York: Prentice-Hall.

Sandler, Kevin. 1997. "Pogs, Dogs, or Ferrets: Anthropomorphism and 'Animanaics.'" *Animation Journal* 6, no. 1 (Fall), 44–53.

———. 1998. "Gendered Evasion: Bugs Bunny in Drag." In *Reading the Rabbit: Explorations in Warner Bros. Animation,* ed. Kevin Sandler, 154–170. New Brunswick, N.J.: Rutgers University Press.

Sax, Boria. 2007. "Animals as Tradition." In Kalof and Fitzgerald 2007, 270–277.

Schickel, Richard. 1986 /1968. *The Disney Version.* London: Michael Joseph.

Shapcott, Jo. 2000. *Her Book: Poems 1988–1998.* London: Faber and Faber.

Shay, Don, and Joel Duncan. 1993. *The Making of Jurassic Park.* London: Boxtree.

Sherman, Tim. 2005. "Video/Intermedia/Animation." In Gehman and Reinke 2005, 189–197.

Sibley, Brian. 2000. *Chicken Run: Hatching the Movie.* London: Boxtree

Snyder, Gary. 1990. *The Practice of the Wild.* San Francisco: North Point.

Solomon, Charles. 1987. *The Art of the Animated Image: An Anthology.* Los Angeles: AFI.

Tezuka, Osamu. 2003. *Tezuka School of Animation.* Vol. 2, *Animals in Motion.* Carson, Calif.: Digital Manga Publishing

Thomas, Frank, and Ollie Johnson. 1981. *Disney Animation: The Illusion of Life.* New York: Abbeville.

Thomson, Robert, Nicholas Mitchell, and Lyn Miles, eds. 1997. *Anthropomorphism, Anecdote, and Animals: The Emperor's New Clothes?* New York: NYU Press.

Von Franz, M. L. 1964. "The Process of Individuation." In Jung 1964, 158–229.

Wake, Jenny. 2005. *The Making of King Kong.* New York: Pocket Books.

Warner, Marina. 1994. *From the Beast to the Blonde: On Fairytales and Their Tellers.* London: Chatto and Windus.

Wells, Paul. 1998. *Understanding Animation.* London and New York: Routledge.

———. 2002a. *Animation and America.* New Brunswick, N.J.: Rutgers University Press.

———. 2002b. *Animation: Genre and Authorship.* London: Wallflower Press.

———. 2006. *Fundamentals of Animation.* Lausanne: AVA Academia.

———. 2007. *Scriptwriting for Animation.* Lausanne: AVA Academia.

Williams, Richard. 1984. *Orwell.* London: Fontana.

Williams, Zoe. 2006. "Political Animals." *The Guardian G2 Magazine,* December 12, 4–7.

Woods, Paul A., ed. 2005. *King Kong Cometh.* London: Plexus.

FILMOGRAPHY

Abu's Poisoned Well (Halas & Batchelor, UK, 1943)

Alice in the Jungle (Walt Disney/Ub Iwerks, USA, 1925)

Anancy the Spider (Moving Still, UK, 1996)

Animal Farm (Halas & Batchelor, UK, 1954)

Animal Farm (John Stephenson, USA, 1999)

Animated Matches, The (Emile Cohl, France, 1908)

Antz (Eric Darnell, Tim Johnson, USA, 1998)

Aviation Vacation (Tex Avery, USA, 1941)

Babe (Chris Noonan, USA, 1995)

Bambi (David Hand, USA, 1941)

Band Concert, The (Wilfred Jackson, USA, 1934)

Barnyard (Steve Oederkerk, USA, 2006)

Bear That Wasn't, The (Chuck Jones, USA, 1967)

Beauty and the Beast (Kirk Wise and Gary Trousdale, USA, 1989)

Believe It or Else (Tex Avery, USA, 1939)

Biswas the Bull (Moving Still, UK, 1996)

Britannia (Joanna Quinn, UK, 1993)

Brother Bear (Aaron Blaise and Robert Walker, USA, 2004)

Bug's Life, A (John Lasseter, USA, 1997)

Bunny (Chris Wedge, USA, 1998)

Butcher's Hook (Simon Pummell, UK, 1995)

Cameraman's Revenge, The (Ladislaw Starewicz, Russia, 1911)

Cat Came Back, The (Richard Condie, Canada, 1988)

Cats and Dogs (Lawrence Guterman, USA, 2001)

Ceiling Hero (Tex Avery, USA, 1940)

Chang (Merian C. Cooper and Ernest B. Schoedsack, USA, 1927)

Charge of the Light Brigade (Tony Richardson, UK, 1966)

Charley (Richard Taylor, UK, 1970)

Charlotte's Web (Gary Winick, USA, 2006)

Chicken Run (Nick Park and Peter Lord, UK, 2000)

Cow, The (Alexander Petrov, Russia, 1989)

Crab Revolution, The (Arthur de Pins, France, 2004)

Creature Comforts (Nick Park, UK, 1990)

Creature Comforts [series] (Richard Goleszowski, UK, 2003–present)

Cross-Country Detours (Tex Avery, USA, 1940)

Crouching Ox, Crowing Rooster (Martin Pickles, UK, 2005)

Cultured Ape, The (Halas & Batchelor, UK, 1960)

Dad's Dead (Chris Shepherd, UK, 2004)

Day at the Zoo, A (Tex Avery, USA, 1939)

Deputy Dawg (Terrytoons, USA, 1961–1962)

Detouring America (Tex Avery, USA, 1939)

D-Fightin' Ones (Friz Freleng, USA, 1961)

Dinosaur (Eric Leighton and Ralph Zondag, USA, 2000)

Dog (Suzie Templeton, UK, 2001)

Ducktators, The (Norman McCabe, USA, 1942)

Dumbo (Ben Sharpsteen et al., USA, 1941)

Father of the Pride (Various, USA, 2006)

Felix Doubles for Darwin (Otto Messmer, USA, 1924)

Finding Nemo (Andrew Stanton and Lee Unkrich, USA, 2003)

Fox Hunt (Anthony Gross and Hector Hoppin, UK, 1934)

Free Jimmy (Christopher Nielsen, Norway, 2006)

Fritz the Cat (Ralph Bakshi, USA, 1972)

Gertie the Dinosaur (Winsor McCay, USA, 1914)

Goofy Groceries (Bob Clampett, USA, 1940)

Grass (Merian C. Cooper and Ernest B. Schoedsack, USA, 1925)

Grasshopper and the Ant, The (Ladislaw Starewicz, Russia, 1911)

Grasshopper and the Ant, The (Lotte Reiniger, Germany, 1954)

Guard Dog (Bill Plympton, USA, 2006)

Happy Feet (George Miller, Australia/USA, 2006)

Hen Hop (Norman McLaren, Canada, 1942)

Hill Farm, The (Mark Baker, UK, 1988)

How a Mosquito Operates (Winsor McCay, USA, 1912)

I Am Not an Animal (Baby Cow Animation, UK, 2004)

Ice Age (Chris Wedge, USA, 2002)

I Like Mountain Music (Bob Clampett, USA, 1933)

Isle of Pingo-Pongo, The (Tex Avery, USA, 1938)

It's Tough to Be a Bird (Ward Kimball, USA, 1969)

Jungle Book, The (Wolfgang Reitherman, USA, 1967)

Jurassic Park (Steven Spielberg, USA, 1993)

Just Dogs (Burt Gillett, USA, 1932)

Kimba, the White Lion (Osamu Tezuka, Japan, 1965)

King Kong (Merian C. Cooper and Ernest B. Schoedsack, USA, 1933)

King Kong (Peter Jackson, New Zealand, 2005)

Klunk (Walter Lantz, USA, 1933)

Land Before Time, The (Don Bluth, USA, 1988)

Lion King, The (Roger Allers and Rob Minhoff, USA, 1994)

Little Nemo (Winsor McCay, USA, 1911)

Little Rural Riding Hood (Tex Avery, USA, 1949)

Lost World, The (Willis O'Brien, USA, 1925)

Madagascar (Eric Darnell and Tom McGrath, USA, 2005)

Metamorphosis of Mr. Samsa, The (Caroline Leaf, Canada, 1977)

Monsters Inc. (Pete Docter, USA, 2001)

Mr. Bug Goes To Town (Max Fleischer, USA, 1941)

My Neighbor Totoro (Hayao Miyazaki, Japan, 1988)

One Froggy Evening (Chuck Jones, USA, 1955)

One Hundred and One Dalmations (Wolfgang Reitherman, Hamilton Luske, and Clyde Geronimi, USA, 1961)

One Million Years b.c. (Don Chaffey, UK, 1966)

One Rat Short (Alex Weil, USA, 2006)

Pet Store, The (Walt Disney, USA, 1933)

Pinocchio (Hamilton Luske and Ben Sharpsteen, USA, 1940)

Plague Dogs (Martin Rosen, UK, 1982)

Plane Crazy (Walt Disney, USA, 1928)

Playful Pluto (Burt Gillett, USA, 1934)

Pocco Rosso (Hayao Miyazaki, Japan, 1992)

Pokemon (Satoshi Tajiri, Japan, 1999–present)

Poulette grise, La (Norman McLaren, Canada, 1947)

Princess Mononoke (Hayao Miyazaki, Japan, 1997)

Rabbit (Run Wrake, UK, 2006)

Ratatouille (Brad Bird, USA, 2007)

Saludos Amigos (Bill Roberts, Jack Kinney, Hamilton Luske, and Wilfred Jackson, USA, 1943)

Scooby Doo (Raja Gosnell, USA, 2002)

Shoemaker and the Hatter, The (Halas & Batchelor, UK, 1949)

Shrek (Andrew Adamson and Vicky Jensen, USA, 2001)

Silly Goose, The (Hans Fischerkoesen, Germany, 1944)

Sinbad and the Eye of the Tiger (Sam Wanamaker, USA/UK, 1977)

Snow White and the Seven Dwarfs (David Hand, USA, 1937)

Spirit: Stallion of the Cimarron (Kelly Asbury, USA, 2002)

Steamboat Willie (Walt Disney, USA, 1928)

Sullivan's Travels (Preston Sturges, USA, 1941)

Tale of the Fox, The (Ladislaw Starewicz, France, 1930–1931)

Tango, The (Gianluigi Toccafondo, Italy, 1991)

Tarzan (Chris Buck, Kevin Lima, USA, 1999)

Terror on the Midway (Dave Fleischer, USA, 1941)

Tide Table (William Kentridge, South Africa, 2003)

Town Rat, Country Rat (Ladislaw Starewicz, France, 1926)

Toy Story (John Lasseter, USA, 1995)

Valley of Gwangi, The (James O'Connelly, USA, 1969)

Wacky Wildlife (Tex Avery, USA, 1940)

Walking with Dinosaurs (Tim Haynes, UK, 1999)

Watership Down (Martin Rosen, UK, 1978)

Weather-beaten Melody (Hans Fischerkoesen, Germany, 1942)

What's Opera, Doc? (Chuck Jones, USA, 1957)

When the Day Breaks (Wendy Tilby and Amanda Forbes, Canada, 1999)

Wild Thornberrys, The (Klasky Csupo, USA, 1997–2004)

William's Wish Wellingtons (Hibbert Ralph, UK, 1999)

Wrong Trousers, The (Nick Park, UK, 1993)

Yellow Submarine, The (George Dunning, UK, 1968)

INDEX

ABOUT THE AUTHOR

PAUL WELLS is the director of the Animation Academy in the School of Art and Design, Loughborough University, United Kingdom. He has published widely in the field of Animation Studies, including *Understanding Animation, Animation and America, Animation: Genre & Authorship, Fundamentals of Animation,* and *Halas & Batchelor Cartoons: An Animated History.* He was series consultant for the BBC's "Animation Nation" and is an established scriptwriter, broadcaster, curator, and speaker worldwide.

Printed and bound by CPI Group (UK) Ltd, Croydon, CR0 4YY

07/07/2026

14916209-0001